Asiwinarong

Asiwinarong

Ethos, Image, and Social Power
among the Usen Barok
of New Ireland

ROY WAGNER

PRINCETON UNIVERSITY PRESS

PRINCETON, NEW JERSEY

"The Onlyes Power Is No Power"
Russell Hoban, *Riddley Walker*

CONTENTS

CONTENTS

ILLUSTRATIONS AND TABLES

TABLES

PROLOGUE

WHETHER they have approached the study of Melanesian peoples in a self-justifying quest for the "primitive other," or in an honest search for the social "basics," Western social scientists have seldom been disappointed. They have generally found the Enigma that is all things to all. And if reciprocity turns out to be something subtler than mechanistic, nonabstract economics, gender conceptions somewhat differently situated than where the current craze would have them, "big men" and millenarian movements rather more complexly contextualized than expected—all the more reason to pursue them with renewed vigor. Melanesia lends itself to ethnographic clichés and eclectic stereotypes for the same reason that it drove a Malinowski or a Bateson to inordinate labor and introspection: either the Enigma is plastered over with easy answers or it totally absorbs one.

Much of Melanesian ethnography, like much of ethnography in general, can be fairly accused of setting up a bogus "establishment" to explain indigenous culture in heuristic Western terms. Africa had its "corporate lineages," its "juropolitical systems," its barristers and "kings," much as its colonizers did. In a somewhat lower key, making allowance for the passage of time and a more eclectic state of theory, Melanesia has systems of finance and conspicuous consumption called "reciprocity," entrepreneurial "big men" who may also be political bosses, class actions called "social control," and sometimes even energy programs. Of course, Melanesia really does "have" reciprocity, and often big men, just as Africa has at least courts and possibly kings, though they are only recognizable as such (rendered "theoretically comparable") when framed or bracketed heuristically as "systems" or "institutions."

The problem is not with the ethnographic usages, which

xi

might prove as much (or as little) if heuristically labeled "secondary pig markets" or "social welfare systems," but with the practice of naively adducing and emphasizing social systems and institutions while ignoring subtler and more basic cultural motivations. Functional, institutional, and ecological heuristics ask the question "How do these people solve our problems within their means?" rather than "How do they resolve and transform our meanings within their problems?" Such heuristics are conceived of, tested, and "proved" in terms of *facts*—meanings that have already congealed around particular interpretations—instead of the more elemental possibilities afforded by interpretation itself.

Fact is a point of negotiation, a "known quantity" in the solution of the enigmatic "X." But what we find in anthropological theory is that the known quantity is often the most variable of all. It is, paraphrasing Nietzsche, "a mobile army of metaphors," deployed so as to outflank the Enigma from a particular position. In the early years of Melanesian ethnography, in the historical surveys and synopses of Codrington and Seligman, Haddon and Rivers, fact corresponded to the rigid and rational orders of Western secular and natural history. The Enigma took the form of Melanesian "history," and of its peculiar cultural forms as reflections of historical and geographical evolution.

With the waning of colonial powers as agents of historical "evolution" and "diffusion," fact assumed the synchronicity of system in the mobilizing nation-states. History, for Malinowski and Radcliffe-Brown, was all too enigmatic. The solvable Enigma was that of systemic integration, still tinged with the aura of "savagery" and evolutionary basicness. For the British, functional school, it was a social and particularly a Durkheimian Enigma; for those influenced by Ruth Benedict, such as Margaret Mead and Gregory Bateson, it was psychological (though Bateson was able, in his schismogenesis model, to show something of its depth and universality).

It was in the newly pacified highlands of New Guinea, after World War II, that the facticity of social integration encountered the next redeployment of the "known." As against the dogmas of the corporate group, residence and land tenure, and social control that guided colonial administrators as well as fieldworkers, R. F. Salisbury introduced, in the context of Siane cross-cousin marriage, the significance of the indigenous conceptualization of things. For "alliance theory," as for the structuralism that stood behind it, fact was now the determination of cultural concepts by conventionalized classifications and frameworks. The Enigma, then, became cognitive, as perhaps an Enigma should be, though the structuralist presumption was that cognition itself is procrustean and structural.

However we may choose to deploy our modern "knowns" of production, gender relations, or poststructuralism, the character of the enigmatic "other" will retain these tinges of primitivism, system, and cryptostructure. The Enigma has been shaped by its interlocutors. And if prudence, if not outright skepticism, suggests that even pure Enigma would be preferable as a starting point, then the findings of recent researchers in the central, "Mountain Ok" region of New Guinea are encouraging. Among other "min" peoples, the Telefol, according to Dan Jorgensen, articulate their lives around the power of Enigma itself, in the form of men's cult-house secrets. The deepest of these, as among the Barok, is held as the raison d'être of society.

Whether ethnographic fact is contexted as history, as society, or culture, and whether the context is viewed as historical accretion or productive "system," it is necessarily represented through the meaningful communication of the ethnographer. Whether the meaningful order of ethnography, the ultimate heuristic, represents itself *as* meaning, or as some form of social, cultural, or ecological energetics, it comes down eventually to the question of what this order signifies in terms of the subjects of the ethnography. For the unspoken assumption of much ethnography, grounded in the Western historical experience, is that order is in some sense a constitution, a covenant, a social contract for the people represented. As such, it runs a grave danger of becoming a moral allegory of what *we* consider to be "culture" or "society" (or politics or economics), a bogus establishment indeed, if not a rustic "law and order" view of life.

The Usen Barok understand their lives to be grounded in "power," *a lolos* (Tokpisin *pawa*), that which enables human capability and tests its limits, but also stands outside of it. If power over something is the ability to negate or destroy it, then social power—that which commands society—cannot be merely a function of the social order itself. It cannot, despite Durkheim's assertions to the contrary, amount to society's representation of itself, and it will not suffer itself to be represented as "order" or establishment. It may only be elicited or contained.

What we might call "culture" or "society" is for Barok the containment by human beings of a spontaneously occurring force or power otherwise manifested in form-changing place-spirits, waterspouts, birth defects, or any other unusual phenomena. Contained in the stylized usages, protocols, and iconic or imagistic forms of mortuary feasting, it is called *iri lolos* ("finished," or "immanent," power).

Image, as a means of construing action, power, or effectiveness is profoundly different from verbal explanation: talk, the Barok say, is cheap. An image can and must be witnessed or experienced, rather than merely described or summed up verbally. The Barok, perhaps, are "from Missouri." Image, of course, can be verbal—a trope or metaphor—but then it will retain metaphor's peculiar intransigence to glossing. An example is the Barok image for "clan"—*a bung marapun* ("the gathering in the bird's eye"). This image is in constant daily use by Barok, but only a few older men purport to say or know what it means (gloss it). They say that the "bird" is the *sek*, or colonial starling, whose ruby-red eye symbolizes, perhaps, the blood of the matrilineage. The clustered, domed nests of the *sek* are always made in clearings above human villages or gardens, within view of the people, who are also in the "eye" of the *sek* (*mara* means "epicenter" or "focal point" as well as "eye"). They say that the *marapun* is *not* the eye of the *sek*, but the spot of blood in the fertilized egg of another species of bird, and so on. *None* of these glosses is universally accepted—but, then, none of them has to be. The image presented in the metaphor *contains* or *elicits* them all, and all that is necessary is to retain the image itself. An anthropologist who might set out to get the *real* gloss would be horribly frustrated, because the cultural convention exists at the level of the *image*, not at that of its verbalized gloss.

The key operations here are those of elicitation—a use of the image to provoke an appropriate response or understanding—and containment, the facility of an image to encompass a number of possible interpretations. Barok claim that their *kastam* (a loanword from English) or *talien dek*, their ritual life, is based on the propriety of their kin taboos. This might ordinarily be seen as a difficult sort of inference or "leap" to deal with, but it is integral to the model I have developed. Here, the key is elicitation; the rigid kin taboos can be understood as special applications of a generalized ethic called *malum*, forbearance or personal restraint out of respect or sorrow for the dead. It is *malum* that rules the protocols of mortuary feasting, the epitomizing rite of the men's house. A taboo, an enjoinment of respect, or a formalized joking relationship is a formally structured and expected injunction for personal behavior. It elicits some form of response, and the way in which the kinsman responds—appropriately or inappropriately, as the case may be—serves to realize or create the relationship itself. (Joking or banter in our own culture might serve as an example here; a gibe or quip at someone can be seen as an attempt to "violate" one's relationship to that person. If the victim "takes it as a joke," laughs it off, he or she acknowledges that the relationship is stronger than the attempted violation, and thus reaffirms the relationship.)

Bateson has pointed out that joking, respect, and avoidance can all serve to provoke responses, each in its appropriate way, and that the particular response occurring in any given situation (whether appropriate or not) becomes, as it were, the next installment of an ongoing (or just terminated) relationship. Because it is indirect, but nonetheless effective, this mode of kin interaction can be spoken of as elicitation, and it is a behavioral analogue of the elicitation of glosses by an image. Thus the Barok assertion of continuity between kin protocols and the ritual elicitation of meanings can be incorporated within a general model of how Barok enact, and conceptualize, their culture. The complex of kin restrictions compels the actor to *show* himself or herself as moral or immoral, appropriate or inappropriate to the ideal of *malum* (and here the powerful notion of *a minenge*, or "shame," comes to the fore); the complex of ritual images manifests and demonstrates (contains) the ritual meanings.

Just exactly how does this model "put together" the meanings of Barok social life? The Barok are organized into two moieties, "halves" of society, affiliation to which is traced through maternal descent. Members of each moiety regard one another as maternal kin, and regard the other moiety, in a general sense, as being related paternally to them. Paternity is the superordinate means through which these moieties interact, and paternity carries powerful symbolic associations of creation or nurturance. In the Barok idea of human procreation, a father, through acts of coition, first conceives his wife's ability to produce offspring, and then conceives the offspring. When children are born, the father is also responsible for nurturing them. Paternity, then, is a matter of inception and nurturance, and each moiety claims the role of creator and nurturer of the other. The father, it is said, did not *have* to give his gift of life and nurturance to his wife and children, their clan, and the moiety that contains it. He gave it freely, of his own will, and therefore paternity is treated as an honorific role—an act of giving and creativity. The ultimate sense of this is summed up in the ethic of *malum*, respect accorded the other moiety out of sorrow for its bereavement (in the general sense, over the deaths of all who have served as vivifiers of one's own moiety).

Since all persons in the society are products of the "elicitation" of paternity and the "containment" of maternity, the ethic of *malum* prevails on all formal occasions that touch upon life crisis, epitomized in death. Moieties contain their own, but each is created out of the substance and work of the other. The icon or image of this is the layout of the *taun*, or men's house, and is implemented in the feasting that takes place there. All transfers of property, title, or status *must* be legitimated by a feast in the *taun*. Even feasts not connected with a death enact the deep meanings encoded in the *taun*'s layout. The rear part of the enclosure contains the bodies of the deceased; the forepart is where members of the opposite moiety are entertained in communal feasting. When a person is newly deceased, and the body is interred in the *taun*, all food for the feasts is brought in by the opposite moiety, pigs are placed facing *inward*, toward the burial section, and no food may leave the *taun*. When the body has decomposed, and its substance is fully contained in the clan (moiety) ground, the image is reversed: the clan has fully contained the nurturance of the clan and moiety of the father. After this, the moiety of the deceased may extend its nurturance to the other; the feasts that follow are provided by the deceased's moiety, the pigs face outward, and food may be removed from the enclosure. In the first series of feasts, the moiety of the deceased enacts its claims on its own: it contains the nurturance of the other. In the second series, the moiety of the deceased reciprocates—it elicits the growth and well-being of its "children" in the other moiety.

Barok liken the rear part of the *taun* to the rootstock of a tree—the burial of ancestors who are "roots" of the present clan and moiety takes place there. They liken the forepart of the *taun* to the limbs of the tree, and in fact the gate to the feasting area is formed by a V-shaped branch—this is the part where the "shoots" are nourished. The great, final mortuary feast, the *kaba*, honors all who have died over a number of years, and is given ideally to install a new *orong*, or ritual leader. The *kaba* cannot be held within a taun, for its imagery dramatizes the power *over* society coincident with the installation of a new leader, and involves the overturning of the *taun* imagery. In the definitive form of this feast, a giant *kaba* tree is dug up by the roots and moved into the village. The tree is then upended, so that the roots form a table on which the pigs for the feast are arrayed, whereas the branch part is buried in the ground. Barok speak of this as "cooking the pigs on top of the ancestors," or "cooking the souls" of the deceased. Burial and feasting, elicitation and containment, moiety and moiety, are shown to be one and the same in a rite that witnesses the sovereignty of power through the negation of social meaning.

What we call "meaning" is but the rhetorical effect, so to speak, of the larger, holistic phenomenon that Barok treat as power—meaning, too, suffers only elicitation and containment. In the final analysis, power is not an accomplishment of Barok society or culture; it is not "the social," in the Durkheimian sense of religious forces as society's refracted perception of its own influence, and it is not social interest. What is liberated in the *kaba* is a negation of social symbolism and category: pure relativity. Power can only retain its force, as a guarantor (or whatever else) of the social, if it can be shown, through its ability to negate the social, to be something greater—the ground of being. In their recognition and witnessing of this, through its activation, the Barok both transcend the social sciences that would make of them puppets in a Western morality play and elude the forces of the developing world that hold them in fee.

ACKNOWLEDGMENTS

THE RESEARCH on which this study is based was undertaken as part of a project, funded by the National Science Foundation (Award no. GBNS 78-06193), entitled "Generating Meanings for Rules: The Necessity of Contextual Contrast in Human Social Organization." Salary provided by the University of Virginia, while I was on research assignment, also contributed significantly to this project's execution, and the support of both institutions is gratefully acknowledged. Dr. Brenda Johnson Clay, of the University of Kentucky, and Ms. Marianne George, a graduate student at the University of Virginia, participated in the project at other field sites.

The Barok were considered intermittently by a number of scholars during the Imperial German administration of New Guinea, though the theoretical interests of the period did not necessitate the objectification of a Barok "culture." The first anthropologist to undertake extensive fieldwork among the Barok was Ms. Carol E. Ballingall, in the early 1950s. Her work was concentrated in several settlements on the west coast. Dr. Owen D. Jessep has carried out extensive fieldwork at the northern (Nabo-speaking) Barok village of Lokon in 1974-75 and subsequently, dealing with general ethnographic subjects and specializing in land tenure. His work, his presence in the field during December 1979 and January 1980, and his continuing interest have been of considerable assistance in the preparation of this study. My own fieldwork was carried out between July 1979 and March 1980, at Bakan Village, where I lived, and also at Kolonoboi (Lulubo) and Ramat villages. Ms. Marianne George worked at the west coast Barok village of Kokola; her insights into the Barok language and its power-related usages have been especially helpful.

In June and July 1983, I was privileged to spend another month in the Barok area, and made use of the opportunity to substantiate a number of points that had come up in the course of analysis. I was fortunate to obtain a point-for-point confirmation, in the most enthusiastic terms, for the iconographic analysis of Barok feasting presented here, from an *orong* of Bakan Village, Mr. Tadi Gar. This includes the model of "open" and "closed" feasts, and of the negation of social meanings in the *kaba*.

Research among the Usen Barok was carried on in association with the Institute of Papua New Guinea Studies and in liaison with the Department of Anthropology and Sociology at the University of Papua New Guinea. I am grateful to both institutions for their assistance, and owe special gratitude to Dr. Maeve O'Collins and William Heaney for their assistance. The Provincial Government of New Ireland responded with warmth and enthusiasm to my proposed research, and extended comprehensive assistance in facilitating it. Among many officers who gave of their time and consideration, I should mention especially the Honorable Mr. Robert Seeto, Mr. Patrick Gatfunmat, and Mr. Jori Sumati in my expression of thanks. No anthropologist ever found a more supportive administration than this government of a free Melanesian people. The interest and concern of two local representatives of that government, Mr. Andrew Rondeau and Mr. Maik Kanin, make them also special objects of my thanks.

On the practical side, my fieldwork would not have been possible without the trusting and sympathetic assistance of Mr. Grahame Goodman, then Manager of the Bank of New South Wales branch at Kavieng; his efforts deserve my warmest thanks. Thanks are also due to Merv and Greg Dunn, Ross Ervin, and the late James Arbuthnot, for aid rendered in adversity; to Terry Needham, for his hospitality; and to Father Joseph Gloexner, at St. Martin's Parish, Namatanai. Mr. Bernard Gash, a good friend and neighbor, was a gracious host during my 1983 visit.

ACKNOWLEDGMENTS

The interest and cooperation of central New Irelanders both within and outside the study area are gratefully acknowledged: I should especially thank Mr. Francis Luttam of Pinikindu Village. My respectful gratitude is extended to Messrs. Polos, Burutle, and Togan, of the Unakulis Clan at Pire, for their fosterage and generosity. All the people of the Usen study area—Ramat, Bakan, Kanapit, Kolonoboi, and Belik—were unswervingly supportive of my presence and work. Special acknowledgment is due to Mr. Mesak Sumati, Mr. Kaminiel Kurus, and Ms. Apollonia Malawa, as well as to Messrs. Param, Opat, and Siwin (of Ramat), Tadi Gar, Babo, Ngangala, Makati, Sition Kesno, and Siwin (of Bakan), John (of Kanapit), Bubulo, Tabagase, Bongian, Pokbulu, and Raragot (of Kolonoboi), and Pokpok (of Belik). The statesman and traditional leader Mr. Nicholas Brokam, of Lokon, rendered invaluable aid, as did Headmaster Charles of the Logogo Community School.

The interest and inspiration of Dr. Brenda Johnson Clay, the Co–Principal Researcher in our project, has been a major impetus and guiding influence in this research. My children and I give thanks to Brenda and Berle Clay, and to Torsten and Severn, for their companionship. And I can only hope that Jonathan and Erika will have received some token of wonder or understanding in return for all that their presence meant for me. Special thanks must go to Nancy-Sue Ammerman, a friend in good times and bad, and special gratitude to Gail Ullman, of Princeton University Press, for her sympathy and support.

A NOTE ON BAROK PHONOLOGY

WORDS in Usen Barok are pronounced with a fairly even stress on all syllables. The English sounds represented as "p" and "w" are allophonic in Barok, and thus to some degree interchangeable. The voiced velar fricative (a gutteral "g"), conventionally transcribed by linguists as gamma (γ), is represented here as G or g. Terminal vowels are pronounced with a final glottal stop, *bara˘*, such that all words can be understood to conclude with a consonant. Vowels are rendered with relatively pure sounds, as in Spanish or Italian, with the exception of the letter "o," which is pronounced like English "aw," the vowel sound in "caught" or "brought."

Asiwinarong

ONE

Bakan Village

ACCORDING to local tradition, at a place called Selpuspusuk ("pull it and it breaks off") just south of the Barok area, where New Ireland is barely more than five kilometers wide, stands a tree called Adi'. The tree blocks the sea, holding New Ireland together at a point where it might otherwise be cut in two. The Barok people inhabit the narrow isthmus of land to the north of this point. It is a low, hilly land, with the highest crests rising over the west coast; on the east coast, the land rises in cliffs (*o-gono wat*, "rockheads") and steplike terraces of ancient seashore from the Pacific Ocean. The coastline is punctuated by many creeks and small rivers issuing from the interior and forming small estuaries that are often identified with *masalai*, tutelary clan spirits. Most of the unoccupied coastal land, even where it has not been claimed by planta tions, is planted in coconut.

Aboriginally, Barok settlements were located inland as well as along the coast (and even some of the "coastal" settlements seem to have been situated somewhat further inland than at present), but the policies of the successive German and Australian colonial regimes eventually brought about the establishment of the entire population along the coasts. Approximately 2,000 Barok now inhabit nine villages along the east coast and six along the west coast. The villages vary in population from about 50 or so to over 200; Bakan, with somewhat over 100 permanent residents, is about average in this respect.

3

Barok is an Austronesian language, assigned by Lithgow and Claassen[1] to the Patpatar family, which includes most languages in New Ireland and the surrounding islands. Barok shows a high degree of cognacy with the languages of Rabaul and the Duke of York Islands, from which Tokpisin (Neo-Melanesian or Melanesian Pidgin) acquired much of its Melanesian vocabulary, with the result that a great many Tokpisin words are identical, or nearly so, with their Barok counterparts. Phonologically, the language is quite distinctive,[2] marked by an extensive use of the fricative g[3] and contrasting markedly with Mandak to the north and the "simplified"-sounding Patpatar languages to the south. Though the intonation pattern of some words seems quite complex, a good rule of thumb in pronouncing Barok words is to give an equal stress and weight to each syllable.

Modern Barok consists largely of two dialects: Usen (said to mean traditionally "where the sun rises") and Nabo ("where the sun sets"), which Lithgow and Claassen term "Central."[4] A third dialect, Gobin (or Gabin), said to have been the standard speech of the west coast villages in the past, has been superseded by Nabo in most places, though according to Marianne George there is a small group of speakers at Kokola. Although Lithgow and Claassen include Loloba and Kokola, as well as the Sokirik village of Rebehen, within the Usen region, these villages are marginal to the dialect, which, for purposes of this study, will be understood to include Ra-

---

[1] Lithgow and Claassen, *Languages of the New Ireland District*, p. 11.

[2] It has a somewhat "oily" sound, in contrast to the staccato of Patpatar and the rolling Mandak polysyllables.

[3] The gutteral, fricative "g" contrasts phonemically with "g" and "k," at least in Usen. The people often complain of the absence of an English orthographic symbol for the sound, which is often rendered as "k" (e.g. Bakan). Many Barok were surprised to learn that the sound occurs in other languages, such as Russian.

[4] Lithgow and Claassen, *Languages of the New Ireland District*, p. 11.

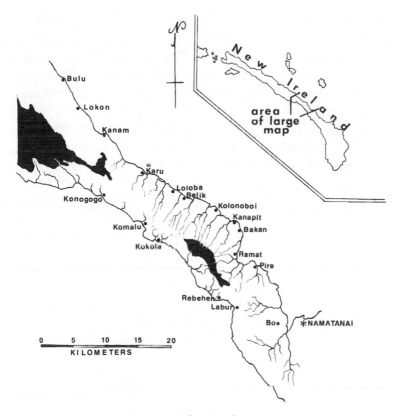

MAP 1. The Barok Area

mat, Bakan, Kanapit, Kolonoboi (Lulubo), and Belik. (See Map 1.)

Surprisingly enough, this complex, which can scarcely number more than 600 inhabitants, also shows linguistic variation at the subdialect level. A senior man of Kolonoboi once told me, "We here at Kolonoboi speak true Usen; the people down at Ramat and Bakan change it a bit, and up at

5

Belik they 'turn' it again." The variation has doubtless little if any statistical significance, though it occasionally involves terms of some symbolic importance. Barok and Tokpisin are the languages most frequently used in village life (the former predominating in private or domestic usage, whereas the mix is about equal on public occasions). Roughly 10 percent of the adult males speak English with some fluency, but even educated professionals will shift to Tokpisin in a village context.

In formal terms the Barok seem never to have been involved in the *malanggan* complex of mortuary art found among the Mandak, Notsi, and other peoples to the north. Ritually, its place might be said to have been taken by the *kaba* mortuary feast. Beyond this, the men's house and its associated customs probably reach their apex in terms of elaboration and significance among the Barok, the Sokirik, and the inhabitants of the Lihir Islands. As against the high degree of localism evident in dialect, variation in broader cultural emphases tends to be gradual, and graded differentiation in a number of ethnographic particulars runs the length of New Ireland. In the Kavieng area, for instance, the matrimoieties and heavy, woven carrying baskets found farther south are unknown, and fishing and sago cultivation are far more prominent than they are among the Barok.

In addition to the influx of in-marrying settlers (often from the Sepik or Madang areas, but sometimes from the highlands or from Buka Island) encouraged by assimilationist tendencies in the culture, several strains of regional cosmopolitanism have figured prominently in the Usen area. One, dating at least from the Reverend George Brown's evangelical efforts, stems from Rabaul and the Duke of York Islands; it provides much of the nomenclature, imagery, and content for sorcery and "power" practices, and serves as the source for exotic cult and "singsing" importations. Another, perhaps associated with the proximity of the regional center of

Namatanai (Barok: La Marana),[5] involves a lingua franca based on Patpatar and known as Laur.[6] The overlapping of these influences in communities that are already polyglot in dialect as well as in language can be bewildering, particularly in some west coast villages.

Most prominent Usen clans have extensive representation on the offshore islands of the Lihir group, and visits between mainlanders and islanders appear to have been even more common in precolonial times, when the Barok went by outrigger canoe, than at present. The fact that Lihir has been a center for the manufacture of *mis* predominates in this mutual interest, as well, perhaps, as the circumstance that the Barok area is Lihir's nearest landfall, and the two peoples enjoy playing "city" and "country" cousins, respectively. Barok seem to prize these contacts all the more for the opportunity to patronize the islanders, as the following anecdote suggests:

Lihir has only a few kinds of birds and insects. Once a man from there came to New Ireland and was fascinated by the variety of fauna here. He was intrigued by the miniature cockroach called *iwis*, which is not found on Lihir. He caught two of them to take back with him, but could not think of a way of keeping them safe during the journey. He thought and thought, and finally hit upon the idea of tying them in his foreskin. He did this, but the creatures began to get hungry en route. They began to gnaw on his penis, and he writhed in pain, shouting "pull! pull!" to the paddlers in the canoe. When he arrived, however, his glans was a bloody pulp. Remembering this incident, we like to tease Lihir men and call them *iwis*.

As well as with Lihir, Barok have extensive clan and marital ties with the Mandak people to the northwest, and with

---

[5] This is apparently a Barok version of the Patpatar name, roughly "(at) the (generic) eyes," or perhaps "the very epicenter."

[6] It includes such important terms as *palik* ("opposite moiety joking" or "-joking partner"), *likura (kaba)*, and *kolot* (basket for *mis*).

the Sokirik and Patpatar peoples to the southeast. There are also "visiting" ties (accompanied also by droll anecdotes) with the remote offshore islands of Tangga, far to the southeast.

History

Bakan Village (pronounced Baɡan) has occupied the stretch of coast between Cape Bakan and Cape Kono since precolonial times. A familiar locus for several generations of natives in the area, Bakan is now the site of the Logogo Community School, which serves the east coast Usen speakers, and during the period of my fieldwork there was a government fishing trawler named *Bakan*. There are two significant traditional caves, Komarabeɡe and Somun, in the low rockface behind the village; in several places the remains of old men's-house enclosures may be seen in the low scrub just back of the shoreline.

The significance of the name "Baɡan" is not known. It may possibly be a contraction of an old designation of a place presently within the "camp"—*Bak Maɡat*, the "young bake" (a figure of speech indicating the undercooked contents of an earth oven)—but this is purely conjectural.

The ground at Bakan has been traditionally associated with the Malaba (Tokpisin *bik pisin*), or Sea Eagle, Moiety, though elements of the other moiety have always been present. The remaining tracts of unalienated land at Bakan (land, that is, which has not been purchased by in-marrying groups) belong to two clans of the Guoɡo complex, or phratry: Wutom (Wuntom Guoɡo) and the "true," or "unmarked," Guoɡo. The *masalai* places of Wutom lie to the north of the village (and its neighbor, Kanapit); those of Guoɡo lie to the south, at the small hamlet called Ralum.

According to a generally accepted tradition, Bakan was founded by Wutom Clan, its major branch (there are others at Kolonoboi, Ralum, and Matakan, on the west coast, and there is a men's house at Kanapit), as it moved southward from Kolonoboi just before the colonial period. The original home of the clan was at a place called Ololobo, at Kolonoboi; the specific, or "small" name of the place is Un no Pere, or Gun no Pere. Wutom lived at this place, back in the bush, during the time of warfare and cannibalism. It is associated with Magalik, the great Umri, or fight leader, of Wutom. It is said that, at Un no Pere, Wutom and Guogo were one line, and it is likely that Wutom's long association with Luage (a clan of the Tago Moiety descended from the mating of a wallaby and a human-headed python) dates from this period. It was to Un no Pere that the python brought his gift to his offspring and to mankind, the marvelous, mealy yam (o-gaubo).

Magalik, whose name means "tomorrow" (indicating the promptness with which those seeking his help could expect action),[7] was famous for helping the unfortunate by killing troublemakers along the whole Barok coast. He learned to fight while throwing grass spears as a child, and he killed the pigs of his adoptive line, who told his natal clan, "come and get this child, he has finished off all of our pigs." The following is typical of the accounts of his prowess:

At Pire there were no warriors, and a man came from Bo to kill the people at Pire and steal their food. The Pire people sent a man named Kis to Bakan in a canoe, carrying half of a pig and a string of *mis*, to come to talk to Magalik at Bakan. He was a man of the Nakela Clan. He came at night, and Magalik asked him what he wanted. He said, "A man has come to kill us all at Pire." Magalik said, "Well, let's go *now!*" and he left with Kis that very moment. They arrived at Pire when the people were cutting up a pig. Magalik sat near the door in the *taun*. Kiabgas, the warrior of Bo, came into the *taun*. Magalik said, "Brother-in-law, come here." They chewed be-

---

[7] Although formally equivalent, this usage has the opposite intent to the Mexican "mañana."

tel nut, and Magalik drank a green coconut. When Kiabgas went to drink, Magalik jumped on him and wrestled him to the ground. He killed him, and then chased all the Bo people down to a foul place. This was at Matanangas.

The name "Magalik" is at present held by Siam, the "big man" of Wutom, who holds in his house the *mis* of the whole clan.

Roughly at the time of pacification, Magalik and the Wutom people moved to a place called Komarapu, or Omarapu, back of the present Bakan, in the hills. After this, they relocated to Kinanamulus, under a cliff near the present road. A cave called Lieng a Kis Gaga ("the cave that sits crazy"), in the bush back of Somun, served as a Wutom *taun* during this "bush period." Then Wutom shed a line and went to live at the site of the present hamlet Kopurus, on land that was subsequently purchased (for one *pram* of *mis* and the head of a pig) by Unakulis, which had buried a "big man" there. Afterward, Wutom moved to Balum, on the beach at Bakan, where they were living in 1916 when Ngangala, the second-oldest man in order of seniority, was born. Later they relocated to the present site of the *taun*, at Baliklet, in the Bakan "camp."

The social and structural complexity of these movements, which were certainly something more than a mere "wandering," might easily be missed in an abbreviated account. Wutom was associated, in these movements, with a number of other clans, which it had "pooled its *mis* with" or was "taking care of." Wutom traveled together with Guogo, with which it shared *mis*; it "looked after" the Malaba clans Tinan Gunun and Banban, and was apparently also associated with Luage, in its travels. It is said that the tailless shark Bemut, a manifestation of the Wutom *tadak*, or *masalai*, and the iridescent, offshore rock Torodege (the "home" of Bemut) themselves moved from the Kolonoboi area to a position off Cape Bakan when Wutom relocated in the region.

At Bakan, Wutom was joined by Nagira, a Tago clan fleeing from a massacre at Tala (Buraibore), among the Patpatar speakers at Cape Namarodu.[8] Wutom intermarried with Nagira, which claims to have cleared off much of the original forest cover at Bakan. Nagira had also intermarried with two Malaba clans, Balage and Komagas, and these shared *mis* with Wutom at Bakan. Unakulis, another Tago clan with land at Namarodu (though it is centered among the Sokirik speakers at Pire), intermarried with Wutom and, coming from the Ramat area, eventually established itself at Bakan. Unakulis has made considerable land purchases at or near Bakan in the past decade or two.

Many of the lines formerly associated with Wutom at Bakan have diminished or have been absorbed. Isnamarun, a Malaba line that had a *taun* near the beach between the Bakan "camp" and Karitis Hamlet, has died out at Bakan. Some survivors of Tinan Gunun live south of Namatanai and visit Bakan for ceremonial feasts. Balage and Komagas, affiliated with the Wutom *taun* at Bakan, are now referred to as "Wutom." The last issue of Luage, a boy born at Punam, south of Namatanai, was "purchased" by a man of Wutom and brought to Bakan to live. He, too, has been merged with Wutom, and the clan now claims the extensive bush territories of Luage, stretching from Kolonoboi to the country behind Bakan, on the strength of this.

Modern Bakan is thus composed of the two Malaba clans from Kolonoboi, Wutom and Guogo, and two Tago clans, Nagira and Unakulis, that had moved up from the Patpatar and Sokirik villages to the south to live with their Malaba affines at Bakan. Additional to these are the in-marrying affines from other clans, or from other parts of Papua New

---

[8] The Nagira people were surrounded and massacred at Tala by the Matandudugia, and fled to Bakan. The Nagira land at Namarodu directly adjoins some of the Unakulis land there, some of which, at Kadawn and Tonare, has recently been purchased by Nagira.

Guinea, or members of such incorporated lines as Balage, whose presence complicates, but does not alter, the basic pattern of clan association. In recent decades the Unakulis lineages, by far the most numerous, have taken the lead in professional achievement and commercial development, forming a contrast to the more traditional Wutom.

From 1700, when the hull of William Dampier's *Roebuck* rang with the volleys of slingstones launched by warriors around Slinger's Bay, as he named the Nambuto estuary (north of the present Namatanai),[9] to the last decades of the nineteenth century, when the Reverend George Brown's Fijian Methodist evangelists made their first incursions into the region, the Barok area must have seen sporadic landfalls by explorers, whalers, blackbirders, and others. But little or nothing of this era of the *trimas* ("three-masts") remains in the native tradition. At Ramat it is recalled that in the time of the great-grandfather of a rather old man (perhaps in the middle years of the last century), many "stone bottles" (*koro-got-wat*, from *koro*, an old word for trade bottle-glass) fell from the sky, causing terrific earth tremors that destroyed houses and extinguished all fires in the area. The earth movement was also said to have created the "*masalai* lake" Tudamo in the bush back of Bakan, whereas the impact of the object itself formed the crater Marakoro back of the hamlet of Ralum.[10] In 1892 the Belgian planter J.B.O. Mouton, visiting the west coast Barok village of Kokola for purposes of labor recruitment, witnessed the slaughter and cooking of a young boy who had been captured in a retributive

[9] Dampier was the second known European explorer to have made contact with New Irelanders; he was preceded by Schouten and La Maire in 1616, who also gave iron and beads to the natives. Hughes, *New Guinea Stone Age Trade*, pp. 20, 22.

[10] Tradition speaks of the "smooth, glasslike stone" (meteoritic iron?) found around the crater; the stone was heavy and "killed people when thrown at them." Another tradition speaks of a "star" (*ti*) that fell into the Gogo River near its estuary.

raid against some enemies who had been causing depreda-
tions with a German rifle.[11] Not much is recalled of German
colonial times, except that the Germans held themselves very
erect, called themselves "doits," and brought large ships into
Ramat Bay.

The German administration's establishment of a regional
center at Namatanai in 1904, and its plans for incorporating
the natives into local "public unions," doubtless had their effects in the area, but the impact is difficult to gauge from
modern indigenous sources. What did register, on both the
native imagination[12] and memory, was the harshness of
working and living conditions during the plantation period
that followed, and the restrictions that mission groups were
said to have imposed upon native ceremonial. An important
factor in the development of New Ireland has been the east
coast highway, which, begun by the German District Officer
Franz Boluminski, made its way along the coast as the century progressed. By the time of the Australian military occupation, in 1914, it extended to Kimadan, in the central
Mandak-speaking area, and the pre–World War II Australian
administration extended it as far as Karu,[13] in the northern
Barok area. Only in recent decades has the section from Karu
to Namatanai (and beyond) been made passable for motor
traffic. Adults recall the slender bush road of their younger
days, dark with overhanging trees, as well as the chore of carrying the cargo of the Australian patrol officers from village
to village, and across the flooded, unbridged estuaries.

The Japanese invasion and occupation of the area during
World War II was still, in 1979, a major subject of reminis-

[11] Biskup (ed.), *The New Guinea Memoirs of Jean Baptiste Octave Mouton.*
[12] Several "stories about white men," said to be traditional Barok tales,
depict the harshness and cruelty of European "masters" in elaborately
imaginative form.
[13] Chinnery, *Studies of the Native Population,* p. 11.

cence and speculation. Many Barok had served the Japanese as soldiers or laborers, or had suffered under the exacting discipline enforced upon villagers by the occupation, only to become fugitives and refugees during the bombing and demoralization by the occupying troops who followed. A number of men's houses were destroyed in the war, the *balat* dismantled by the Japanese to provide pavingstones.

Following the close of hostilities, from the late 1940's to 1963, Bakan, like other New Ireland villages, was reorganized into a "camp," a compact, orderly settlement surrounded by a low wall of loose coral (largely the same *balat* stones that the Japanese had used for pavement). The general outlines of this camp (as well as a few portions of the old wall) survived to form a core for the Bakan of 1979—a kind of double hamlet, still called the "camp," accommodating Wutom and Unakulis as well as the adjacent Nagira hamlet at Belamaket. Otherwise, in the years since 1963, what seems to have been the traditional settlement pattern has reasserted itself, and the remainder of the village occupies a string of hamlets along the highway.

Bakan Village, 1979

The hamlets of Bakan stretch 1.68 km (1.05 statute mi) along the east coast highway. Counting the camp, there are seven hamlets in all, named as a rule for the ground they occupy. The village includes the Logogo Community School, two trade stores, a United Methodist church, two or three copra dryers, and nine *taun*. At the south end of the village, near Karitis Hamlet, are the modern home and outbuildings of an expatriate Englishman who has married into the Unakulis Clan. Excluding the school and the expatriate's homestead, the village includes seventy-four buildings. With a few exceptions, these are of "bush materials" (fresh tree-trunk frame covered with woven bamboo matting) and corrugated

14

iron (*kapa*) roofing. Rainwater is collected in metal water tanks from the iron roofing.

Although the village could be said to have several functional "epicenters," the broad, open center of the main camp, with its *tawan* trees, maintains a historical as well as a demographic precedence. Stretching between the door of the Wutom *taun* and the road, it takes the form of a large rectangle, surrounded by dwelling houses. On one side, near the highway and partially surrounded by living hedges, is the village courthouse, a small, open-sided structure where the circuit court periodically convenes. Just behind the Wutom *taun* is a gentle slope down to the reef, a site where men often make the earth ovens for steaming festive pigs. The beach-and-reef (*logon*) beyond this is somewhat informally divided into men's (from back of the *taun* southward to Balum) and women's (northward from back of the *taun*) bathing areas.

The rectangular layout of the main camp is replicated, more or less, in the plan of each of the other hamlets. Each hamlet includes at least one *taun*, belonging to the predominant lineage in residence, as well as dwelling houses. The land at Bakan is made up of named tracts, which owe something of their rectangular regularity to the recent work of Land Demarcation Committees. Claims to the land, and to some degree the boundaries themselves, are based on long-term traditions of occupation, use, or purchase, known recent purchase, or on the symbolism of spaces surrounding former *taun*. In no case were claims or boundaries predicated upon association with a clan *tadak*, or tutelary spirit; in the few cases where the presence or influence of a *tadak* was noted, the spirit belonged to a lineage that was defunct or absent. Thus the situation confirms Owen Jessep's conclusion that only at Lokon Village, in the Nabo dialect area, does association with a *tadak* serve as a "title" to a tract of land.[14] Bound-

---

[14] Jessep, "Land Tenure in a New Ireland Village," p. 170.

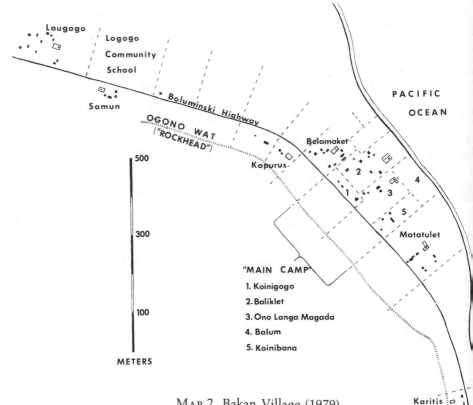

MAP 2. Bakan Village (1979)

aries within the camp are complicated by the *lu naraman*, "doorways," of *taun* formerly sited about the area, whose significance (and, to some degree, prohibitions) remain in force, although the structures have been removed. The tracts known as Koinigogo, Ono Langa Magada, and Balum (see Map 2) correspond with *lu naraman*. Although most ground names are in the Barok language,[15] some of the tracts at the

---

[15] Thus Ono Langa Magada means "the horsefly bake," and Karitis,

camp, Baliklet, Belamaket, and Matatulet, bear names in the Lihir language that were bestowed in the past by members of Guogo Clan from that island group. Another recent usage, which has resulted in the naming of several hamlets at Ramat (e.g. Ralum, Ramok) for notable localities in the Rabaul area, can be detected in the designation of Koinibana as "Rakunai."

Of the nine *taun* at Bakan, three belong to Unakulis and three to Nagira, whereas Wutom and Guogo have one apiece, and a senior traditional leader, Tadi, a member of the Malaba clan Palarauo who is married to Unakulis at Karitis, has built one there. In addition there are two *bang*, men's houses without a surrounding enclosure: one situated next to the church, where it serves as a sort of male "ready room" before and after services; the other providing a ceremonial center for the Unakulis people living at Laugogo Hamlet.

Excluding employees at the school, and local families whose permanent, employment-linked residence is outside the Barok area, the total population of Bakan Village in late 1979 was 117. This figure is subject to considerable fluctuation as relatives employed elsewhere enjoy periodic vacations, and as the normal flow of kin-related settlement and resettlement takes its course. If we count the camp as a single hamlet, as in Table 1, the average population of a Bakan hamlet is 16.7; if the camp is counted as two hamlets, the average is 14.6. A glance at the raw figures shows that, excepting individual family settlements such as Kopurus and Somun, the hamlets, as localized lineage settlements, vary between 15 and 20 inhabitants. Descriptively such a hamlet amounts to a matrilineally oriented extended family, centered upon the *taun* that the dominant (usually senior)[16] male member

---

named for a freshwater spring that enters the sea at the shoreline, means "at the mixed water."

[16] There is no exact title or description for this position, which is often referred to in Tokpisin as *bikman* ("big man"). The Barok term *orong* is also applicable, but as the status connoted is largely a relative one, its use is frequently a matter of courtesy alone.

TABLE 1. Demographic Structure of Bakan Village (Late 1979)

	Camp	Belamaket	Matatulet	Karitis	Kopurus	Somun	Laugogo	Total
MEN								
Married, virilocal	7	3	1	2	1	0	1	15
Married, uxorilocal	0	0	3	1	0	1	2	7
Unmarried	5	3	3	1	0	2	1	15
WOMEN								
Married, virilocal	5	3	1	2	1	0	1	13
Married, uxorilocal*	1	0	4	3	0	1	2	11
Unmarried	1	0	1	1	1	1	4	9
CHILDREN								
Boys	12	6	4	3	0	0	4	29
Girls	7	0	3	4	1	1	2	18
HAMLET TOTAL:	38	15	20	17	4	6	17	117

* Includes several women whose husbands, if still married, live elsewhere. In one instance, where two clans live together, the husband lives virilocally, the wife uxorilocally.

"bosses." This basic pattern is subject to many variations and often incorporates a fair number of in-marrying affines from outside the Barok area, or even from beyond New Ireland.

Other forms of irregularity are apparent in the listings for postmarital residence of adult men and women: in one marriage, made within the camp, the couple lives bilocally;[17] in another, the wife lives (uxorilocally) in Karitis, and the husband (virilocally) at the camp; and one Guogo woman, living at Matatulet, is uncertain as to the whereabouts of her husband. Thus the percentage of virilocality among men is 68.2, whereas that among women is 54.2. Of the men of marriageable age, 59.4 percent are married, as against 72.7 percent of the women of marriageable age. These ratios are by no means unusual for a Melanesian population. Native recollection suggests that the present pattern of monogamy, however much it owes to missionization, was only slightly altered by occasional polygyny or polyandry in the prepacification and plantation periods.

The settlement pattern at Bakan reflects the modern political situation of domination by the originally immigrant Tago clans, Nagira and Unakulis. (See Map 2.) Of the hamlets, only the main camp, with its Wutom complement, and Matatulet, where Guogo is centered, are not completely dominated by one Tago line or the other. The *taun* at Belamaket and Laugogo are those of Nagira lineages, with another managed by a Nagira family at Somun. The Unakulis residents at Karitis and Laugogo hamlets, and at the camp, constitute the children (and their families), respectively, of three sisters in the present grandparental generation. A fourth sister lives with her children and grandchildren at Ramat, and a first cousin of the sisters manages the small Unakulis *taun* at Kopurus.

---

[17] In this case, as in the other, residences were coded simply as "uxorilocal" and "virilocal."

Although few of the surrounding villages are without their examples of professional achievement—sons or daughters who have become teachers or high ecclesiastical or government officers—Bakan is exceptional in this regard. A high proportion of the adult Nagira and Unakulis men are both fluent and literate in English, and a number of clan members or their children or affines hold high positions in the provincial and national governments, or in higher education. While this professional record is quite remarkable in itself, it is supplemented by the fact that most of the copra marketing at Bakan is carried on by either Nagira or Unakulis, and that all of the other commercial activity is carried on by Unakulis. This includes two trade stores at Bakan[18] and, during the period of my fieldwork, the operation of a Japanese Dyna truck for passenger and freight hauling.[19]

Lest this picture of "bourgeois Bakan" present an all too facile image of "instant modernization," the account requires clarification on two points. First, as in Finney's studies of local entrepreneurs in Goroka,[20] the commercial enterprise is neither simply an adoption of Western practices nor an adaptation of native usages, but is a "preadapted" amalgamation of both. Second, no commercial enterprise is easily or completely separable from the resource base of the sponsoring kin group. Typically the bank account that such an enterprise often opens in Namatanai may be drawn upon indiscriminately to meet business expenses, such as restocking a trade store or vehicle repair, or to provide for kin obligations and customary feasts. A withdrawal of almost the whole ac-

[18] Members of Unakulis Clan maintain two trade stores at the Sokirik village of Pire as well, so that, although the four stores are in competition, and are owned by different lineages, Unakulis has held a monopoly on retail sales from the Gogo to the Bopire rivers.

[19] The truck, which was sold in 1980, was hired out for profit and also put at the personal disposal of members of the Unakulis sibling group at the camp, as well as being used to prepare for ceremonial feasts at their *taun*.

[20] Finney, *Big-Men and Business*, especially chap. 6.

count will be made—perhaps 400 *kina* or so—to purchase wholesale merchandise for a store. Later, as the goods are sold, the gross cash receipts will be deposited, building up the account until another drastic withdrawal, perhaps for a mortuary feast, is warranted. Much the same practice is followed with regard to productive resources, such as coconut plantations. Ripe coconuts are gathered and cut, and copra dried, when cash is needed to meet some long- or short-term expense; periodically a day's labor or so will be done on behalf of the church, or to fill some other community need. Once when I was temporarily out of funds, concerned lineage-mates offered to spend a day cutting copra for me (I gratefully declined).

Resources, profits (*ogagawa*), and capital belong—like the "pool" of traditional wealth, *mis* or *mangin*, held by an *orong* on behalf of a clan—to a kind of validational fund, a manifestation that is at once moral and powerful, of the ascendancy of the owners. The difference is that commercial ventures are seldom carried on at the level of the clan, and do not seem to be bound by the strict ideology of matrilateral succession that governs the *taun* and its ceremonial functions. Although the support base of an enterprise can vary widely, an example might be furnished by the most successful operation in Bakan. This is managed by the six sons (and one daughter) of Lote, one of the three Unakulis sisters. Its resources include extensive coconut plantations inherited from the father, Sumati, of Maranat Clan. The commercial enterprise is identified, for purposes of banking and vehicle registration, by an acronym compounded of the father's and mother's name: "Sumalote Baron Group," the "Sumalote Brothers." The usage follows both that of Papua New Guinea, in which the father's name is adopted as a surname, and that of the Barok, which gives special recognition to patrilateral ties and inheritance. But the crosscutting ties also serve to individuate this group and render its "ascendancy" distinct from that of other Unakulis in the area.

Business and professional achievement mark the salience of Bakan in a consciously "development-oriented" society. But the more general aspect of modernization, which touches every family, is education. The Logogo Community School is, together with the school at Karu, one of two elementary schools (first through sixth grades) serving the east coast Barok. Unlike the earlier regional school operated by the preindependence regime at Kolonoboi, where much of the present adult generation acquired some degree of literacy, Logogo maintains a uniformly high educational standard. Although much of the credit for this is due to a dynamic headmaster, the school enjoys a degree of community support that would be remarkable anywhere in the world. There is an active School Committee made up of leaders from nearby villages, and the extensive front lawn that occupies most of the school grounds is landscaped by a border of decorative plants and ceremonial markers—traditional Barok elements that otherwise occur in *taun* enclosures.

The school year enjoys a preeminence in the regular cycle of activities at Bakan that must, in bygone decades, have been the prerogative of the United Methodist church calendar and, perhaps, in the era before that, the old gardening "calender." The regularity of Sunday services, along with Sunday school instruction for the children, and the Friday tradition of refurbishing the church grounds and buildings, still punctuates the weekly round, though it shares prominence with the Monday morning "line" meetings to discuss community affairs and organize collective tasks, and with the less formal copra marketing on Wednesday and Thursday. Major church holidays such as Christmas are celebrated with special services and much informal festivity, but their social and financial impact is neither as intensive as that of the formal feasting system, nor as comprehensive as the responsibilities imposed

22

by schooling. In addition to the small fees paid at the opening of the school year, in early February, parents (i.e. most adults) must see to it that their children are in a position to attend classes regularly throughout the year. The year culminates with "Breakup," in mid-December, when all parents attend ceremonies for the closing of the year, partake of a festive meal, and witness the awarding of prizes for academic excellence. Parents are expected to present gifts to their children on this occasion—generally items of clothing—in appreciation of their scholarly efforts, and frequently outings or class picnics will be organized. In the six weeks following Breakup, schoolchildren enjoy a vacation, while the parents of children going on to one of the high schools launch all sorts of projects to raise the necessary tuition (100 *kina* or more per child). It is the busiest time of the year.

In its superimposition of the modern school calendar upon the older colonial cycles of mission and government obligation, and in its spatial syncretism of hamlets, "camps," and traditionally hallowed places, Bakan is a complex historical accretion, a cultural "text" or inscription. If only the sources were forthcoming, or the native "reading" were itself historical, what a history it could tell! But, despite many suggestive allusions, the purport of this inscription is not historical, and its reading takes us into regions where even the finest documentation would only be supplemental.

TWO

The Barok World

THE LONG, slender expanse of New Ireland, extending more than two hundred miles northwest-southeast, lends itself very easily to a unidimensional mode of reckoning. The poles of the continuum, at least for the bulk of the population, which lives between them, are the provincial capital, Kavieng, to the northwest, and the modest center of Namatanai, in the south-central portion of the island. This polarity has completely supplanted the "right/left" frame of reference familiar to Westerners: a driver, backing his car along a difficult stretch of village road, is told to go "Namatanai! Namatanai!" by anxious onlookers; an old man, fiddling with the dial of his shortwave set, is directed to turn it "Kavieng."

As is so often the case with habits as ingrained as this one, there is evidence that the bipolar scheme predated considerably the founding of Kavieng and Namatanai. Moroa, the Creator, traditionally began New Ireland at its southeastern tip (called "the eye of the place") and worked northwestward. Other accounts also incorporate this directionality. According to a tale from Siar:

Once all the saltwater was confined in a hole beneath the ground, and capped by a stone. An old woman would come and remove the stone in order to obtain saltwater in which to cook her *kumu* [greens]. Two brothers, Silik and Kambadarai, would season their *kumu* simply by urinating on it. Silik encountered the woman one day and, tasting her *kumu*, found it to be delicious. He followed the woman, secretly, and observed how she removed the stone and took

24

saltwater. He did the same, and brought some home to cook with his *kumu*. When he did so, he offered some to Kambadarai, who asked him why his *kumu* tasted so good, whereas that of Kambadarai still smacked of urine. Silik explained to him about the old woman and the stone. The two decided to remove the stone. They retraced Silik's steps to the place of the hole and removed the stone; when they did so, the saltwater began to boil up and soon the flood rose everywhere. The old woman was very angry with them when she saw this, and told them that since they were responsible, they must run as quickly as possible and dam up the water. They were to run and throw down stones to hold it back. Silik tried to show Kambadarai how to run, but he only replied, "I know, I know, you needn't show me." Silik ran straight as he threw down the stones, and the place where he ran became the coast; Kambadarai ran crooked, and the place where he ran became the central mountains of New Ireland. When they came to the region of Kavieng they were running very fast, and the stones they threw down had spaces between them. That is why there are so many islands lying close together offshore at Kavieng. Lihir, Tabar, Tangga, and all the other islands are stones that they hurled out into the sea. Silik later made the first ship, and traveled on it to the place of the Europeans; Kambadarai made the first *mon*, the large canoe of the Siar people, and remained with them.

Traditionally the southeast, or "Namatanai," direction was called *mara bo*, the "eye" or "hole" of the pig; the northwest, or "Kavieng," direction was the *mara mangin*, the "eye" of the *mis* (strung shell-disk currency). Possibly this reflects an early specialization in trade commodities, for the first known manufactories of *mis* were on the offshore islands of Tabar, to the northwest of the Barok area. The widespread legend of Lunganga, the giant, man-eating pig that ranged over New Ireland in the past, situates Lunganga's home at Siar, in the *mara bo*, "where it can be seen today."

In a more localized frame of reference, this geographic polarity is supplemented by another distinction, itself widely distributed in New Ireland. This is the opposition of "bush"

25

(*pirogo*, literally "weeds" or "undergrowth") and "beach" (*logon*) or "sea" (*lamo*). While the dichotomy is an important one, it does not seem to have the explicit sexual and spirit associations described by Brenda Clay for the northern Mandak.[1] Although Barok fishing and seafaring activities are exclusively male, and although the men's earth oven for steaming the festive pigs is invariably sited along the beach (whereas the women steam vegetables at the *pan*, the women's cookhouse, in the hamlet), Usen Barok do not make an ideological association of men's houses with the beach. Significant as the bush/beach opposition is in cult and in folklore, its application is not systematic.

Both polarities, however, that of the northwest/southeast and that of the bush/beach, are encoded within the linguistic conventions of ordinary discourse. One goes *uruso* to the bush (*e onan uruso go pirogo*), or arrives *meruso* from the bush; to the beach and (at least on the east coast) to the southeast, one goes *uruo* (and returns *meru*),[2] and one goes *uri* (*meri*) to the northwest.[3] These are obligatory direction markers that follow the verb and precede the preposition in a sentence involving locomotion.

The prevailing seasonal winds are also aligned on a northwest-southeast basis. From May to September the *taubar*, or southeasterly trades, dominate the weather, bringing clear

---

[1] Clay, *Pinikindu*, pp. 85-87.

[2] There is some confusion as to whether *uruo* and *uri* have identical or opposite applications on the west coast. Some informants recalled disagreements between east and west coast Barok as to whether *uri* was in the direction of Kavieng or Namatanai. Were the markers used to designate the same direction on both coasts, then the system would accord with the *mara bo / mara mangin* polarity; were they to designate opposite directions, it would register the right/left dichotomy. Unfortunately, rapid language change and considerable linguistic diversity on the west coast make this a difficult matter even for natives of the region to resolve.

[3] The suffix *-enge* may be added to indicate a short distance, a few meters or so: *E onan urenge go gunun te e*, "I am going *urenge* over to my house."

skies and fine, dry days. Offshore, trees and flotsam are carried by, and Barok say that the strong winds blow the rain-
clouds away. The *taubar*, which may recur fitfully at other
times of the year as well, is often invoked magically to clear
the skies for a feast or a dance. From September to November
the relatively weak *tunumat* blows from the northeast,
bringing debris and the drifting "trees of the sea" into shore.
In late November the gusty squalls of the *labur*, the
northwesterly (or Southeast Asian) monsoon, bring the region its heaviest rainfalls. These may last, on a more or less
intermittent basis, through the end of March, and the gusts
may reach higher velocities than the heavy *taubar* winds of
July and August. Two successive *labur* months were given
the folk designations *polo wi-i ngas* ("green coconuts blown
on the road") and *o soro kalang* ("running crazy in the taro
beds"). The *labur* is followed, in late March and April, by a
period called *mamat* ("calm"), after which the southeaster-
lies gradually blow back the days of halcyon weather.

For all of their uncertainties and inaccuracies (for the *tunumat* and *mamat* are barely noticeable, and the *taubar* can
blow any time of the year), these directions, winds, and sea-
sons present a conventionalized frame of reference for everyday life. But they are scarcely more than that; apart from occasional folkloric reference (only the *masalai*, it is said,
worship Moroa anymore), they do not belong to a cosmol-
ogy. Indeed, the Usen Barok do not, even to the extent that
the neighboring Mandak do, recognize or deal with a symbolic geography of circumambient spaces. Although a Barok
legend situates a "land of the dead" somewhere on an offshore island, and although the *yuo*, ghosts of those who have
died violently, can be seen fishing, like their Mandak counterparts, in the form of waterspouts or rain squalls on the sea,
the dead are not especially associated with the sea or with any
other direction.

The symbolic valences of the Barok world are more explicitly centered upon, and reflective of, human concerns, performances, and restrictions. Symbolically "charged" spaces radiate outward from the men's house, rather than from the bush or the sea; ghosts, spirits, the "peoples" of peripheral spaces, and the formidable *tadak* (*masalai* or clan-spirits) represent and entertain the inclinations, jealousies, and ambiguities of the people themselves more than they involve cosmic paradigms. What is modeled in this forceful anthropomorphism is *ethos*—how, when, and under what circumstances one should (or should not) act—rather than structure.

Perhaps the best illustration of this is the articulation of the traditional calendric and ethno-astronomical lore with the gardening cycle. For several reasons gardening deserves our attention, and at least a summary discussion and formal description: it commands—even today, for village people—the largest allocation of working time of any normal subsistence activity; it represents a primary realization of sexual complementarity and the nurturance that eventuates from it; and it remains the elemental productive mode both for the sustenance of everyday life and for the feasting that bestows value upon that life.

Barok Gardening

Gardening seems always to have been the most significant subsistence activity for the Barok. Fishing, hunting and food collecting, and cash cropping, however important the latter has become in recent years, are supplementary in an economic and a moral sense. A village resident who does not garden, who sustains a family on "store foods" such as tinned beef and rice, becomes the subject of gossip and covert, if not overt, disparagement. The government emphasis on traditional gardening, in order to reduce national dependency on imported rice, has served only to strengthen an indigenous attitude.

As a moral act, gardening helps to define sexual roles by apportioning complementary tasks in a joint enterprise according to gender, and serves to resolve, or realize, the sexual specialization through the fact of production. Neither the exclusively male activities of fishing (casually with hook-and-line or torches, or concertedly with nets) and hunting (spearing wild pigs with the aid of ubiquitous packs of eager hounds), nor the largely male operations of copra production, can claim anything like the sense of secular sacramentalism that gardening traditionally commands.

But this significance is better illustrated by counterexample than by direct affirmation. The story of Satele, the man who originated the coconut, and its variants,[4] is widespread in New Ireland. It is obviously an account whose appropriateness has been enhanced by the events of the last seventy years or so. The following Barok version was told to me at Kolonoboi Village:[5]

There was a man named Satele, who lived at Kanam. His wife, Inimtele, belonged to a clan called Winime. All the men and children of Kanam would come down to the bay in the morning and afternoon to catch *tele* fish [sardines] with the traditional net, scooping them up. Satele gained all of his sustenance from the *tele*; he didn't work in his gardens, but caught the fish from morning until night. He would catch fish until evening, then put them all into a large *kis*, and, because he didn't have vegetable food enough for his family,

---

[4] Clay, *Pinikindu*, pp. 81-82, presents a synthesis of several accounts of Solala or Songalarala, the Mandak counterpart of Satele.

[5] This story is said to have come originally from Masiguio, of Kuniime. It was told to me with great care, and, upon completion, the narrator presented me with a "Satele" coconut, from a grove at Kolonoboi said to have been planted with the original coconuts received from Kanam. For whatever reason, this remarkable fruit bore a "face"—two "eyes" and a "mouth" centered upon a noselike convergence of sutures—two or three times as large as that found on ordinary coconuts.

he would carry the fish from door to door. When he came to a house, he would give *tele* to the people there, and the woman would bring cooked vegetable food for him. When the fish were finished, and the basket was full of cooked tubers, he would carry them home for his family to eat. He would do this every day, and soon everyone heard of his habits. "Say, this man doesn't work in his gardens; don't give him any food! Tell all the women to say to him, 'Oh, we haven't had time to cook—we've worked all afternoon in our gardens.' " When Satele next came around to the houses, the women all told him this story—at every house the response to his gift of fish was the same. He thought, "Oh, what will my family eat now?" Now there is a kind of tuber that grows in the bush; it looks like sweet potato, but it is poisonous. We call it *a sawa, a sawa re gileba*. When it was quite dark, Satele cut a long, dry coconut frond for a torch and thrust it into his belt in the back. He lit it for a light, cut a long stick, and went back into the bush to where the *sawa* grow. He dug them up, and as he did, the sparks and ashes from the torch fell about his shoulders as if to spell out his laziness. He brought the *sawa* back to his place, cooked them, ate them, and his death began then. His family, who knew about *sawa*, hadn't eaten any. When he became ill, he told his family, "If I die, you shall not bury me in a burial place; you must bury me right here at my place. And after you have buried me, keep watch at the place and see what grows here." Then he died, and his family buried him. His firstborn child remembered the words of his father. But the family left his place and went to their own lands. Later on, there was a drought and a famine, and the mother of the family went off to the bush with all the people to get *aila, kulis*, and other bush foods. The children stayed at the village. The mother went to a place in the bush back of Konabuso, where they lived, where there is a kind of red earth that people eat. It is molded into spherical lumps and roasted in the fire; when the outside turns white it is eaten, and has a texture much like cooked sago. The mother would bring this as food for her children. One day when the mother was away, the firstborn son took his younger brothers, including the small lastborn one, and, remembering his father, followed along the beach until they came to their father's burial place. When they arrived, they began

to clean the place. As they were cleaning, they noticed that something had sprouted there, but they did not disturb it. They left it
there. In fact, the shoot had come up together with a letter [histry]
giving instructions for the working of copra. But because the boys
had not visited the site earlier, a European was able to steal the letter
before they saw it, and thus it was Europeans, rather than the people of Satele, who set up the copra industry. The next day the
sprout had grown quite large—perhaps God assisted it. The day
after, when they came, the tree was ready to bear. By the next day,
it had borne small fruits. They did not tell their mother of this,
though. After a while, the coconuts were dry [ripe], and the boys
took one of them. They shook it, and heard water inside. Then they
broke it open and gave it to the small, lastborn brother to eat. They
wanted to see whether it would harm him. The brothers watched
him, and he was happy, he played. When the mother arrived, the
little one would not eat earth like the rest. Then they all went to try
it; they took a green coconut and drank it, then they ate it, and it
was good. The firstborn told the others, "You cannot tell other people about this; our father gave it to us." They did not tell their
mother, either. But she noticed that, although they refused to eat,
their skins were healthy. She asked what they had been eating.
They told her she should not go with the others in the morning, but
follow them instead. They saw that the ripe coconuts had all fallen
down. The mother thought, "This should belong to all the people."
Now they decided to make a large kaba; the clan Winime made a
huge platform, gathered up the ripe coconuts, and piled them on the
platform until it was full. They sent ginger as a message to all people, to the east coast, west coast, islands; all the fish of the sea, all
the birds, all creation came. The firstborn of Satele stood up on the
platform and told everyone about the coconuts. Then they distributed them to all who came. They gave them all away, and after that
Kanam itself didn't have any coconuts. There were only three that
grew at Konabuso; the coconuts at Kanam now have all been
planted since the war. The face of Satele may be seen on the coconut
itself.

   Satele (sa-tele, the "fisher of tele") is so fond of fishing for
sardines, and so skillful at it, that he would rather exchange

the fruits of this masculine activity for tubers than make the effort to cultivate them in his garden. He thus opts out of the sexually complementary production of gardening, substituting instead an exchange of products between the sexes, and a kind of individual division of labor. This inversion of the accepted productive mode, with its implied disdain for the moral relations of gardening, provokes a jealous reaction, and Satele and his family are deprived of sustenance by women who claim that garden work has left them no time to cook. Driven to despair, the unhappy fisherman goes to the bush and gathers the (poisonous) wild tuber *sawa*, which he eats, causing his death. Dying, he tells his family to watch his grave and see what sprouts there. After he dies, the family leaves, and soon a great famine descends upon the area, forcing people to eat bush fruits and the very earth itself. His firstborn son, however, returns to the grave, and notices the tree growing there; when it bears, he tries it as food and induces his brothers to keep it. But Inimtele, discovering it, decides that the coconut should belong to all people, and she holds a *kaba* (the final death feast for a relative) to distribute it.

Thus Satele's failure to gain sustenance from the sea alone leads first to his death, through the partaking of wild bush crops, and finally to the origin of a food crop that grows *between* the bush and the sea, and bears its fruit neither on land nor in the water, but in the air. The coconut, moreover, is a special food, the "refresher" at the beginning of a feast and source of the coconut oil that is essential to many of the festive delicacies. It was the legacy of a man who, providing only seafood for his family, met his death by eating poisonous tubers of the bush, but who gave his body as refreshment (via a death feast, hence the first distribution of coconuts at such a feast) to his countrymen when famine had forced them to subsist on the earth itself. Even traditionally, then, the coconut was peripheral to gardening and to gardens; modern

New Ireland has seen Satele's breach of morality compounded, as the coconut, the basis of cash cropping, becomes
a way *out* of gardening altogether.

The Barok think of themselves as gardeners primarily of
yams (*o*), for which small platform-houses are made in the
gardens, and of a related tuber called *mami* in Tokpisin (*guogo* in Barok). Some taro (*pas*) is also grown, but the most
commonly eaten tuber was, in my experience, the recently
introduced sweet potato (*Ipomea batatas*, Barok *patete*).

Usen Barok gardens are made nowadays just inland of the
sandy beach area, typically (on the east coast) on the "bush"
side of the Boluminski Highway. At Bakan they were made
immediately above or below the *ogono wat*, the "rockhead"
of short, steep cliff running parallel to the shore a few
hundred meters inland. Gardening is of the bush-fallowing
or slash-and-burn variety, and seems to be carried forth in an
entirely traditional manner. In selecting a garden site, one
looks for land that has healthy trees and good undergrowth.
A condition called *konis*—"a sickness of soil"—is especially
to be avoided, for crops will not grow well there. *Konis*
ground is covered with grass and dead trees; the *ules*, or
"sandpaper tree," is common there.

The first step in preparing a garden is *arok a pininik*, clearing off the brush. This is done by men, sometimes with the
help of women. Weeds and grass are pulled up by the roots
and laid down again on the spot. Next the men cut the saplings (*sasala*), laying them down at the places where they are
cut, and then (*buburung*) they cut the large trees. After this
comes *miria*, the men cutting the felled trees into sections; in
the next step, *kaus*, they cut the tree foliage. When *kaus* is
finished, the wood and dead foliage are left to dry, and people
wait for sunny weather for the firing.

When the foliage is dry, and the weather looks promising,
the next task, *igarai*, piling branches at the bases of large,
standing trees, is in order. Then the brush is fired (*ogat*).

33

This is followed by fencing, which again is exclusively male. The tasks in fencing, or *toboro*, include *ulen a toboro*, driving in sets of parallel stakes (*ti*—the same word as for "stars"); *e tuo*, laying branches horizontally between the stakes; fetching *olo*, the vines for fastening the fence; and *kut*, fastening the vines. When this is finished, the garden is said to be *ire bok a komo*, or enclosed.

A garden, *komo*, is divided into a gridwork of regular, rectangular sections, called *omo*. *Omo*, which are demarcated by laying out lengths of dry wood, taken from the felled trees, end to end on the bare, cleared earth, measure roughly 5 × 8 m. The dividers along the longer sides are called *wapang*; those along the shorter sides are *burutukus*. *Omo* do not constitute separate areas of ownership, and may only occasionally or incidentally segregate plantings of different crops. In addition to imparting a sense of order to what would otherwise be a tangled profusion, they seem to be most effective in apportioning, and setting limits to, the tasks of gardening. This is, however, merely an outsider's observation, and my informants could not think of a specific "reason" why gardens are laid out this way—it is just the way gardens are made.

When the *omo* have been marked out, the women enter the garden to weed—a first weeding called *wa pagu*. When this is finished, the men *ruprup*, loosening small patches of earth every few feet by thrusting in the sharpened end of a long, heavy dibble (*a si*) and pulling it to the side with a levering action. Yams and *mami* are planted then, as women bring the shoots in baskets (*kis*) and scatter them (*raravi*) over the loosened earth, after which they plant them in the ground (*sisinge*). Sugar cane (*tu*) is planted together (*sul arigen*) with the *mami*, and taro (*pas*) is sometimes planted in its own *omo*. Perhaps a day or so later, bananas (*a un*) are planted, by the men and women together, along the inside of the fence, especially in places where there is ash. At this time, too, edible greens, or *paluo* (Tokpisin *kumu*), are planted, as well as such crops as *paragum* (a long-leaf taro), *goru* (a kind of yellow taro), pineapple, beans, tomatoes, and onions.

Traditionally, many of the steps in Barok gardening were accompanied by spells, rites, and other ministrations to ensure a successful crop. These were for the most part private and secret, and they have largely dropped out of use. Planting was a special focus of these spells (*mameng*). For *mami*, people called out the names of *orong* who had died; tree leaves were wrapped around powdered lime (*kabak*), ground together in the hands, and put on the shoots to be planted. For taro, a vine was worked together with earth, wrapped with betel nut in a *laplap*, and washed in water.

When the planting is finished, the "door" of the garden is "fastened" (*bagot a marami*). A large, forked tree-crotch in the shape of a Y like the one at the entrance to the men's house, is set up inside; and another outside, the gate of the garden. *Nganga*, a vine with needles on it, is stretched across the opening of the *marami*, near the top, and leaves of the *pirien* tree are fastened to it. This is to protect the garden from malign influences. Vines and leaves are also put at all corners of the garden fence, and a kind of "watch vine" is often placed at the *marami* to neutralize the pollution of menstruating women who might enter. After closing the door, it is taboo for people to enter the garden, which must remain undisturbed for three to four months.

After this period, the first entry, *pit buon* ("breaking the vine") is made into the growing garden. The women weed (*kip pirogo*) and replant crops that have died; when they have finished, the door is fastened once again. On the fifth month another entry, *kip mu*, is made to weed the garden. On the sixth month, *kip sawang*, or opening the garden, takes place. The maker of the garden may, if he chooses, hold a feast in the *taun* for *kip sawang*; the feast is called *wunam wunam* ("the saplings are growing well"), and the owner must furnish a pig for it. After the garden has been opened, crops such as bananas may be harvested from it. When the leaves of the yams and *mami* become dry, about eight months after planting, the *ora matagen*, the "bed" (actually a small platform-house) for tubers is built. This is generally raised a meter or more above the ground, and encloses a long, shallow sitting or crawl space between low walls, in which the ripened tubers are stored after harvesting. A shallow-pitch roof, usually gabled, is made of sago leaves. The "power" that is made when putting tubers into the bed mentions the names of trees, and is done to keep the food from finishing quickly, and to make it "sit down."[6]

Both traditionally and (in a pragmatic sense) today, the cycle of gardening activities described here could not operate as an isolated undertaking. Some form of sustenance—i.e. a producing garden—is necessary during the months of planting and waiting for the crops to mature. Moreover, even in the summary description offered here, it is obvious that some accounting of lunations must be kept if the cycle is to be carried forth on schedule. It is difficult to speak with an older Barok man or woman on the subject of gardening without some mention being made of the heavenly bodies. People say that crops will do well only if one "plants by the moon" or "by the sun" or stars, as the ancestors taught, for they knew far more about such things than the present generation. What they are referring to, in the largest sense, is the calendric cycle by which the making of gardens has been controlled.

Awat: The Celestial Mechanics of Gardening

There are traditionally two gardens made, in alternation, so that the produce of one will sustain the people while they pre-

[6] This seems to refer to the notion that yams may "travel" of their own

pare and wait for the other. The "first garden," said to be the smaller of the two (there do not seem to be any differences with regard to crops), is called *a lua*. The "second," and larger, garden is called *a sinam*. Apart from the flowering of certain plants and trees, which is supplemental (or even contingent—if the *lua* is not planted, some say, the *banbun* tree will *not* flower), the timing of these gardens is regulated by three celestial indicators: the moon, the sun, and the Pleiades. Because these constitute a sort of celestial idiom for the larger gardening cycle, I shall consider each at length, and separately.

The moon, *a tege*, is significant to the Usen Barok for its monthly cycle, for its ecliptic opposition (when full) to the position of the sun, and for its tendency to go into eclipse. Until a decade or two ago, it was a special duty of an *orong* to be alert for the signs of a lunar eclipse. When these appeared, he was to stand up in the *la gunun* and call out, *A tege erabo met* ("The moon is about to die"). At this signal the children would cry out, *a tege met* ("the moon is dead"); dogs would be thrashed to make them howl, and men would call out (*kup*) and, *segen gamut*, beat the slit-gong (*garamut*). The noise was made "so that the moon's light would return," or "so that the moon looks back, and does not go away." It was said that the moon had tried to follow "the sun's road" (identified with *kubu*, "the smoke"—i.e. the Milky Way), which is too hot for it, and must be called back lest it burn up completely (an allusion, probably, to the dull red glow of refracted atmospheric light that suffuses the moon in total eclipse).

In earlier times the consequences seemed even more catastrophic. The moon, in one version, is a woman, and when it goes into eclipse its deep red color goes to the women, causing

---

accord, familiar from the Trobriand area. There is a kind of yam, called *balus*, which is said to send its "head" above the ground to peer about, like the periscope of a submarine. If the coast is clear, the yam will emerge and walk about at night.

their menstrual bleeding. (This does not mean that menstrual flows necessarily occur during or after eclipses, but that the eclipsed moon "pictures"—*a baliklik de pere tege*—or exemplifies the bleeding of the women.)[7] Were the eclipsing moon allowed to "die" altogether, the account continues, all women would also die out, and only men would be left. Hence women would call out the ancient name for the moon, *intugalapit*,[8] to "call it back" during an eclipse.

A cycle of six named lunations seems to have been recognized, and used in conjunction with gardening, in pre-European days, though it is no longer used or even generally known at present. According to my informant,[9] the Barok of the precontact period had not even suspected the possibility of a longer (twelve-month) calendric cycle; speaking of the number of cycles in a year, he commented that "we thought there was only one, but the evangelists came and taught us there were two." After contact with the mission evangelists,[10] the traditional calendar was amended to include twelve months, retaining only the name of the first lunation of the Barok stellar year, Marana-kai, and merely numbering the remaining eleven (*sesion ninong ni tege*, "the second of the moon"; *sesion narun ni tege*, "the third of the moon"; and so forth). The lunations of the original cycle, in the order in which they were given to me, are shown in Table 2.

[7] The implicit suggestion of a connection between female sexuality, via the lunar cycle, and garden fertility might receive some support from a variety of "power" made during tuber planting. An *orong* would dress in female attire, lime on his face, and, shouting spells, throw tuber cuttings around the garden while another man would throw down tubers in a great hurry.

[8] An archaic name for the sun was said to be *langen*.

[9] An old man, quite disdainful of what little others could remember of the subject, he also showed an astonishing recall of many details of the German administration period.

[10] These were most likely Fijian evangelists of the Reverend George Brown's Australasian Wesleyan Methodist Missionary Society, which be-

TABLE 2. The Traditional Barok Calendar

Lunations	Coordinate Events	Gardening
Matana-aler	sun rises "in the middle"	"first garden" planted
Murung-aler	—	—
Tege ni Kuka	crab hunting	—
Tege Gowo	—	"second garden" prepared
Marana-kai	Pleiades on meridian	garden planted
Muruna-kai	Pleiades *pi la bidede**	bananas planted

* "Turn their bottom."

I was able to obtain translations for two of the names for lunations: Tege ni Kuka ("Moon of the Crabs") and Tege Gowo ("Moon That Is Left," or "Moon That Remains"). Beyond these, the comments volunteered along with the names are of some help in reconstructing the calendric operation of the gardening cycle. It would seem that Matana-aler, when the sun rises "in the middle," should correspond more or less with the equinox.

In fact Barok seem always to have noted the seasonal variation in the points-of-rising of the sun and moon, and to have coordinated this information with their other calendric observations. The northern solstice occurs when "the sun rises over Lihir and the full moon rises over Namarodu" (i.e. when they rise at the points relatively closest to these landmarks, depending upon one's position on the coast), and the southern solstice when "the sun rises over Namarodu and the full moon rises over Lihir."[11] The northern solstice is identified with the *awat ni nien*, the "year of food," or "year of

<hr>

gan operations on the Duke of York Islands in 1875. The Methodists had an important station at Kolonoboi (Lulubo) Village in the Usen area.

[11] These descriptions were given to me by natives of the east coast of New Ireland, from which both Lihir and Cape Namarodu are visible, and from which celestial objects can be seen to rise over the sea. In their sea-

plenty," and the southern with the *awat nere long*, or *sam awat*, the "year of hunger." Otherwise the sun (*gaken*) serves to mark the time of day, "sun" being "noon."[12]

The term *awat* is sidereal in the strictest sense, and its overlapping with lunar and solar reckonings testifies to the coordinate nature of the Barok calendar. It is used both in the sense of "year" and in that of "the new year" or "the turning of the year." The *awat* occurs when the *bungli* (probably a contraction of *bung-lik*, "little bunch" or "grouplet"), the Pleiades, are "on top." Since being "on top" is contrasted, in Barok sky-lore, with both "rising" and the position *pi la bidede*, "turning its bottom" (*i tanim as*), it would appear likely that one *awat* occurs at that time of our sidereal year when the Pleiades are on the meridian at sunset (as one informant suggested) or in the early hours of the evening. Since, moreover, one *awat* is identified with the traditional cycle of six lunations, and two *awat* are encompassed by the sun's annual circuit of the ecliptic, it follows that *another awat* must occur at the *opposite* time of the year—when the Pleiades are on the zenith at sunrise, or in the early hours of morning just before sunrise.[13]

How does all this relate to the gardening cycle? A precise relationship would be difficult to fix, though sufficient material is forthcoming to provide a general picture. We know that the equinox occurs sometime during Matana-aler, the third month after Marana-kai, the month of the *awat*. The Pleiades transit the meridian at 6:00 P.M. (close enough to

---

sonal determinations, west coast observers reckoned the shadow of the land cast over the sea at sunrise.

[12] "Morning" is *pugu*, "afternoon" is *gaien*, and "night" is *domun*. As elsewhere in Papua New Guinea, these terms have come to be used as greetings, in imitation of Tokpisin and ultimately English.

[13] When I interviewed him regarding this analysis in June 1983, Mr. Bubulo of Giligin, Lulubo Village, confirmed that the morning transit of the Pleiades (*long tulait*) is known to Usen. He commented that the morning transit signaled the making of the *a lua*.

Matatulet Hamlet, Bakan (1979).

At left, New Ireland from the Air. Above, a Barok Garden. Below, *Ruprup*: Breaking the Ground.

Above, Consecrated *Taun* with Heirloom
Mangin. Below, Erika Learns *Malum*.

Above, the *Bun*, a Clan Treasure. Below, the Author "Buying the Shame" of the Name "Sogang."

Above, Namatanai Town (1983). Below, *Tinie* Hut, Kolonoboi (1979).

Above, Mimetic Arm and Body Gestures, Lokon (1979). Below, *A Tinie*, Lokon (1979).

Above *Olagabo*, the "Gate of the Pig." Below, Interior of the *Gunun*.

Above, *Pan* at Karitis Hamlet, Bakan. Below, the *Konono*, or Feasting Space.

Above, Areca Nut and Green Coconuts atop a *Butam*. Below, *Da Go Baliklik*, the Women's Bake.

Above, the *Olagabo*: A Huge Pig for the Feast. Below *Ma Palas A Bo*: Laying Out the Pigs.

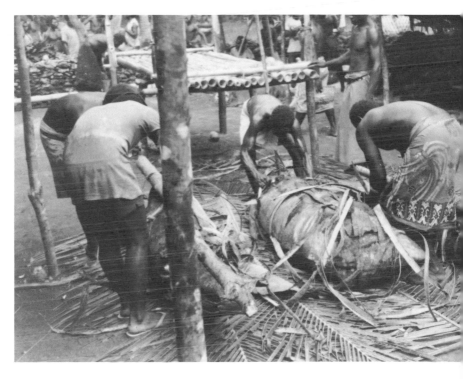

Above, Slapping a Pig at Purchase (view from *Gunun*). At left, Mr. Tabagase Talks over the Areca Nut. Below, Claiming the "Head" of the *Tunan*.

Above, Preparing the *Kun* for Bananas. Below, Sealing the *Kun*.

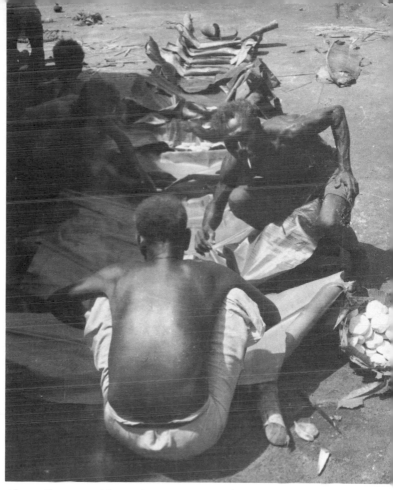

Above, Preparing *Olos*. Below, Removing *Olos* Packets from the Stone Oven.

Above, Taro "Bed" for a Feast. Below, Mr. Polos, *Orong* of Unakulis, atop Sogang's *Una Ya* at Pire.

sunset around the equinox in a near-equatorial latitude) on February 21, and are prominent near the zenith in the early hours of the evening for about a month before. They again transit the meridian at 6:00 A.M. on August 22, and are prominent in the predawn sky for a month or so afterward. If we choose January 21, when the point of sunrise is still tolerably close to Namarodu and the Pleiades transit at 8:00 P.M., as a date for the *awat*, then the following two lunations should bring us just a few days short of the March equinox, and the sun will indeed "rise in the middle" during Matana-aler. But of course this is a mere approximation—based on Western concepts of precision and timekeeping—ventured as a kind of "bracketing" of native parameters. What is more likely is that Marana-kai, a lunation, began at the new moon closest to the *awat*—anywhere from late January through the month of February—so that all of the "dates" reached in this system of reckoning were functions of the conjunction of lunar, solar, and sidereal events (and therefore quite variable). The fact that two of these factors, the solar and sidereal, as epiphenomena of the earth's rotation, are relatively constant, makes the system self-correcting to a degree. Thus the "shortfall" of about a fortnight between the cycle of six lunations and the six months between evening and morning *awat* would be more obvious at some times than at others; but the name of the final month in the series, Tege Gowo, "the one that is left," at least suggests that one could, in a pinch, add another "one that is left" until the new moon of the *awat* was reached. Thus corrected by its sidereal component, the calendar could then incorporate the September equinox within its third lunation.[14]

---

[14] According to Ms. Marianne George, a "line of stars" called Dako, running along the Milky Way ("the sun's road") in the northern sky, transiting the meridian on August evenings, is taken on the west coast as a sign of the *mamat*, and as a signal to begin planting. It serves, according to Mr.

Industrious gardeners though they may be, the Barok do not (and probably never did) make four gardens a year, so the comments on gardening accompanying the lunation cycle deserve qualification. Fortunately, both the words of informants and my own observation can be of help here. Although the association of planting with certain lunations must invariably lead to some ambiguity no matter what the actual arrangements, and although the ambiguity of the earlier system was doubtless compounded, for purposes of reconstruction, by the adaptation to a twelve-month cycle, it is clear that only two gardens were made during a standard (Western) year. The "first garden," *a lua*, was made during a "time of food" (*awat ni nien*), after the northern solstice; that is, at the Matana-aler of the September equinox, or, as my informants volunteered, simply "in September." This was to provide sustenance for the planting of the larger garden; but, as a small garden, it would yield considerably less food. It takes at least six months for a garden to ripen, and it is said that the "second garden," *a sinam*, was planted at "the hungry time" (less than six months after the September planting) of the *labur*, just after the (evening) *awat*, but before the Pleiades *pi la bidede*. This would be in January or early February, as the Barok themselves affirm, and would take advantage of the torrential rains of the northwesterly monsoon for the largest crop. In traditional terms, then, we could surmise that the "first garden" was planted in the Matana-aler following the morning *awat*, and the "second garden" (begun, perhaps, in the Tege Gowo immediately preceding) was planted during the Marana-kai after the evening *awat*.

If this assumption is correct, then it is not difficult to see why my informant chose to begin his series of lunations with

Bubulo, as an evening correlate of the morning *awat*. Dako would seem to correspond with the long axis of our constellation Cygnus.

Matana-aler rather than with Marana-kai, the "first" month. For Matana-aler marks the planting of the "first garden," and this sequence provides the best illustration of the use of the calendar to regulate gardening. No garden is planted during the Matana-aler of the following *awat* (March), for then the largest garden, the *sinam*, is already in the ground!

Modern Barok would seem to retain the rhythms of this system, as well as some of its ideology. The largest gardens made during my fieldwork were planted in late January and early February, and most older men could readily recount the injunctions about planting when the *bungli* are on the meridian (significantly, in the evening), and leaving off planting (or planting bananas) when they *pi la bidede*. So it has been the *sinam*, like Marana-kai and its (evening) *awat*, that survived evangelism and the modification of the calendar.

For some Usen Barok, at least, the heavens still model the gardening cycle, however anecdotally. What is intriguing, however, is the degree to which sky-lore is in turn modeled (again anecdotally) upon gardening, the food quest, and the preparation and consumption of food. The full moon, *tege gudun* or *tege ben*, is heralded as a sign of plenty: people say, *O, a tege ben* (There is good food, our food is plenty"). The crescent, half or gibbous moon is the *subuna tege*. When the young crescent moon appears tilted in the sky, the direction toward which it tilts (the side on which "its mouth is heavy") is said to have food, whereas that toward which the horn is raised is supposed to suffer famine. A level crescent indicates universal abundance.

The predawn appearance of Venus is called the *sorotonoe*, "deceiver of the fish traps." This image dates to the days when youths were secluded in a small house on the beach and given instruction in the use of a fishtrap (*a tonoe*) incorporating a vine with long needles. The brilliant "morning star" led them to believe that dawn had arrived, and they would put out the traps too soon, so that sharks would take the fish before they could get to them. The difficult and elusive Mercury is also known, from its morning appearance just before sunrise, as *tinan*. The appearance of Venus as an "evening star" is sometimes known as *sili-lagon*, "giving light to Lagon," alluding to an anecdote in which the women of a clan of this name used the illumination to flatten taro tubers so they might be cooked in *sumo* packets. More commonly, and vulgarly, however, the postsunset Venus is called *burbur tapis* ("fearing flatulence"), the "star" that goes away quickly to avoid the flatulence of the men, settling down after their large evening repast. The imagery of the food quest is borne out, rather diffusely, among the few fixed stars that can claim a general recognition. The three conspicuous stars forming Orion's Belt are known as the *tala narun*, the "three canoeists," and the somewhat sketchier asterism (including the Great Nebula) that we call Orion's Sword is the *tala narun a une*, the "three female canoeists." The star Sirius, also nearby, is *ku*, "the pigeon."

Elicitation and Ethos

The cycle of gardening and food production, on one hand, and the movements of celestial bodies, on the other, stand as controlling analogies for one another. Because food production plays a central role in gender relationships, in defining and realizing the moral complementarity of men and women, however, the *awat* is something more than a mere speculative analogy. As a means of correlating concerted human activity through the observation of external events, and of focusing human concern on an image of productivity in the process, it becomes in fact a means of eliciting, or indirectly bringing about, the social and moral relationships of gardening.

The *awat* is a part of the complex of usages that Barok call *kastam*, along with their moiety organization, kin restrictions, and the protocol and symbolism associated with feasting in the men's house. Introduced here in the context of gardening, the *awat* provides a first example of the role of *kastam* in eliciting the significant relationships of Barok culture. The following sections of this work will consider the ways in which such elicitation occurs: first with respect to social and kin relationships; then, following a discussion of the centrality of the nonverbal, perceptual image in Barok ideas of spirit "power" and efficacy, with respect to the imagery of formal feasting in the men's house.

The object of elicitation is a pervasive, fairly self-conscious ideal or standard of comportment and interpersonal relationship that I shall call "ethos." For Usen Barok, this ideal or standard is vested in the range of recognized kin relationships, and in the more abstract ethics that they call *malum* and *malili*; they generalize the concept most often by using the English loanword "respect" (the Barok equivalent is a transitive verb, *yii*). Although it furnishes a criterion for morality, the Barok ethos is intrinsically "public" and relational; the enactment of *malum* or *palik* (the heavy joking that takes place between certain relatives) makes no sense when carried on in solitude.

If we follow Geertz's definition of a people's ethos as "the tone, character, and quality of their life, its moral and aesthetic style and mood,"[15] and consider that this tone, character, and quality takes on a special inflection when it is made self-conscious, then perhaps a brief characterization of Usen Barok ethos might help prepare the reader for the ensuing account of its elicitation.

It was several months after I had settled in at Bakan Village and begun my work that I came to a rather disquieting realization: although my children and I had been accepted in the village, and although we had made many friends, I had never seen the inside of a village house. And no one, with the exception of a very good friend (and he had hovered near the door), had made so bold as to enter the semiopen "dining

---

[15] Geertz, *The Interpretation of Cultures*, p. 127.

area" of our two-room house. This seemed unusual to me because, during my earlier fieldwork in the highlands, I had been welcomed into every dwelling in the village (and had come to habituate several) within the first week. Even more unsettling was the realization that it had taken me so long to notice this, that I had learned and internalized a code of expectations apparently without conscious effort.

Usen Barok generally referred to their avoidance of dwelling houses in the context of certain (affinal) kin protocols, which forbid one to enter the house, go beneath the house, or even touch or pass beneath the drying laundry of certain categories of relatives. Similar kin avoidances are, to be sure, found elsewhere in New Ireland. But among the Barok they seem to be extended more widely, and so the more general comment on the subject, that houses are avoided out of respect for the person, seems to fit the situation better. At all events, persons—whether man, woman, or child—simply do not go into the house of another, unless they are intimate companions (Tokpisin *poroman*) or members of a young, unmarried age set.

Modern Barok houses generally consist of two or three rooms, built a meter or so above the ground, on pilings, or else with an earthen floor. They are made for the most part with "bush materials," woven, split-bamboo walls on a pole framework with a half-pitch roof of corrugated iron (*kapa*) or of sago leaf or kunai grass thatch. A smaller, earthen-floored cookhouse is generally built nearby. Although the main house may or may not have a roofed veranda, one of the rooms is invariably what I shall call an "open room," with a wide outer doorway and large open spaces in lieu of windows in the other walls. The open room serves as a sort of informal sitting area for the family, and may be visited by an outsider "who has come for a very definite purpose." The closed rooms, used for sleeping and storage, are never visited.

The dwelling house (*a gunun*) is a very visible sanctum of personal inviolability, to be approached by a nondweller with caution and formality. Any assertive or aggressive intentions displayed by a nondweller in its vicinity are understood as violations of the inhabitants' personalty. One may not, for instance, go to a house—particularly that of someone in another clan—and, without explaining the reason or excusing oneself, shout at or strike a child or spouse. This would be interpreted as anger against all those present, or those of the house, and would cause them great shame. It would, indeed, oblige the *offended* parties to "buy" their shame by presenting the offender with a length of *mis*. An incident of this sort that occurred during my stay at Bakan created a considerable scandal (it was one of a number of events that caused witnesses, according to their idiom, "such shame that I was unable to sleep all night"), and ultimately found its way into the village court.

Another, unrelated scandal, quoted here from my field notes, provides an illustration of how the "shame" of entering a house is treated in this court, which adjudicates strictly according to local, traditional custom:

A youth from the offshore island of Tangga was brought to Bakan by a local lineage head. But the youth did not stay with him; he wandered about, living some of the time at Kolonoboi, and sometimes with P—— and his family in the main camp at Bakan. P——'s wife's sister, a schoolgirl of 11 or 12, was said to have "aroused the belly" of the youth by standing on a rock above him while he was bathing. Encouraged by this, the young man went in the evening to a nearby house, where the schoolgirl was staying with a high-school student on vacation. The youth bolted the door of their sleeping room from the outside, then climbed in the window and hid beneath the girl's bed. When she lay down to sleep, the girl sensed his presence and called out. The older girl turned her flashlight beneath the bed and discovered the youth, who struggled out and managed to escape through a window. He went to Karitis Hamlet, where he slept in the *taun* for a week without eating, feigning illness to cover his shame. The magistrate, hearing the case in the village court, fined the youth 50 *kina* for entering the house and 2 *kina* for his attempt on the girl. The youth went to Kolonoboi to try and find money with which to pay the fines, but was charged again for some bottles of water he had drunk at the *kaba* at Lokon, and had failed to pay for. A village woman married to a local expatriate finally paid his fines, and allowed him to work off the money by building a pig enclosure. Then the youth left for Tangga, ordered out of the village.

Perhaps the severity of the fine, in this case, resulted from the youth's violation of the sleeping room. But even the open room, that frontier of personal propriety, has its moral accounting. Who visits there, what they do there, and how long they stay are carefully noted and speculated upon. When a young Daribi laborer, whom I had befriended at Karimui many years before, took several meals with my family in our open room, it was tactfully suggested that he might sleep and take his meals henceforth in the *taun* of my clan, lest he place an undue strain on my resources.

Person, family, and clan are surrounded by an invisible wall of reserve and sanction, objectified in the dwelling house and its immediate surroundings, and extended to an ultimate, and ceremonial, significance in the case of the *taun* and its circumambient spaces. These spatial constraints are but the physical projection of a thoroughgoing regime of behavioral taboos, an emphatic "marking" and exaggeration of the boundaries of human action. The sense of exaggeration is not diminished when we turn from the heightened respect exacted by some protocols to the avoidance or heavy joking demanded by others: all are equally means of marking, provocation—and elicitation. Exaggerating the seriousness or nonseriousness of a place, person, or action is a style of social rhetoric and motivation that is perhaps found universally in human kin relations; among the Usen Barok it is the fundamental means of eliciting social ethos. The moieties, to which we shall now turn, are central to that elicitation.

THREE

Moiety and Relationship:
The Core of *Kastam*

THE CORE of Usen Barok *kastam*, in its conceptual as well as
behavioral elicitation of ethos, is the system of mutually and
dialectically opposed moieties, and the system of key relationships that their existence and interaction bring about.
The moieties are counterposed against one another in a con-
flictive and even paradoxical manner: each claims the absolute propriety of its own matrilateral membership, but also
claims the inception and nurturance of the membership of the
other—"what's mine is mine, and what's yours is negotia-
ble." The moieties are mothers to their own, and fathers to
each other; they both contain and nurture, and in the final
stages of the *kaba*, when the nurturance of containment is
shown to be the same thing as the containment of nurturance, the hierarchical claims of one over the other are finally
established. The moieties stand in a relation of asymmetrical
and perpetually unresolved hierarchy to one another.

This stance, and its competitive implications, are scarcely
incidental; they are rather the means, the definitional "load-
ing," by which the elicitation takes place. And the elicitation,
rather as in Bateson's concept of "schismogenesis," is a matter of challenge and response, of how the actor or actors rise
to the situation posed by an alter. It is for the most part (except insofar as words are used in cues and explanations) nonverbal, dependent upon learned responses and "self-reveal-

49

ing" images. The behavioral core is a matter of the differentiating elicitation of kin relationship (respect, joking, and avoidance); the ritual and conceptual elicitation and resolution is a matter of iconographic image—most especially that of the feast in the men's house. But the same dualistic mechanism pervades and governs both modes of elicitation. A comprehensive discussion of moieties in their elicitation of ethos will occupy much of the present work; in this chapter, I shall address the eliciting of specific kin relationships and the recognized ethical modes *malum* and *malili*.

Usen Barok share a system of exogamous moieties, as well as the specific "totemic" designators of those moieties, with their Mandak and Sokirik neighbors, and with many peoples of south and central New Ireland and adjacent New Britain. Usen call their moieties Malaba (*bik pisin*, "the big bird" in Tokpisin) and Tago (*smol pisin*, "the smaller bird"); Malaba is the white-bellied sea eagle (*Haliaetus leucogaster*, Tokpisin *manigulai*), sometimes featured, with his magical pig, in folktales. Tago (Tokpisin *taranggau*) is a white-headed sea hawk, possibly[1] the Brahmany kite (*Haliastur indus*). In addition to these birds of prey, the moieties are sometimes identified with distinctive traits (Malaba people have three creases on the palm of the hand, Tago people four) or with other natural species (Malaba with a large white butterfly; Tago with the *roro*, the splendid *Ornithoptera* butterfly).

Each moiety claims to nurture and vivify the other, to be, literally, its creator; and each also claims and contains the nurturance of the other as its own, by act of uterine birth, containment in the clan lands or *taun* (or within the protection of its *tadak* spirit), and, most significant of all, in the mortuary feasts and the final incorporation by burial of the body in the *taun* enclosure. The ritual containment enacted

[1] Clay, *Pinikindu*, p. 36, identifies Erangam, the Mandak equivalent, as *Pandion leucocephalus*.

in the men's-house feast serves ultimately as the culture's rite of validation, but this ritual may be used to validate paternal as well as maternal successorship. In the end the moieties cannot adjudicate or settle things; they are less a means of organization than one purely of elicitation.

Cross-Moiety Relationships

Usen Barok are conscious of relationship as such, and recognize a number of terms for specific relationships. Most of these are specifically linked to kinds of kinsmen, though there are also more abstract ethics, such as *malum* and *malili*, which will be considered at the conclusion of the present chapter. Barok people consider these relationships to entail certain restrictions, or limits, in the nature of taboos or constraints on behavior. In approaching the Barok relational system as the elicitation of ethos, I shall consider the various relationships as being brought about, differentiated, and also actualized by and through the taboos and constraints associated with them. Certainly, I think, the relationships are learned in this way by individual Barok as they grow up, and Barok also learn to associate particular sets of restrictions with particular named relationships, and with particular individuals. Thus a certain adult woman, my adoptive sister, was presented to my children: "This is your *tau*; she can look after you with good food. You must never call her anything but *tau*."

Anthropologists have traditionally approached kin relationships as consequences of given consanguineal or affinal connections, facts that are said to be the same in every culture because human beings everywhere recognize something like marriage, have mothers, fathers, siblings, and so forth. The generalized frame of reference provided by a range of relatives has thus served anthropology as a point of comparison among the varying modes of cultural kin categorization.

Such a standard of comparison certainly makes things easier for the comparativist; the difficulty is that it can also misrepresent the cultural emphases of the people under study. *Their* "facts" of relationship may be different from our standard assumptions; their emphases may be different from ours, to the point of regarding relationships, rather than relatives, as the basic factor. I shall, accordingly, note the "genealogical intercepts" of the relationships discussed here, for purposes of identification, and also make use of English relational terminology, except where the use of Barok terms is advisable for conceptual reasons or in order to familiarize the reader with them.

Writers such as A. R. Radcliffe-Brown and his followers in the "functionalist" approach promoted a conception of kinship and kin relationship as a kind of juridical institution, a basis of legal order grounded in the rights of persons over other persons, or in rights regarding property. This may not seem very different from kin relationship as "the core of *kastam*." But there is a real difference in the respective priorities assigned to "relatives" as against "relationships": if relatives are taken as invariant "facts," then "kinship" is the charter that a particular culture has made of those facts, and the special characteristics of relationships are of secondary importance. For Radcliffe-Brown and his followers, such features as joking, respect, and avoidance were seen as functional correctives, to ease the stresses and strains brought about in an *already existing* system of rights and privileges; they were derivative devices, applied within an institution to keep things running smoothly. If, however, we take relationship and its nuances as of primary significance, as in the elicitation of ethos, then the characteristics of relating can scarcely be derivative "functions." We are concerned with the way in which the "charter" itself is generated.

Relationship, in very much the sense in which I use it here, has been a central concern in the work of Gregory Bateson.

Among a number of insights into the subject communicated in his writings, the approach taken in his paper "A Theory of Play and Fantasy"[2] is remarkable for its simplicity and directness. Commenting on the play of nonhuman animals, he notes "the bite that is not a bite" as an example of play behavior, for an attempted bite that turns out to be a playful nip negates its ostensible intention, and relays what Bateson calls a "metamessage" about the character of the interaction. It conveys the message "this is play," that "these actions in which we now engage do not denote what those actions *for which they stand* would denote."[3] Play, then, is paradoxical, for it sets out to violate a relationship, and succeeds in affirming or even establishing the relationship through the negation, or failure, of that violation.

How does this work in a human situation? As among animals, joking that is appropriately *accepted* works upon the context, or "frame," of the interaction. A dig in the ribs, a just-sufficiently uncouth word at the right time, hazards or ventures the possibility of a relationship sufficiently close and trusting that this kind of violation can be accepted. And the other, to whom the venture is made, is given the opportunity either to affirm the "framing" relationship by taking the joke as a joke, or to deny the relationship by taking the "violation" seriously. Every trying or hazarding of a relationship in this way leads to its renegotiation, and the normative means of elicitation, the taboos and restraints customarily imposed in kin protocols, are the techniques by which the renegotiation is effected.

The range of changes that can be rung on this essentially simple principle, its transformations, permutations, and elaborations, are comprehensive through a broad cross-section of human and nonhuman activity. Bateson observes that such

---

[2] See Bateson, *Steps to an Ecology of Mind*, pp. 177-93.
[3] *Ibid.*, p. 180.

ploys as deceit, bluff, threats, responses to threats, and histrionic actions can all be seen as forms of a single phenomenon. We can also see relationships involving an exaggerated respect or avoidance as examples of this phenomenon, for the particular form of emphasis through which the relationship is hazarded—the manner in which the gauntlet, so to speak, is thrown down—is less important than the fact that it *is* hazarded. Suppose, instead of testing my relative's indulgence (and commitment to our relationship) by venturing a playful violation, I demand of him, under the appropriate circumstances, an exaggerated degree of respect. My relative has the option of yielding to my demand, and affirming the relationship, or of rejecting the demand and calling the relationship into question. And avoidance, which substitutes the pose of not interacting for the attempted violation of joking, or for the exacting distortion of respect, offers the same option for testing and renegotiation.

Relationship is elicited by challenges that force it into consciousness and set up its renegotiation; the most vulgar and unseemly conduct, or, under the appropriate circumstances, the most circumspectly *proper* conduct, can serve as a challenge. To the degree that others respond to the challenge, and in the manner that they respond, the elicited relationship can be seen as affirmed, or at least as commented upon in such a way that the relationship is tacitly acknowledged. Whether a relationship is initiated in this manner, or sustained, or perhaps reinstituted or taken up again, is less important than the fact that all such constitutive ploys are a means to its continual re-creation.

There are three major modes of cross-moiety relationship among the Usen Barok: those involving marriage, *nat* (or paternity), and the *naluwinin* relationship. They are centered, respectively, around avoidance, respect, and joking, and—given the fact that they follow a temporal progression, paternity following upon marriage, and the cross-consanguineal links of *naluwinin* upon paternity—the succession from comparative restriction to comparative familiarity bespeaks a certain order, or continuity. Let us consider cross-moiety relationships in that order.

All Barok of normal birth belong by birth to the moiety of their mothers, and moieties are strictly exogamous. The breach of moiety exogamy is called *leges*. Those guilty of marriage within their own moieties are subject to social disapproval and humiliation: their names, as well as all kin terms, are not used, and they are simply addressed and referred to as *leges*. The usages through which the ideal of forbearance, or *malum*, is elicited between the moieties, are also dropped, and each member of a *leges* union is required to "buy the shame" of his or her act with ten *pram* of *mis* or a pig. It is said that in traditional times *leges* was punished by public strangulation. Children of a *leges* marriage would automatically be assigned to the opposite moiety and would be called by name alone, without recourse to kin terminology.[4]

In declassing offenders from kin relationship and from *malum*, *leges* amounts to a kind of punitive inversion of the avoidance that normatively plays a constitutive role in Usen marriage. Instead of eliciting a relationship by carefully heeding certain prohibitions, *leges* are placed in an ostracism wherein the terms and actions that would ordinarily serve to elicit relationship must themselves be avoided. Avoidance, for *leges*, becomes an end rather than a means to an end.

What is the appropriateness of avoidance, per se, to marriage and affinal relationships? A link can be seen in the privilege of option, or preferment, the right (often bargained for) to marry a certain person. In this respect a bride, for instance, is given over as against the possibility of *not being given*. Avoidance, eliciting a relationship through not "relating" in

---

[4] Children of a *leges* marriage are distinguished from illegitimate children, *naron ni ngas* ("brothers of the road") who are treated with a more covert disapproval.

certain respects—relating by demurral—is the opposite of preferment, and its appropriateness as a means of elicitng the affinal relationship (as against joking) is that of "marking" or encoding the favor of preferment within the relationship itself. By not speaking with, not imposing upon, not mentioning, or even totally avoiding the benefactors involved in the gesture of preferment, one elicits the spontaneity of granting the preferment again and again.

Traditionally, Usen Barok marriage is contracted through betrothal, or else at the initiative of the woman. Marriage partners are not specified by category of previous relationship, though an alliance strategy between clans (to be discussed later) involves marriage within the *goko* and *nawiligen* relationships. The right of a man to betroth his daughter to his own maternal uncle (her *goko*) is recognized, though this *should* be done only when the prospective groom has no siblings (left), and needs someone to look after him. The exchange of sisters between men as wives (*kinis ne wunuwuo*, "reciprocating the sitting down") is not only acceptable, but is deemed highly appropriate. Bride price is given in sister exchange, though the amount is less than what is given otherwise.[5]

A daughter may be "promised" (*konge-wi*, "pointed out") to a man as a future wife by placing her on top of his head. This practice is called *olo-wi*, and a promise or request made in this way may not be refused.[6] A betrothal may also be contracted through the presentation of *mis* by the father of the

[5] Elopement with a woman without the permission of her line would expose a man to the invective of his wife's people, and he would be obliged to "buy" her with two or three *pram* of *kuwas mis*.

[6] Often among Barok drinking together, a man's *tamasik* ("brother-in-law") will offer him a bottle of beer after first placing it on top of his own head. Refusal would be tantamount to touching the head or skin of the *tamasik*, something that is explicitly forbidden. Should the refusal occur, the giver could draw a charcoal streak down his forehead, which would not be removed until the refuser had paid him however much he might request.

prospective husband to the father of the girl. This "tabooing" of a future bride, as Barok like to put it, is called *isik-pi*, "fastening the gift," and it involves a *pram* of valuable *kuwas mis*, which is later discounted from the amount required for the bride price.

Although marriage by betrothal is seldom practiced at present, negotiation is still a factor in the arrangement. Barok prefer marriage partners to be roughly equal in age and experience. A woman who wishes to marry a man will choose one of his age-mates or confreres (*a ile go losarige*) as an intermediary. The intermediary may approach the man directly, or go to his *orong* and request that he assemble the payment. The man's *orong* (his maternal uncle or lineage head) will assemble the *mis* at his house and transfer it to the *orong* of the woman (at a later time the husband is expected to find the *mis* with which to make restitution to his *orong*; often others will contribute).

The bride price, *mangin ni kun balikilik*, or *mangin ni kun une*, consists of payments for *kunu minenge* ("buying the shame") of various relatives of the bride, and *kun tus* ("buying the milk") for the nourishment given her daughter by the bride's mother. In the minimal case, as between parties to a sister exchange, one *pram* apiece of *mangin dek* will go to the brother(s) and maternal uncle of the bride as *kunu minenge*, and one *pram* to her mother, as *kun tus*. Otherwise, the traditional payment for a bride is understood to be about five *pram* of *mis*, and at present this is supplemented with 300 to 500 Papua New Guinea *kina*.

The bride's people reciprocate with a payment, generally smaller, called *ta lar* or *tin tar*. It is given to "open the clan" to the new bride, and to "end all worry," and also to pay (in advance) for the care and support she can expect from her husband's line. The *ta tar* includes the *lege marami* (one *pram* of *mis* given by the bride herself to her husband's *orong*, to pay for her right to enter the husband's *taun*) and

57

the *ta tar* proper (sometimes called *ine belaure*), payments to "buy the shame" of the husband's relatives. Generally this involves a *pram* of *mis*, given to the husband's sister, and varying amounts to his other relatives.[7]

Nothing could be more misleading than to imagine that these arrangements are carried out automatically, or in a programmatic way. Usen Barok say that a man should conceal his marriage choice and that, when a man marries, his wife should not come quickly to his house. Often enough the exchanges are not made until after the couple has been living together for some time, or even until the birth of several children to the union.

Avoidance, in other words, extends to the admission of the fact of marriage itself; it is a "taboo" subject. For the Usen Barok, as in Tokpisin generally, affinal kin are *tambu*, that is taboo, people. [8] The most crucial relationships, those involving the spouse's parents and siblings, are elicited by an almost total avoidance. The most highly restricted of these are the *nataon* relationship, between a man and his wife's mother, which precludes any sort of bodily contact and requires name and general proximity avoidance, and the *na-inison* relationship, relating a woman to the spouse's matriline (and a man to a "matriline" spouse) via the *"orongship"* of the maternal

---

[7] The exchange of *ta tar* (and of the bride price) should ideally occur at a feast given on the occasion of bringing the bride to the groom, called *a eni erili*, or sometimes just *tin tar*. The groom's line kills a pig and cooks it, providing vegetables; the bride's line should provide at least some food also. The bride's people should also contribute all the things used by a woman: tongs, tools, cuttings for planting food crops, and coconut shoots. Most important, however, is a small, live pig given or promised by the bride's people to the groom. The pig is to be raised by the husband so that he may sell it when it matures and use the profits to repay his *orong* for the "loan" of the bride price, as well as to repay his wife's line for the piglet.

[8] *Tambu*, of course, means both "affine" and "taboo" in Tokpisin, and probably for good reason. The Usen words *tamasik* and *tamtam* (a mortuary food taboo) are probably cognate with the Tokpisin term, and with each other.

uncle. (Recall that it is a woman's *inisote*, her husband's maternal uncle, who provides her bride price.) In addition to a name taboo, a man cannot eat food that has been carried by his (female) *inisote*, and may not walk beneath her house floor, her serving basket, her carrying basket, or her clothes hanging on the line. As the same restrictions apply to man and his maternal uncle's wife, and as it is generally felt that no man called *orong* should be allowed to sit beneath baskets or clothing, the explicit nature of this restriction seems to acknowledge the maternal uncle's status as the *"orong"* of his sister's children.

Usen Barok affinal relationships are listed in Table 3. Barok tend to consider relationship as a reciprocal, encompassing condition, and to treat the individual kinsperson as somewhat of an accessory to that condition. The "reciprocal" sense of a relationship (for the minimal two parties) is distinguished by the prefix *na*, the "plural reciprocal" (for three or more parties) sense by the prefix *ba*, and the final, or "exhaustive reciprocal" (all those in the relationship) by the prefix *bunbun*. The individual kinsperson is indicated by an often variant form with the suffix *ke* or *te* (*re*) added.

In addition to the parties to the marriage itself (terms for spouse or co-spouse, the latter involving instances of polygyny or polyandry in which two inseparable same-sex companions marry a single person), the terms include their parents, siblings, and maternal uncles. This list is practically coterminous with the set of persons involved in the bride-price payments and their reciprocation: the two *orong*, maternal uncles who respectively give and receive the payments, and the close kin of bride and groom whose "shame" is bought via the component payments of the bride price. In particular it is those closest to the bride, linked to the groom in the *nananan, namaraton, nataon,* and *nanumunin* relationships, whose consideration and whose "shame" is in-

TABLE 3. Usen Barok Affinal Kin Relationships

Relationship	Singular Reference	Taboo	Genealogical Intercept
nasuon	*isuoke*	—	H, w (spouse)
naturan	*turan-ke*	—	male co-spouse
nalaba	*alaba-re*	—	female co-spouse
nananan (natamasik)	*tamasike*	name, proximity	WB, ZH (m. sp.); bw, hz (f. sp.)
namaraton	*maratoke*	name, proximity	wz, bw (m. sp.); ZH (f. sp.)
nataon	*taon-te*	name, touching, proximity	wm; DH (f. sp.)
nanumunin	*numuke* (m.), *numuke a une* (f.)	name, proximity	WF, wfz, DH (m. sp.); BDH (f. sp.)
nainin	*ananake*	name	hm, sw (f. sp.)
natamarin	*tamarim*	respect, careful banter	WMB, ZDH (m. sp.)
na-inison	*inisote*	name, food, clothing, position	mbw (m. sp.); zsw, HMB, HZS (f. sp.)

ABBREVIATIONS: F, "father"; M, "mother"; B, "brother"; Z, "sister"; S, "son"; D, "daughter"; H, "husband"; W, "wife"; m. sp., "male speaker"; f. sp., "female speaker." Hence WMB is "wife's mother's brother." Male referents are abbreviated in upper case, female in lower case.

volved in the preferment of her bestowal, and it is precisely those relationships that carry the most severe taboos.

An Usen Barok marriage is created and sustained through relationships whose elicitation reiterates the challenge of the initial preferment: the bride could as well *not* have been given. Marking their interactions by pointedly *not* interacting in certain specific and familiar ways, those in the relationships tacitly acknowledge the limiting condition of their relationships and, therefore, also acknowledge the relationships. The marriage itself is kept secret as long as possible, and co-residence and even payment are preferably delayed, surrounding the very act with the acknowledgment of its potential nonfulfillment.

Usen Barok feel that a man has precedence and authority within a marriage; they say that this is because he has given payment for his wife. He thus has the option to determine the postmarital residence of the couple, and very often the residence is virilocal (this is, if not a norm, at least an *expectation* among the Usen). On the other hand, there is no real sense here, as often in the New Guinea highlands, of the necessity (or capability) of a man to *control* his wife. Should the wife try to "boss" her husband, therefore, or if she plays around and acts up at his place, the man often decides to take up residence at her (parents') place, because people there can hold her to her duty. By virtue of his authority over the woman he marries, a man is often spoken of as the *orong* of the women who marry her brothers (women, of course, who will be in his own moiety). This distinction has a special force if his wife's brothers' wives are living virilocally: if he should share clan affiliation with one or more of them (even broadly interpreted), he could assume the prerogatives of the women's maternal uncle(s) in those cases, and set and receive bride price for their daughters.

Marriage involves the two moieties in their role as regulators of connubial availability; they are *available* to each other, and affinal relationships are elicited through the actualization of one of the possibilities thus made available. Paternity, necessarily also a cross-moiety relationship in a system of matrimoieties, involves much more; for it establishes the claim of a moiety to what we could call the inception of the other, "causing it to arise" in the Tokpisin idiom or, in other words, creating it. The members of a moiety are all begotten by those of the other, who are "fathers" (but also paternal offspring) to it.

Usen Barok, like many other Melanesians, claim that a child is conceived by the interaction of semen (*a peʒe*) with maternal blood (*a de*). But, they say, the maternal blood cannot be menstrual blood, which is "dirty," but must be *clean* blood. A couple must have sex perhaps six or seven times, in the opinion of my informants, before the "bad" menstrual blood comes out, and "good" blood appears. The man's semen, in fact, *causes* the clean blood to arise in the woman; it is "the strength of the man" that brings it about. What is meant here is actually a notion of transubstantiation: a woman herself cannot create a child, for her blood runs; to make a child, the blood must be contained within the uterus. This is accomplished by the action of the male semen upon the female vaginal secretion, *peʒe a une* (literally "female semen"), which is turned into "clean blood," which, in turn, seals the uterus. When this occurs, the embryo (*karlo*) begins to form. If the firstborn child resembles the father in its face, people will say that the blood of the father "won out" over that of the mother, that the father worked hard, his blood was "big."

This usage of the word "blood" in a special, marked sense to refer to a father's substantial or nurturant relation to his offspring is shared with the northern Barok[9] and the Man-

---

[9] Jessep, "Land Tenure in a New Ireland Village," pp. 68-71.

dak.[10] In fact, according to my informants, "blood" (*de*) used in this way is a euphemism for "semen," which is not a "nice" word, though a woman, particularly when angry and speaking to her husband, will refer to their children as *pege te nongon*, "your semen." The phrase *e-de-re*, "of my blood," may be used either by a mother or father in reference to their children.

A more general term for paternal offspring, and one that partakes of a widespread Austronesian root, is *nat*; it is used in reference to the clan of the father, to the children fathered by men of a clan, or to one's patrimony. Thus the child of a Wutom man is *nat wutom*; of a Maranat man, whatever the child's own clan, *nat maranat*. All the children (born to other clans) of the men of a particular clan are the *nat* of that clan. A feast held by a clan to honor its *nat* is a *tabanat* ("giving to the *nat*"), and the *nat* of a particular clan are related to one another as *nat arige* ("*nat* together") or *bak arige* ("children together").

The stipulated inheritance received from one's father is one's *nat lo*, and whatever a man might promise to his *nat* in this way is inalienable from them. This might include any sort of property or possession: land, wealth, or even his *taun*. The *taun*, of course, is intrinsically linked to the lineage and clan as a ceremonial center and point of definition; to transfer a *taun* as *nat lo* is to alienate it from the clan whose *mis* decorated it at the feasts for its consecration and refurbishment, and whose members donated labor, wealth, and services to its constitution and upkeep. Thus, although a man with aspirations will often raise a *taun* at the place of his uxorilocal residence, far from the lands or dwelling areas of his clan, the alienation of even such a peripheral center will count as a substantial loss to the clan. Yet they can do nothing about it, and the fact that a man will (and frequently does) initiate such a

[10] Clay, *Pinikindu*, pp. 39-41.

transfer is emblematic of the male situation among the Usen.[11]

Nat is the dialectical counterstroke to clan and moiety, the point where moiety impinges creatively upon moiety, and where an individual, of "some other clan," bestows a line of offspring upon a clan. It would be fair to say that everything that a clan or moiety *contains*, in its grand icon of containment, the *taun*, amounts in one sense or another to the proffered nurturance, the *nat*, of the other moiety; but it is equally true that *nat* can realize itself only within and through matriliny. A *taun*, or any sort of property given as *nat lo*, simply passes from one matriline to another, and the father who deeds it over never has any expectation to the contrary; the inheritance never becomes "patrilineal," for instance.

The authoritative role of the father within his marriage and family is very much the same thing as the effect of his substance in conception: he is the outsider who organizes and commands the family, as his substance, which does not itself block the uterus, acts upon his wife's substance to cause it to seal the uterus and begin conception. And yet the fulfillment of his role as father, should he decide to honor it to the utmost, occurs at the expense of his own matrilineage; for, to the extent that he enriches his *nat*, he impoverishes his matriline. The contingency in which a man, as father, acts is that of being a benefactor to those under his own authority, rather than a resource to those under another man's; the mode of elicitation toward this role, or contingency, is that of grateful respect.

This respect characterizes the two principal relationships

[11] The Unakulis *taun* at Bakan, with which I was associated, was thus transferred by Sumati, of Maranat Clan, in his terminal illness in 1973, to his *nat*. They "thanked" him, while he was still alive, with a large *mile nien* payment. There were numerous other instances of *taun* transferred in this way.

associated with *nat: narama*, with the male father (and his brothers); and *nawiligen*, with the *tau* (or *un tamana*), the "female father," or paternal aunt. The relationships are alike in that the parental role involves nurturance and support: "My *tau* is my father; she can care for me with good food, and she can find food for me." A man inherits his father's responsibility to look after his *tau*. But it is also true that the father's sister is subject to the authority of another man besides father, and bears children for another clan—that of father's birth. Although she shares his nurturant role, she has neither the freedom nor the motivation that father has to favor her *nat*. A *tau* is to be respected, and the term *tau* must be used in place of her name, but the appropriate elicitation of a relationship with her must acknowledge and incorporate the ambivalence of her situation. It is a violable relationship, and so it is renegotiated as against the possibility of violation, through joking and the "snatching" of property.

The issue of paternal nurture is seemingly resolved by indemnifying exchanges made upon the death of the father by the Mandak and the northern Barok. Brenda Clay suggests that a final indemnification for nurture extended across unit boundaries is made in the *embinou-egursay* payment of a pig, and in the smaller monetary payments, *erutuma* or *erumu* ("throwing out food"), that take place at the *ekarambis* death feast among the Mandak.[12] Owen Jessep speaks of the Barok custom of *milc nien* (likewise "throwing out food") as compensating a father's lineage for the food and care given to his children among the northern Barok, and mentions the giving of a pig as *mile nien*.[13] There is no reason to doubt the judgment of either ethnographer, nor the veracity of their informants, but the Usen Barok I spoke with regarded the payment of more than a small amount of money or *mis*

[12] Clay, *Pinikindu*, p. 118.
[13] Jessep, "Land Tenure in a New Ireland Village," p. 235ff.

as *mile nien* as an instance of Mandak influence. They spoke of *mile nien* as a payment of one *pram* of *mis* or 10 *kina* given on behalf of a deceased parent to *his or her* line by the surviving spouse and/or children.[14] In 1979, an attempt to raise *mile nien* by public contribution at a death feast at Belik scandalized most of the Usen present. We can conclude that the indemnification of paternal nurture by exchange is not a definitively important resolution of *nat* among the Usen.

Certainly it is another facet of this problem—that of reconciling paternal nurture within a well-articulated matrilineal succession—which frames the ambivalence of the joking relationship with *tau*, who must be "mother" to others even as she plays "female father" to ego. And this ambivalence reaches its climax in the third of the cross-moiety relationships we shall consider—*naluwinin*. It is for the males of father's matriline, those who stand in the line of authority and succession with father—his maternal uncles and sisters' sons—to embody and express the ambivalent implications of *nat*, in the case of a male ego. For a woman, this relationship, *naluwinin*, involves father's mother and her sisters, and fathers's sisters' daughters; though in all cases the relationship is reciprocal. *Lawuke* are persons of the same sex who are related (and sundered) by making differential—"patri" as against "matri"—claims on the same person. *Pit la ne naluwinin*, "the manner of *naluwinin*," is not simply a joking relationship; rather it is the epitome of joking relationships, and the generic term for them. The very ambivalence that characterizes the situation of *naluwinin* with respect to one another—that of people with equally valid, but structurally different, proprietary claims on the same man—becomes the means by which the relationship itself is elicited. Like the *tau*, the *lawuke's* name is tabooed, and the taboo is sanctioned by a fine of *mis*, or of a pig. Whereas *nawiligen* can

---

[14] Villagers from Bakan and Ramat claimed that the term for this payment in their area (subdialect?) is *sigorop nien* ("throwing up the food") and scorned the term *mile nien* as meaning "sour food."

and do avail themselves of one another's possessions, *naluwinin* carry this to the point of provocation and plunder: a *lawuke* does not merely appropriate an ax or a tin of fish; rather, he or she will come and take all of one's clothes, or *mis*, or even a car or radio. Revenge is considered perfectly legitimate, and is in fact the appropriate response—except that taking back one's own is considered contrary to the spirit of the relationship. One should, after a lapse of time, take something else, money for property, or one can take *lawuke* to the bar in Namatanai and get him drunk.

Usen often use the "Laur" (Patpatar "Pidgin") word *palik* in reference to either the *lawuke* or the mode of provocative interaction that the relationship has come to metonymize.[15] *Palik* behavior, characteristically the means of eliciting the *naluwinin* relationship, becomes generalized as the principal idiom for moiety interaction on ceremonial occasions, especially mortuary feasting. *Palik* is elicitative provocation and, on the most general level, in the public arena of feasting, identifies the impasse of conflicting *nut* and matrilateral obligations in *naluwinin* with the ethic of *malum*, or respectful forbearance toward those of the opposite moiety.

Persons of contrasting gender who share the circumstances of *lawuke*—the opposite sex siblings of one's *lawuke*—are in the *nagoko* or *nagogup* relationship with one, and are called *goko* or *gogup*. The dynamics of the relationship are similar to those of *naluwinin*, except that *nagogup* treat one another with somewhat more of the distance and respect that opposite-sex siblings do. *Goko* should not use one anothers' names, and should refer to one another with the kin term; in strictest terms they should not speak with one another at all, nor speak ill of one another. Though one may avail oneself of *goko*'s possessions, the restraint in the relationship prevents such "snatching" from reaching the extremes of the *naluwinin* practice.

[15] Clay, *Pinikindu*, pp. 42-43.

The message, at any rate, is clear: marriage, transformed into *nat*, develops a kind of cross-moiety kin elicitation, in which parent and sibling ties are replicated through relational combinations that combine matri and patri ties. Thus *tau*, being female, is a kind of "cross-father," and *lawuke* and *goko* play the role, as cross-cousins, of highly ambivalent "cross-siblings." The most interesting development, however, involves a man and his *goko's* children, who stand in the relationship *namurlik-gogup*, or "*gogup*-maternal uncle." More commonly, the children of a *gogup* are called *bak ni ausagit*, "children of outrageous talk," because the restraints applied to *gogup* no longer are in force here, and heavy joking, property confiscation, and even marriage become possible. But it is also said that if *nagogup* are like siblings, then the male is in the same way a maternal uncle to the children of the female, a *maruak-gogup*. Thus, in addition to a "father" and "siblings" via *palik*, or *malum*, Usen also have a "cross-maternal uncle."

One might conclude that, given father's sister acting as a kind of matriclan proxy for father, Usen Barok "play" the set of crucial authority and family roles—father, maternal uncle, and siblings—through the cross-moiety dimension as a form of fictive kinship. Ambivalent and seemingly derivative as these relationships may be, however, they are certainly not fictive. They are grounded in the claims of *nat* and, ultimately, in the claims each moiety makes to the inception of the other. And given the necessary dialectical tension between the moieties—the fact that what each moiety must ultimately "contain" as its own can only be the nurture of the other—the relationships developed around *nat* are as basic, and as real, as any in the society.

Same-Moiety Relationships

I have presented these obviously "made" relationships of affinity, and the apparently "fictive" ones of *nat*, in order to exemplify an important point: that there are no kin relationships that are not "made" or "fictive" in the sense that they must be learned, and their motivations renegotiated, by purely cultural means. "Basic" matrilineal relationships, such as those with the mother, sister, and maternal uncle, are as much derived from, and developed out of, the relationships of *nat* as the latter are based on them.

In his introduction to *Matrilineal Kinship*, David M. Schneider observes that matrilineal descent groups depend for their continuity and operation on maintaining control over their male and female members.[16] He goes on to state that this dependence "might be phrased as an interdependence of brother and sister."[17] Since a man depends upon his sister to perpetuate his lineage, Schneider continues, "*there is an element of potential strain in the fact that the sister is a tabooed sexual object for her brother, while at the same time her sexual and reproductive activities are of interest to him.*"[18] Taboos, of course, are the subject, and not a self-evident presupposition, of our discussion here. And although Schneider continues with the very cogent observation that respect and avoidance would serve very well in this context to minimize the strain between brother and sister, it also becomes apparent that, in this respect at least, the relationship resembles those of affinity. Why not assume here, as we did in the case of affinal relationships, that the avoidance is the means of eliciting the relationship, rather than a device for avoiding conflict? As such, it might be thought of as "anti-affinity," for its object is to symbolize and realize the solidarity and common interests of brother and sister as against their necessarily separate marital destinies. As the wife's mother, for instance, is avoided on behalf of someone else, namely her daughter (and the preferment of her daughter),

[16] Schneider and Gough, *Matrilineal Kinship*, p. 8.
[17] *Ibid.*, p. 11.
[18] *Ibid.*, p. 13. Emphasis in original.

so the sister is avoided on behalf of *her* children, her brother's heirs.

The strong affinal avoidances among the Usen make use of the fact that the bride *could* have gone to someone else as a foil or challenge against which to continually renegotiate the respective relationships; the bond between cross-sex siblings is elicited by renegotiating against a different, but analogous, sort of threat—that brother and sister are destined to be separated by their marriages. Thus two crucial avoidances control, respectively, marriage and the lineality that anchors marriage: the "shame" of the affines creates the nurturant interaction of the moieties, and the "shame" of the *sista*, or *nasiginin*, constitutes the moieties themselves.

Opposite-sex siblings, *nasiginin*, stand in a relationship of almost painful restraint, self-denial, and respectful consideration to one another, especially on the part of the male *sagake*. It is unthinkable that he should go against his sister's word or cause her displeasure. And yet any sort of bodily contact or even obvious proximity is forbidden (they must not "smell one another's skin"), and those in the relationship should not call one another, or one another's spouses, by name.

The mutual interests of brother and sister are not limited to the offspring of the woman, the man's matrilineal heirs; rather, as we have seen in the preceding section, a woman stands as *un tamana*, "female father," to her brother's children as well, and thus plays a major role in the nurturative relations of *nat*. The generative force of *nasiginin* is therefore reciprocal: brother and sister each serves as a kind of parental proxy to the children of the other, as if they were "back-to-back" parents. Father's sister, as the *tau*, represents a supple, nurturant, somewhat permissive father, whereas mother's male proxy (for her own authority is compromised by her husband's) is her children's ultimate authority figure.

The *maruam*, or maternal uncle, is spoken of as the

orong—the "boss," or ultimate holder of authority, over a person. Although the term also has a more general significance, it is noteworthy that Chinnery recorded "Orong Kanu" as the term for "mother's brother; mother's brother's daughter's husband" at the northern Barok village of Karu in 1929.[19] Qualified as *orong-iang* (perhaps "*orong*-one"), the term may also be used by a woman for her brother, despite the colloquial identification of a woman's husband as her "*orong*." The austerity and the formal, respectful tone of the *namurlik* relationship between a man and his sister's children certainly reflects the restraint and circumspection of the male role in the *nasiginin* relationship. The senior *maruake* is in this regard the converse of the *tau*, demanding obedience rather than proffering nurturance. The relationship is one of punctilious respect; and excludes familiarity; a person should respect, and obey the directives of, the maternal uncle. A woman's *maruake* sets and receives payment of her bride price; a man's *maruake* should provide the *mis* for his bride price, and may contract his marriage for him as well.

The authority of the *maruam* is "real," insofar as it involves recognized responsibilities and a sense of respect that every Usen will own up to. But it is also heavily compromised by the authority of a father over his children, and over their mother. Given that every Usen male participates in the organization of a *taun*, the icon of matrilineal containment, under the supervision of his *maruake* and perhaps a higher-ranking lineal authority, the formal aspects of the relationship lend the weight of conviction to the sense of authority. But in more realistic terms, the impression of overweening awe and respect here is the artifact of an elicitational ploy, in every way analogous to the avoidance among affines or between brother and sister, or to the joking among *naluwinin*. Exaggerated respect within the *namurlik* relationship

---

[19] Chinnery, *Studies of the Native Population*, p. 23.

71

amounts to the elicitation of responsibility within the lineage, clan, and moiety. A most punctilious respect is exacted of a person by his or her *maruake*, whether within the context of formal *taun* ritual or outside it, and the response to this elicitation, as in the case of joking or avoidance, constitutes the individual's acknowledgment of (or acquiescence in) the relationship. Respect is essential to the constitution of clan and lineage, and to the elicitation of the relationships that activate them; it is crucial to the expression of Barok ethos. Yet it should not be understood, on that account, to be more "genuine" or "social" than avoidance, as practiced between brother and sister, or than the joking of *naluwinin*.

Respect extends to, and perfuses, the *naninen* relationship with mother and her sisters, and the *naron* relationship among same-sex siblings: in both cases the sense of solidarity, nurturance, and support is more taken-for-granted, and the strain of authority less emphatic, than in the *namurlik* relationship (mother and siblings share with ego the dual authority-claims of father and maternal uncle). In the case of the maternal relationship, mother takes the role of the "nurturant" counterpart to *maruake*, as *tau* does in *nat*. Same-sex siblings, like their cross-sex counterparts, share the same matrilateral as well as *nat* relationships, a feature that both makes for a sense of solidarity and egalitarianism among them and tends to isolate them as a set. We shall return to this shortly, because it is of considerable significance structurally. The *narum* relationship is basically unrestrictive, an indulgent grandparental tie mediated with ego through some more formidable respect figure: mother, father, maternal uncle, or *tau*. (Usen Barok consanguineal kin relationships are listed in Table 4.)

A final same-moiety relationship is traced through fatherhood, itself of course a cross-moiety relationship; this is the bond that Usen call *bak' arige* ("children together") or *nat arige* ("*nat* together"), "siblings" related through the circumstances of fatherhood. Technically any person whose father is of the same clan as one's own father is one's *bak arige*; this is especially significant for those who are children of full brothers, or for men related as maternal uncle and sister's son (*namurlik*). *Bak arige* should treat one another as full siblings, using the proper terms for same-sex (*toke*) or cross-sex (*sagake*) siblings. In the case of the latter, all the restrictions bearing upon *nasiginin* are in force: they may not call one another or their spouses by name, nor approach one another, nor speak at close quarters. A person may not marry the offspring of his or her *bak arige* (though others of the clan may); and a man takes a share of the bride wealth given for female *bak arige* (about one *pram* of *mis*, or perhaps 20 *kina*), and might contribute the same amount or a bit less to the *tatar* payment made by her line. *Bak arige* may also bring pigs for one another's death feasts.

Bak arige are members of the same moiety who share a single *nat*; the strength of the bond itself may vary according to personal predilection and accessibility. The *nat* of an entire clan may be honored as a collectivity at a special feast held in their honor, called a *tabanat* ("giving to the *nat*").[20] This, however, marks the broadest *formal* extent of *nat* as a recognizable tie; its practical effect is measured by intensity. As a potential channel for the transmission of a man's entire inheritance, *nat* can acquire a significance equal to that of matrilineal connection. Even where this potential is only partially realized, the structural effect of *nat* is to segregate out the set of siblings who share (and/or suffer) in common the same combination of inheritance decisions: those of the fa-

[20] A *tabanat* is a formal feast, with many imaginative embellishments, held in a *taun* of a clan in honor of its *nat*. The *nat*, generally children or young people, are entertained, decorated, then brought to the decorated *taun* by a messenger (*ninut*) and allowed to enter on payment of a nominal fee. They are seated together in the *taun*, then feasted lavishly from an assemblage of specially marked food (clan members are feasted free of charge). Firstborn *nat* are expected to give *mis* instead of money.

TABLE 4. Usen Barok Consanguineal Kin Relationships

Relationship	Singular Reference	Taboo	Genealogical Intercept
narama	mama(re), tamam	respect	F, FB
naninen	neneke, nago(re)	—	m, mz
nawiligen	tau	name	fz, bd, BS (f. sp.)
namurlik	maruam, maruake	respect	MB, ZS, zd
naron	toke	—	B, MBSS, FZSS (m. sp.); z, mbdd, fzdd (f. sp.)
nasiginin	sagake, sagam	name, touching, proximity	z, mbsd, fzsd (m. sp.); B, MBDS, FZDS (f. sp.)
nagogup	goko, gogup	name, touching, proximity	fm, zsd, mbd, fzd (m. sp.); SS, MBS, FZS (f. sp.)
naluwinin	lawuke	(palik behavior)	FMB, ZSS, MBS, FZS (m. sp.); fm, sd, mbd, fzd (f. sp.)
narum	pupu(re)	—	mm, mmz, MMB, MF, MFB, FF, FFB, HMF/m, dsw, dd, zdd/S
namurlik-gogup	maruak-gogup	—	MMBS, MFZS; MBDS/d, FZDS/d (m. sp.)
	baroke	—	S, BS, MBDS, FZDS (m. sp.); ZS, MBSS, FZSS (f. sp.)
	balike	—	d, bd, mbdd, fzdd (m. sp.); zd, mbsd, fzsd (f. sp.)

ABBREVIATIONS: F, "father"; M, "mother"; B, "brother"; Z, "sister"; S, "son"; D, "daughter"; W, "wife"; m. sp., "male speaker"; f. sp., "female speaker." Hence MBSS is "mother's brother's son's son." Male referents are abbreviated in upper case, female in lower case.

ther and of the maternal uncle(s). A very noticeable consequence of this is the degree to which *agana*, or lineages—particularly wealthy ones—tend to isolate themselves and retain
exclusive claim to their holdings.

As generalized kin relationships, *nat* and *namurlik* (with
its attendant matri relationships) resonate the respective implications of interaction between and within the moieties in
terms of claims, prerogatives, and networks of people. But
the opposed stances of self-abnegating nurturance and containment of one's own are also capable of a more direct realization in terms of ethos, and it is to this realization, that of
malum and *malili*, that we now turn.

Malum and *Malili*

A well-educated Barok man once explained to me, as we were
waiting for a mortuary feast to begin, that the whole of Barok
public life could be summed up in the two concepts *malum*
and *malili*. *Malum* is the ethic of forbearance, of self-restraint, in respect of the bereavement of others; in more general terms, it is the "appropriate response" to any intermoiety joking, or humiliating or potentially shaming
solicitation, however harsh (and the harsher it is, the more
poignant the realization of *malum*). In the context of a death
feast, it is the moral ideal for the behavior of those of the
moiety opposite to that of the deceased. Those who have suffered the loss will "try" the moral mettle of their rivals with
various types of formal and informal hazing. *Malum* thus
epitomizes the ethical ideal of the proper response to the message "This is play," and does so in the face of an elicitation
that, in its forwardness, amounts to a veritable solicitation of
relationship.

In this respect an incident related (with a characteristically
cavalier approach to punctuation) by the labor recruiter

75

J.B.O. Mouton, from an 1892 visit to the west coast Barok village of Kokola, is most interesting:

at about six or seven in the morning there come from the north point of the bay we were in I saw about twenty or thirty natives all painted white from head to foot, brandishing spears and tomahawks dancing and coming toward us, I at once collected my boys and there we were ready for the worst then a native came to me and told me that there would be no harm coming that it was an acknowledgement for the service we did in enabling them to have a revenge against their enemies, in fact as those warriors reached us they said, malummalum malummalum and throw their spears at my feet sticking them in the ground.[21]

As a graphic enactment of forbearance this dramatic, averted onslaught amounts to a superb exemplar of what Bateson called "the bite that is not a bite."

Used outside its ethical context, *malili* refers to a calm, untroubled condition of the sea's surface, to halcyon weather. As an ideal, according to my confidant, it sums up an image of social serenity: "The belly of the people is calm, like the quiet sea." This is the peace of the orderly feast in the *taun*, where a friendly, convivial spirit of good fellowship should prevail. It is to this end that the areca nut and its condiment is distributed, freely and abundantly, at the outset of every feast, for this prized tidbit—the object of innumerable small requests, borrowings, and trades during momentary encounters in the village—brings a warm, relaxed glow to the breast. The rich food, purchased with much display before the "sitting down" of the assembled feasters, is distributed freely and equally to all, and shared convivially among knots of contented celebrants. Any disturbance, loud talking, quarreling, or unseemly conduct in the context of the feast, or in the *taun* itself, is subject to stiff fines.

[21] Biskup (ed.), *The New Guinea Memoirs of Jean Baptiste Octave Mouton*, p. 91.

Malum and *malili* are exemplary—ideals of ethos whose implications for the moral tenor of Usen life are as focal as the exemplary "publicness" of that cynosure of decorum, the *taun*. It might not be altogether inappropriate, then, to conclude my discussion of the ethical dynamic of Usen life as it began, with a circumstantial example from my fieldwork. From the time of their arrival in the village, my children, accustomed to a relatively mild and supportive relationship among playmates, were considerably rebuffed by what we might call the junior rendition of the message "This is play." For a probing, investigative dig in the ribs, or even a healthy swat from a playmate generally receives no more than a glance of acknowledgment in the elicitory ambience of Barok village play. My son, at 6 years, would either react with a tirade of assertion or seek the solace of a compassionate adult. My daughter, at 9, would respond by taking offense ("The kids all hit me!"), crying, and carrying on. Elaborate fatherly explanations in a Batesonian vein at dinnertime did little to bring understanding ("But if they want to be my friends, why do they *hit* me?"). This reaction was even self-reinforcing vis-à-vis the village children, for it became loads of fun to touch off a tantrum simply by jostling Erika in the way that everyone jostled everyone else anyway.

Erika persevered, however, and grew very fond of village food; and the women of the nearby *pan*, or ceremonial cookhouse, often obliged her with choice bits of pork fat, or with tubers steamed in coconut oil. One day, very early in the morning of a climactic memorial feast, Erika dressed in her favorite *laplap* and approached the *pan* for a share of the lavish "breakfast" prepared for the celebrants who had spent the night singing traditional *gogo* laments. On her way she encountered a fond but zealous *pupu* ("grandmother") of the opposite moiety, who, basin in hand, was anxiously looking about for more *Malaba* people to receive their customary dousing. Without further ado, the *pupu* emptied the basin over Erika's head. As Erika stood there, stoically smiling, soundless, and to everyone's astonishment (most especially her own) unflinching, the *pupu* hurried back to the *pan*, refilled the basin, returned and doused Erika again. Then, with enviable decorum, Erika turned quietly on her heel, went back to the house for dry clothing, and proceeded to the *pan* for her breakfast. My day was too busy to ask Erika what had happened, but much later, when I did question her about her behavior that day, Erika said she had taken her dousings quietly "because I wanted to *shame* them for what they had done." She had learned the ethic of *malum*, in the only way one really can.

FOUR

The Clan: Exchange and Alliance

◼

THE SETS of relationships elicited through the interaction of the moieties, including same-moiety relationships, provide the substance for Usen Barok social and ritual life. As I have suggested, these relationships, the attendant means of eliciting them—avoidance, respect, and joking—and their generalized expression as *malum* and *malili*, constitute an ethos, a collectively held and collectively felt motivation and code for the conduct, expression, and experience of social and ritual life. Usen Barok are conscious of the individual performance and experience of this ethos through a social sense of embarrassment, or self-consciousness, which is glossed in Tokpisin as *sem* ("shame") and is known in the indigenous language as *a minenge*. To "have," to experience and respect, *a minenge* is to respond to the ethos and use it as a guide.

The social and ritual structure of the Usen, the aspect of *kastam* in which ethos is organized in terms of social units and social responsibility, and through which the crises and transitions of individual lives are negotiated, is the subject of this and of subsequent chapters. The central focus in the social organization of ethos is the clan, or *bung marapun*, a primarily conceptual unity that serves to fix the cultural person as actor and as identity into the responsibilities of collective life. The present chapter describes and considers the clan as a social unit, which means largely its role in holding and exchanging traditional wealth, and its role in marriage alliance.

Considerations of *kastam* that involve identity, power, and, most especially, the *taun*, and therefore the negotiation of life crises and transitions (including succession among *orong*, or "big men"), are reserved for subsequent chapters. There is good reason for this. Although these topics are crucially involved in the organization of social responsibilities, their understanding is a matter of coming to terms with something less immediately familiar to an anthropological audience than exchange. It concerns the use of the perceptual image, or icon, as an operational unit in ritual and in relations of power and identity. For this reason the discussion of the *taun* and its feasts, in many respects the anchor points for Barok social and ritual life, will be postponed until after the operation of the perceptual image has been introduced, in Chapters 5 and 6.

The Money of Shame

The traditional currency of minute, strung, highly polished shell disks that Barok call *mangin* (Tokpisin *mis*) and share with other New Ireland peoples as well as, generically, with a broad range of Melanesian "island peoples," is an expected component of all transactions involving pigs, land, and other traditional items or rights. It is not at present obligatory, however, and generally the value will be paid off about half in Papua New Guinea *kina* and half in *mangin*. But if a pig, for instance, particularly one that is purchased in a *taun* before an assemblage of feasters (to whom the payment must be displayed) should be bought with *kina* alone, people would talk, and the buyer would doubtless feel conspicuous. There would be a certain sense that *kastam*, the significance of the occasion and the usages that legitimize it, had been violated.

In this regard we could speak of *mangin* as the money of *kastam*.

Since most of the traditional occasions for the giving of *mangin* (including, frequently, the purchase of pigs at a feast) are conceived of in terms of *kunu minenge*, "buying shame," however, we might better speak of the "money of shame," a currency that measures its exchange value, most consistently, in terms of social consciousness.

The shell currency of New Ireland is distinctive, and is rather different from the Tolai *tambu* of the Rabaul area, made of Nassa shell. Barok say that their *mangin* was originally made on the offshore islands of Tabar, but that later manufactories were established on the Lihir Islands as well. It is made of a small (ca. 1.5 cm), salmon-colored shell, probably *Chrysostoma paradoxum*, of the family Trochidae, found on Dyaul (Djaul) Island, off the west coast of northern New Ireland. (Often, jars of them can be purchased in the stores in Kavieng.) Once the shells are obtained they will be given to a trading partner or acquaintance from Lihir, who will undertake to turn them into *mangin* in return for a certain "cut" of the finished product.

Mangin is denominated by grade, or named variety, and by standardized lengths measured on the body. The following measures, listed in progression from shortest to longest, are recognized:

a *eligo na sie*: from the middle of the chest to one breast

mangin a tus: measured between the breasts of a man or woman

mangin sogorobo: from the fingertip to the middle of the chest, "enough to buy a small pig to raise"

mangin sanga sangaie, or *sinangai* ("the hands"): measured between the fingertips of the outstretched hands; this is the Tokpisin *pram* ("fathom"), and is the length intended when *mis* or *mangin* is otherwise unqualified.

On the most general level, *mangin* might be differentiated into what I shall call "heirloom *mangin*" and "circulating *mangin*." The former includes many archaic and unusual varieties (often pure white, and I have seen a brilliant, translucent salmon color) that are no longer made or used. It is held, together with shell ornaments such as the *bun*, as a clan treasure, handed down through the generations. Two kinds of heirloom *mangin* are distinguished: *a menekis*, used to decorate the door of the *taun*, the *kaba* tree, and children at the *kaba*; and *sogoi-segeri*, long strings (I have seen one about twenty meters long) that are draped about the *taun* enclosure on festive occasions. Heirloom *mangin* is "priceless" and without exchange value.

Circulating *mangin* is colloquially graded into *mangin dek*, "fine" or "good" *mangin*, including the best two or three specific grades, and *mangin tunu*, "essential" (ordinary) *mangin*. Specific grades of *mangin* are valued in terms of color, red-orange taking precedence, and size, with larger disks preferred. The following ranking, in decreasing order of value, approximates[1] a general consensus:

1. *pabang*: red-orange, large disks
2. *kuwas*: red-orange, smaller disks[2]
3. *emeras*: red-brown
4. *sili-uro*: alternating bands (10-12 cm each) of gray and pink-white, large disks
5. *lolot*: alternating gray and pink-white, but smaller, disks

The *mangin*, generally in strands of *sinangai* length, is usu-

---

[1] It is the ranking of *emeras* as against *sili-uro* and *lolot* that is in question, though informants listed *emeras* together with *pabang* and *kuwas* as *mangin dek*.

[2] A. B. Lewis, *Melanesian Stone Money in Field Museum Collections*, attributes the terms *mangin, kawas (kuwas?)* and *lolat (lolot?)* to an article in the periodical *Globus* by Dr. Albert Hahl, governor of German New Guinea from 1902 to 1912 (Lewis, pp. 20-21). Hahl wrote about central New Ireland, and it seems likely that he had Barok informants.

ally decorated—with a small *Conus* shell, a costly and specially made ornament crafted from glass beads and a shiny seedcase, or, in some cases, single human teeth. Human teeth may be used to decorate *pabang* or *kuwas mangin*, but not other varieties. The grades of *mangin* are usually mixed when making a purchase; a large pig costing ten *pram* might, for instance, be bought with one *pram* of *pabang*, one of *kuwas*, five of *emeras*, and three of *lolot*. A string ("of *mis*"; it is not known what distinctions were made) could be obtained, or sold, at the Namatanai Council chambers for from 20 to 30 *kina* (U.S. $30-45) during the time of my fieldwork, though the price was said to be inflating.

In its use, Barok *mangin* approximates the functions of three kinds of currency: the "vital wealth," as I have called it, that circulates in the New Guinea highlands, like Nuer marriage cattle or pearlshells as part of an economy of human attachments; "money," in the accepted Western sense as part of an economy of goods or produced "things"; and "money" as a medium of moral merit, or ascendancy. It is the principal marker of exchange in marriage and other rites that comprise the cycle of human nurturance; it is interchangeable for Papua New Guinea currency and for goods, such as pigs and land, that can also be converted into money; and it is the preferred medium for fines, for the "buying of shame," and for all transactions in the *taun*. Thus, in its use, the value of *mangin* approximates a kind of triple metaphor: each standard of exchange draws away from the definitional certitude of the other two. Because this range of valuation includes the "human currency" of bride wealth, death payments, and various retributive assessments, there will be a certain tendency to "convert" *mangin* into "bride wealth" and to analyze the Barok in terms of corporate lineages. And because the credibility of universal value ("property, production, consumption") is bolstered by the "real" credibility of exchange in what Immanuel Wallerstein calls the "world system"—because, in fact, *mangin* may be redeemed by *kina*, and *kina* by dollars—there will be a possibility of redeeming *mangin* theoretically in this way also.

But our interest here is less that of choosing the most profitable "exchange rate" for exploratory analogy than that of discovering the cultural criteria for "internal" convertibility, and so we must return to the matter of moral evaluation. The profits of business dealings as well as the advantages of kin position tend, among the Usen, to be translated into ethical ascendancy. This is why *kastam* is preeminent on the scale of Barok values, why so much money, time, and effort is spent on it. It is not a matter of sentimentality, nor of "conservatism," but of a core of validation that holds the essence of cultural credibility. Property as well as lineal identity and integrity are functions of this credibility.

For Usen Barok, this powerful ethical emphasis serves to resolve the ambiguity of monetary reference, insofar as it may be resolved, in terms of moral valuation. The store of *mangin*, decorative as well as circulating, that an *orong* holds for his clan, a visible objectification of many diverse events and transactions in which claims to honorable standing or restitution are validated, amounts to a hoard of social merit.

We might consider defining the Barok clan in terms of its store of *mangin*, its moral capital of "shame" positively achieved, as the Usen themselves speak of the *bun*, a hanging ornament of twenty or so dog's teeth suspended on strings of *mangin* from an egg cowrie, as the "basis of the clan." Shell wealth is "honor," the transactional increment of a clan, as the *taun* is its focus and its icon, and the *tadak* spirit its power or strength. Let us turn, then, to the *bung marapun* itself.

The *Bung Marapun*

The Barok term *bung marapun* refers to a unit of social conceptualization that natives gloss in Tokpisin as *klen* (sometimes *klem*) or *bisnis*, and that we may following Jessep,[3] identify as "clan." Membership in a clan is by birth, and follows the line of the mother; thus, a given clan will always belong to one particular moiety. Although it is formally possible to split a clan, or to forswear siblingship (*sugurno*), adjustment or negotiation of *bung marapun* affiliation is extremely rare, and in no sense normative.

Bung marapun is a metaphor with a complex range of analogic possibilities, which my informants appeared unable or unwilling to resolve. A *bung* is a gathering or aggregate, as in Tokpisin, a "bunch"; *mara* is a usage of considerable generality or unifying force—it is "eye," but also "vital core" or "epitome." *Pun* is a bird; in the case of this metaphor, according to the east coast Usen, it is the *sek*, a bird that ornithologists know as the colonial starling (*Aplonis metallica*). This is a small, red-eyed blackbird that builds extensive colonies of domed, grassy nests, which have the appearance of arboreal villages or pueblos, along branches overlooking cleared areas or human gardens. Co-workers directed my attention to such a colony one day as I was working in a local garden, and also showed me a type of orange-red berry that they call "the eye of the *sek*." It seems likely that the resemblance of *sek* colonies to human villages (for a village is a kind of "vital core"), their proximity (for a Barok village was often situated in the "eye" or view of its avian counterpart, and a clearing is also an "eye"), and the notable red eye of the bird itself, perhaps suggestive of maternal blood or clan substance, might singly or together have some part to play in the metaphor of *bung marapun*.

Although some may wish to identify it with the politically motivated corporate lineage of social anthropological literature, the *bung marapun* approximates this construct closely

[3] Jessep, "Land Tenure in a New Ireland Village," p. 56. Jessep notes that the term *bung marapun* may also be used in reference to a single lineage, or *gan* in his usage.

only when its holdings are taken out of context and viewed in the Western sense as "property." It is frequently too large and dispersed, and occasionally too small, to operate as the sort of politically interested group that social anthropology requires and postulates, and its lines of inheritance are frequently compromised or dispersed as *nat lo*. A clan may or may not be traceable in its genealogical entirety to some apical ancestress and its various ramifications or may not be capable of articulation in these terms. Many, possibly most, Usen clans have branches in the non-Barok linguistic or cultural groupings; some, like Unakulis, have all of their *tadak* places, and even their *orong*, in such areas. It is, at all events, quite difficult to determine, when an Usen speaker says that two people are "of the same clan," whether a single *bung marapun*, two such units that have allied by "pooling *mis*," or supposedly cognate units from distinct linguistic and cultural areas are intended.

The localized manifestation of a dispersed *bung marapun* is the *aɣana*, or "branch," which may be identified in anthropological terms, again after Jessep,[4] as the "lineage." (If the *bung marapun* is not dispersed, this localized lineage may be identified with the clan itself.) Almost invariably the *aɣana* occupies or dominates a named hamlet (*la gunun*), focused upon its *taun* (better: the *aɣana* is constituted morally by its *taun*, with its cluster of dependent residences). Generally an *aɣana* (which may be as small as a single family) is a cohesive and politically interested unit that holds and utilizes some defined local portion of *bung marapun* land, and holds validating feasts for mortuary and other appropriate public occasions. It is precisely in this concern for moral propriety and feasting, however, that the *aɣana* of a *bung marapun* cooperate, pooling their efforts and sometimes their resources. In

---

[4] *Ibid.* Jessep renders the Barok term as *ɣan*; that is, the central root in *a-ɣan-na*, minus its nominalizing prefix and its suffix. This seems entirely plausible, though I have heard it more often spoken as all one word.

terms of propertyholding, production, and commercial enterprise, they seem far less disposed to do so. Resources and profits were definitely not shared among the four Unakulis *agana*
at Bakan in 1979-80, and those of other lineages wishing to
use the truck belonging to one of them were obliged to *hire*
it.

If all of this would seem to assimilate the *agana* to the social anthropologist's model of a localized, corporate lineage,
committed to Fortesian rites of solidarity at a higher "level,"
then the size and constitution of the *agana* commends our
closer inspection. For it is not its commercial or propertarian
concerns that suggest a reconsideration, but the question of
lineality. The relatively small size and shallow genealogical
depth suggest not only that at this level the influence of *nat*
and patrilateral inheritance begins to be significant, but also
that the *agana* is defined, in its corporate identity, by the
overlapping of *nat* and *bung marapun* affiliations. Thus the
concept of corporate lineality, of "unilineal descent groups,"
is difficult to apply here because "corporateness" comes into
play at precisely that point at which unilineality is compromised, and for precisely the fact that unilineality *is* compromised. The wealthiest and most successful *agana* at Bakan
are, perhaps not surprisingly, those that have received the
more substantial *nat lo*, and in this respect the adoption of the
commercial name Sumalote by the *agana* of the children of
Lote, *nat* Sumati, is eloquent.

In all respects relating to *kastam*—to the traditional validational complex of feasting in the *taun*, moral ascendancy,
and successorship to ancestral holdings—the *agana* is strictly
matrilineal. In this sense, too, it is truly a "branch," for the
true ethical and ceremonial center of gravity is the *bung
marapun*, and any sort of profit or ascendancy that the *agana*
might realize is referred and attributed to its clan basis. This
fact serves to ensnare the model of the corporate, unilineal
descent group in the toils of a paradox, for only when we drop

the utilitarian sense of "property" in terms of which this model was framed can the *agana* possibly be seen as unilineal; it can become "corporate" in the secular sense only by being bilateral. The rites and offices of *kastam* are matrilineal in conception, and their focal articulation is achieved in the cultural unit of the *bung marapun*.

Whatever might be said in this contingency regarding the dispersed nature of the *bung marapun*, the two clans that I knew best, Unakulis and Wutom, had each an *orong* who maintained a *taun* in proximity to its *tadak* place, who held custody of the clan's assemblage of *mis*, and who was accorded the preeminence at least of a primus inter pares by the heads of the other *agana*. *Orong*ship is, of course, a relative term as it applies to individuals, a usage that is common enough in Melanesia. But in a cultural sense the concept of *orong* is a necessary absolute, inseparable from Barok conceptions of moral rectitude and hierachy. The *orong* is the mediator for, and the human counterpart of, the *tadak*, the clan *masalai* spirit; he is the arbiter of protocol and the chief speaker at *taun* feasts, and the custodian of the clan's store of *mis*. *Orong*ship is thus implied in the cultural conception of a *bung marapun*, like matrilineal affiliation; where you find a clan, there you will find, regardless of any considerations of worthiness, an *orong*.

As a cultural unit, the *bung marapun* amounts to a fusion of three symbolic elements, or complexes: *mangin*, *tadak*, and *taun*. *Mangin* is the element of objectified moral standing, of social potential realized as an increment of moral issues resolved in the past. The clan's hoard of *mangin* is retained in one place under the guardianship of its senior authority, or *orong*; it must be formally divided and apportioned if the clan itself is divided, and on certain occasions it may be "pooled" with that of another clan of the same moiety, in recognition of an explicit bond of affiliation or alliance with that clan. *Tadak* is the element of identity and of spiritual, or transcendental, power and efficacy, conceived here as a single quality or dimension. The clan's *tadak* is said to be the "strength" (*a lolos*) of the clan; it is conceptualized and dealt with as an incorporeal, though sentient, spontaneous, and responsive being, who maintains a protective interest in clan members, and should stand in a special relationship to the *orong*. A clan's traditions and given names generally celebrate the unique capabilities, attributes, and manifestations of its *tadak*. The *taun* is the embodiment, at once the symbol and the mechanism, of the act of containment that is the validating feast, and it also encompasses the essence of the ancestors buried within its enclosure, the source of the clan's status and inheritance. A place of sanctuary and hospitality for all men, the *taun* is the supreme artifact and instrument of legitimation in Barok culture; it literally contains the dead, and sustains the living in all their life crises, from childhood feasts through weddings to the mortuary complex.

Although Usen do not systematize elements of this sort, the three that define the formal cohesion of the *bung marapun* can be seen in indigenous terms to nest within one another in a series of progressive inclusions. The *tadak* encompasses the origin-grounds of the clan, extending its power and protection over its lands and members: in a not unrelated sense, it also "contains" the clan as the source of its identity; and in many cases, its origin as well. The *taun*, then, is contained within the *tadak*, and contains, in turn, the lives, deaths, and social ceremonials of the members of the clan. It also contains the store of *mangin*, providing a locus for its display, at special feasts when the structure itself is decorated with *mis*, and also when the *mis* is "cooked," or used in the purchase of pigs, and undergoes obligatory display to the assembled feasters. It would be fair to say that the *tadak* commands transcendental power, the *taun* manifests ancestral authority, and *mangin* objectifies and represents ethical ascendancy and merit.

Alliance

Grounded ultimately in *a lolos*, power in the cosmic sense, and temporally in the protocol of *talien dek* ("correct form"), or *kastam*, the *bung marapun* negotiates its formal standing with other, like units in terms of *mangin*, and in terms of the elements and values for which *mangin* may be exchanged. The formal means by which this negotiation may be effected is defined by the preeminent ideological means of clan definition: moiety alignment. Clans of the same moiety share at least a potential sense of mutual identity and support; those of opposite moieties relate through the (not necessarily less convivial) elicitation of *malum*, as well as through the more specialized kin protocols of affinity, *nawiligen*, and *naluwinin*. On the other hand, diffuse obligations and expectations such as these are universal, and are scarcely tokens of fidelity or commitment; they may be said to obtain even among clans at war with one another, or even among those that were unaware of one another's existence.

Among clans of the same moiety, or their local representatives, however, there is a specific, formal rite for establishing alliance or consubstantiality. This is the public act, on the part of the respective *orong*, of pooling or sharing their *mis*. It is known as *bungim mis* ("joining *mis*") or *tromwe mis wantaim* ("throwing down *mis* together") in Tokpisin, and variously as *teve mangin ari*ɣe, *kubus mangin ari*ɣe, or *ngusun mangin ari*ɣe in Barok, and the lines that participate in it are said to *dobo tuari*ɣe, "stand up together." Units joined in this way thus acquire the right to inherit land, property, and *taun* from one another. The rite itself is generally concluded between *a*ɣ*ana* of the respective clans that are situated in the same village, though the implication is that the entire *bung*

marapun have become "one line," and sweeping generaliza-
tions are frequently made on this basis. The bonds are conceived in dyadic, rather than commutative (i.e. connecting
units through serial attachments) terms, and although most
of the *agana* of a single moiety in a village may be linked in
this way, it must not be assumed that all are. Performance of
the rite is binding, but for the tie to exist at all it must have
been solemnized at some point. Often it originates with a famous traditional incident, as in the following example:

In the time of fighting, the men of [the Patpatar village of] Sohun
went to raid Kolonoboi. When they arrived, the people there were
cutting *kalip*, and the men from Sohun shot a young woman. Her
maruam, Magalik, chased the men back toward Sohun. Retreating,
they came to [the Patpatar village of] Rasese. The *orong* there was
sleeping in his *taun*. The men from Rasese asked the Sohun men
where they had come from, and they told them what they had
done. The *orong* recognized the name of the woman who had been
shot as that of his *gogup*. He arose from his sleep, took his spear
and his ax, and speared and cut the killer from Sohun, killing him.
He told the women to steam-cook the body, and when they had he
ate it. They sent word of this to Magalik: "I avenged the killing of
my *gogup*; we killed the man." Magalik wanted to befriend the
Rasese *orong* (they had previously been enemies); he took a pig and
five *pram* of *mis*, put them into a canoe, and paddled down the
coast. They came to Lagabuo. Magalik spoke to the Rasese *orong*:
"You avenged your *gogup*; here is your pig, your *mis*, [and] now
our clans can join. I will take a girl-child to Kolonoboi and look after
her as a token of our union." She grew up, she married, and bore
her first daughter, who became the mother of this narrator.

Adoption of this sort, which was often done to dramatize and
seal such compacts, can be seen as an equivalent (in "demographic" terms) of the sharing of *mis*.

The symbolic adoption of a (potentially childbearing)
maiden, as well as the joining of *mis*, is of course not worka-
ble as a strategy for alliance across moiety lines. The modes

of alliance and interaction between *bung marapun* of opposite moieties are well understood, for they are simply those of relations between moieties—intermarriage and the eliciting of *malum*. Beyond this, *bung marapun* or *aɤana* of opposite moieties that wish to forge special ties with one another must do so by raising the level of preferment, so to speak—concentrating their marriages with one another. This is done deliberately in some Usen communities through an ideology of "marriage with the *tau* and *ɤoɤup*."

It would be something of an oversimplification to speak of this strategy or policy as a norm, for marriage (or potential marriage) is, if anything, contrary to the spirit and the protocols of the *naɤoɤup* and *nawiligen* relationships. When the issue arises at all, it is generally a matter of ambivalence, one that is related positively or negatively to changes thought to have come about since traditional times. At Belik and Kolonoboi villages, where the practice is recognized, people often maintain that it is *the* traditional form of Barok marriage but that some villages have abandoned it in recent times because of mission disapproval. At Bakan, Kanapit, and Ramat, where the practice is largely disavowed, people say that the moral severity and uprightness in ancestral times would never have condoned marriage within those relationships, and that the practice is a consequence of the general looseness of moral restrictions in recent times. It is interesting to note that Belik and Kolonoboi occupy the northern half of the Usen east coast, and that each is locally recognized as being (sub-)dialectically distinct in contrast to Kanapit, Bakan, and Ramat. Moreover, the practice of marriage with the *tau* or *ɤoɤup* is in each case associated with a long-term association of two *bung marapun*: Maranat and Liengmau at Belik; Guoɤo and Gunaun at Kolonoboi.

Marriage with the *tau* or *ɤoɤup* is termed *pe o bala masa* in Barok. It occurs with some frequency at Belik and Kolonoboi, but also sporadically in the other Usen-speaking vil-

92

lages, where it is noted but its occurrence is often ignored. The most frequently volunteered observation regarding the practice is that it is something of a blessing, because marriage permits two people who otherwise would be restricted by severe kin protocols to relate familiarly ("to speak ill of one another") as spouses. It is recalled that, in earlier times, marriage with a *tau* or *gogup* required a payment of about one *pram* of *mis* and the money equivalent of 2 *kina* by each party to "buy the shame" of the marriage.

Figure 1 presents a genealogical diagram of all the (traceable) marriages that I could locate and which informants identified as instances of marriage "with the *tau* or *gogup*" resulting from three early marriages between the Gunaun *agana* Medalamo and the Guogo *agana* Balitas at Kolonoboi. (The three initial marriages, those of Ariran, Sabual, and Nason, were also thought to be "with the *tau* or *gogup*," but were not traceable genealogically.) All the marriages shown here involve one or the other *agana*, and all but five (those of Kaminiel, Lemen, Marit, Misirom, and Tualir) involve both. Of the nine traceable marriages, none was contracted between persons who would normally call one another *gogup*, and only if we consider the two initial Gunaun sibling sets (the offspring, traditionally, of two sisters) to be a single sibling set, can we speak of one marriage, that of Masingida, as being between *tau*. Allowing for this collapse of the two sibling sets into one, all the remaining marriages except Bongian's (he married his mother's sister's husband's sister's daughter) involve persons connected through ancestral *naluwinin* or *nagogup* (e.g. cross-cousin) relationships. The "closest" of these is that of Kaminiel, who married his *gogup*'s daughter, his *balike ni ausagit*. Marit married the daughter, and Lemen the granddaughter, of mother's *lawuke*; thus, Marit married a woman whom his mother would call *toke*, and whom he should call *neneke*, and Lemen married a classificatory *sagake*. Misirom also married a "sib-

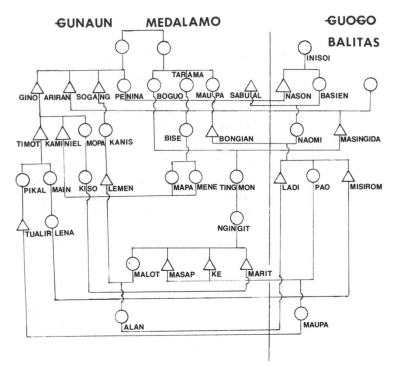

FIGURE 1. Marriage with the *Tau* and *Gogup* between Gunaun Medalamo and Guogo Balitas at Kolonoboi

ling," the granddaughter of his father's *lawuke*; Ladi married a "daughter," the granddaughter of his father's *gogup*, and Masap (daughter of his grandmother's *gogup*) and Tualir (his mother's father's *gogup*'s great-granddaughter) each married a *pupu*.

Certainly the final arbitors regarding relationship terms and their use must be the natives themselves—else the comparative study of kinship would be the preserve of the geneticist rather than the anthropologist. The objectivity, as Lévi-Strauss long ago pointed out, lies not in "concrete relations

94

of consanguinity and affinity," but in the conceptual approach in which relationship is apprehended. That only one of the nine traceable marriages "with a *tau* or *gogup*" involved a *tau*, and that none involved *gogup*, may mean something beyond the fact that Usen kin-term usage is not necessarily based on a literal reading of genealogy. Since the sole collateral tie in most of the premarital relationships traced here is a cross-sex tie (e.g. MoBr., fasi.), and since the valorized relationship for male and female issue connected through that bond is *gogup*, this term may be used here in the sense of the Siane *hovorafo* as described by Salisbury:[5] as a partner in a closely related clan.

The Usen folk tradition concerning the relaxing of stringent kin protocols in "close" marriages has, indeed, little relevance here, for most of the premarital relationships between spouses in Figure 1 are well beyond the degrees of relationship within which such protocols are normally observed. Thus it seems that the alliance of clans, rather than relationships between persons, is the significant consideration here. A relationship term (*gogup*) with a heavy ethical implication is used (hyperbolically) to indicate close intermarriage; this leads to a certain embarrassed disqualification, or even disavowal, on the part of many, and even to speculation that such marriages are made for personalistic reasons—to "get out of" taboos.

There is additional evidence to corroborate the claim that these marriages are part of a policy to cement a lasting alliance between the *agana*. Table 5, based on an unusually well articulated *agana* genealogy, indicates the numerical concentration of Gunaun Medalamo marriages with external units over a span of several generations. Not only are the rates of intermarriage with Guogo Balitas high, but intermarriage of this lineage with Guogo as a whole accounts for roughly 78

[5] Salisbury, "New Guinea Highland Models and Descent Theory."

TABLE 5. Gunaun Medalamo Marriage
Concentration

Number of Men	Married to	Percentage
4	Guogo Balitas	33.3
2	Guogo Atare	16.7
2	Guogo Malaba	16.7
2	Guogo Liengamale	16.7
1	Maranat	8.3
1	Rasese	8.3
TOTAL 12		100.0
Total % men married to Guogo *agana*		83.4

Number of Women	Married to	Percentage
4	Guogo Balitas	20.0
4	Guogo Atare	20.0
3	Guogo Malaba	15.0
3	Guogo Liengamale	15.0
1	Guogo	5.0
1	Palarauo	5.0
1	(Lavongai)	5.0
1	(Kavieng)	5.0
1	(Rabaul)	5.0
1	(Kainantu)	5.0
TOTAL 20		100.0
Total % women married to Guogo *agana*		75.0

percent (83.4 percent of men's marriages and 75.0 percent of women's) of all marriages! (Comparable figures for Unakulis, based on somewhat inferior genealogical materials, show the highest concentration of marriages with any external unit to be 26.7 percent.) It is true that some of the Gunaun and Guogo *agana* at Kolonoboi are comparable in size and significance to *bung marapun,* and have separate *tadak* spirits. It is all the more remarkable, then, to find the high concentration carried over across a number of Guogo lineages, and the genealogical depth might lead us to infer that the practice of close intermarriage has been in force here since before the lineages attained their present differentiation.

As a deliberate strategy of alliance, the concentration of marriages has the potential advantage of concentrating patrilateral ties among the units involved, thus avoiding the dispersal of inheritance as *nat lo.* Two heavily intermarried units would simply pass their *nat lo* back and forth. In this respect, however, this somewhat controversial practice differs from the techniques for alliance among clans of the same moiety that we discussed earlier. For the sharing of *mis* and the adoption of daughters pose no problems for the working-out of relational ideology—the differentiation of clans *within* a moiety is not a moiety concern. But when two units elect to forge an alliance by intermarrying continuously (marrying "their relatives," as the Usen would have it), the "sign" of their interrelationship shifts from the ideologically acceptable one of nurture and *malum* to one of continually revised affinity. And this, in turn, constitutes a very real compromise of *kastam.*

The ethos and the relationships generated by the dialectical interaction of the moieties is integral to Usen Barok *kastam;* the clan is the locus at which that ethos and those relationships are actualized in terms of human affiliation. But this does not mean that the clan (or clanship) or the welfare of the clan (or of an intermarrying isolate of clan units) is what *kastam* is "about." Clanship, the respect of the *maruam,* and the authority of the *orong,* are but one side of a complex equation.

Alliance is an issue in which clan welfare becomes a prime consideration, however. Perhaps if the strategy of "marriage with the *tau* or *gogup*" were accepted, and adopted, more widely than it is, the norms of moiety interaction would be influenced more in the direction of affinal relations, as Clay[6] has suggested for the Notsi of north-central New Ireland. However it may fare politically, the Usen clan is defined as a cultural identity not so much by its size or success in the world, but by its *tadak* spirit. And since the present study concerns cultural meaning, it is to this subject that we now turn.

[6] Clay, *Pinikindu*, pp. 139-41.

FIVE

A *Tadak*

THE TOKPISIN term *masalai* covers an astonishing variety of native conceptions, generally "bush spirits" of one sort or another that are associated with particular places. In some cases, however, as among the Barok, and perhaps in New Ireland generally, the term has a much more specific and exclusive application. No one would think of using it with reference to a *gilam*, for instance, even if the *gilam* were known to be associated with a particular pothole. Among Barok the term *masalai* is restricted to manifestations and beings that are known in the indigenous language as *a na tadak* (sing.: *a tadak*).

A *tadak* is generally, though not invariably, identified with some extant *bung marapun*, or is associated with the *agana* of a *bung marapun* in some more or less derivative fashion.[1] A *tadak* is a form of power (*a lolos*); it is known or experienced through a number of manifestations, the more common or conventional of which are recognized and named in each case, as indeed the *tadak* itself is often identified by the name of its best known manifestation. But that does not mean that any of these recognized or named manifestations

[1] Jessep prefers to associate the *tadak* with the lineage, or *agana*, rather than with the *bung marapun*, and notes that this is typical of Lokon, though he is aware of instances elsewhere where this is not the case. Where I have encountered the association of *agana* with *tadak*, as for instance among the Guogo, it seemed to me that the status of the unit was itself ambiguous, midway between lineage and clan. See Jessep, "Land Tenure in a New Ireland Village," p. 161.

is the *tadak* itself, for the transformational capability of the *tadak* is intrinsic to its power and being. The changing of appearance (*pire wuo*) is coincident with the power that is the *tadak*, as is regenerative ability or immortality—all of these are aspects of a single conception.[2]

A term of "Laur" origin, *a masoso*, is used by Usen to denote the particular manifestations of a *tadak*: *samting i sanap long masalai*, or "that which is animated by the *masalai*." In the strictest sense, however, any of the *masoso* may also be spoken of as *a tadak*, since all are equally appearances taken on by the power. A *tadak* is ultimately the totality of its *masoso*, but at that degree of completeness it approximates a kind of arcane lore, known in its entirety perhaps only to a few clan elders.

A *tadak* is identified in a fundamental sense with at least one locality per named manifestation; the characteristic locality of the best known manifestation is generally spoken of as *the* place of the *tadak* (*a ʒoron tadak; ples masalai* in Tokpisin). This may be a piece of ground, a stream, a cave, a rock or reef formation, or a submerged rock in the sea. It is said to "belong to," to be under the special protection of, the *tadak*, and may also be seen as one of its manifestations. It is often credited with floral, faunal, geological, or marine features that give evidence of unusual or regenerative capabilities. A reflective informant once speculated that *tadak* is actually the effect of a place that has a great deal of power, since none of the more obviously animate manifestations, such as people or animals, could be understood as its essential form.

The association between a clan and its *ʒoron tadak* is a sa-

---

[2] I am grateful to Professor Rodney Needham for calling my attention to some comments by Roselene Dousset-Leenhardt on the Tolai concept of *tabapot*. This is a designation for figure-ground reversal, and the Tolai define man as a *tabapot*. Informants suggested *wewet puo* as the Barok equivalent, and said that it is the means by which power is incorporated in art. *Pire wuo* might be understood, by analogy, as the revelation of hidden appearances through the transformation of known ones.

lient feature of the relation in which identity is generated via the *tadak*. Jessep has demonstrated in a comprehensive study that identification with the *tadak* legitimates claims to a surrounding piece of land among the "beach people" of the northern village of Lokon, but that this type of legitimation is not found elsewhere among the Barok.[3] The material collected by Marianne George at Kokola indicates that accounts tracing clan origin to the impregnation of an ancestress at a *goron tadak* are a significant feature of this association there. Moreover, there is some indication of *tadak* being passed on to successive occupiers of the land. At Bakan, on the other hand, there are traditions of *tadak* that move periodically from one habitual locality to another, or of *tadak* that relocate, together with their *goron tadak*, to follow migrations of the clans with which they are identified. Here, as among the Sokirik- and Patpatar-speaking peoples to the south, the "true" or essential locality of the *tadak* is most often a stream, a "*masalai* water."

A *tadak* is felt to retain a kind of general, tutelary interest in the clan and its members, assisting them with its powers, particularly in collective pursuits. It can also, however, turn on them and harm them if its wrath is incurred, and it may play tricks on them or deceive them for entirely wanton motives. It will react to intrusion or pollution irrespective of the agent's clan status. Thus, anyone who has recently had sexual intercourse, or a menstrual discharge, and goes to a *tadak* locality or washes in a *masalai* stream, will be subject to reprisal, and a man who bathes in such a stream after a menstruating woman has entered it will suffer a swelling of the genitals. If an infant is taken to a *tadak* locality the *tadak* will take its soul, which must be retrieved magically. Likewise if a person throws some of his or her food into the *masalai*

[3] Jessep, "Land Tenure in a New Ireland Village," pp. 172-202.

place, the *tadak* will eat it and cause the person's abdomen to swell.

Clearly, a *tadak* is an entity unto itself and has a generic status. *Tadak* are also known to fight one another, and it is felt that the clan, especially its *orong*, belonging to its locality must know what a particular *tadak* is doing at all times. Traditionally an *orong* was expected to maintain a rapport with the spirit: "the *masalai* talks to the *tanonu*, the spirit of a man, in a dream, and shows it things." A particular *tadak* may also present or reveal new food crops or technological innovations and skills for the benefit of its line or of mankind generally. And, in the following story, told to me by an Unakulis lineage head, *tadak* are by no means beyond human frailty even in this:

The *tadak* of Unakulis lives at the River Dahana at Pire. It can appear as a python, a human being, or a shark. As a python, it is called Manmankaun; as a human being, it is called Singido. It is also called Sangakol. If it comes as a snake you may not speak with it; if it comes as a man, you may talk to it. It makes nets [*a eben*] for snaring fish. It made a kind of fish trap [*a tonoe*], called *sigisigi*, which has needles from a vine in the bush to help trap the fish. Singido went to throw his fish trap into the sea. He threw it in, and it would float out to the point at Namatanai. Then he would go out in his canoe at noon and pull it in. He would go ashore to gut and clean his catch, and then steam two fish, one for himself and one for his mother, who was a death adder [*mo*]. When he gave her the cooked fish together with some taro, his mother would coil around it. Once when Singido was ashore in a cave, a child found his canoe on the beach, crawled inside, covered himself with a *pagum* leaf, and fell asleep. Singido did not notice him; he got into the canoe with his *sigisigi* and did his songs and spells for catching fish with it while the child was lying there and witnessing his magic. Singido then discovered the child and asked what his lineage was. The child said, "I belong to another clan, Marit." Then Singido's thinking went awry, and thinking "this *tonoe* belonged to my clan," he gave the *tonoe* to the child.

102

It is clear that, although Barok say that "the *tadak* is the strength [*a lolos*] of the clan," the identification of *tadak* and *bung marapun* is no simple equation or identity, nor is it a matter of the same entity manifested at different phenomenal levels. Let us, then, consider the relation between them.

Identity

The *tadak* is interstitial to the forms and appearances conventionally known to Barok; it has power over form and can change its appearance at will. Thus *tadak* cannot be defined in terms of any of its manifestations, but only through its capabilities. It is seemingly of a different phenomenal order than mortal human beings and other living things; for that reason, any point of similarity, any resemblance or correspondence, that might be established or recognized between human beings and *tadak* must necessarily be analogical or metaphoric in character. It is a link of analogy, in other words, between two dissimilar beings, and is articulated over and against their differences.

Since relations of power over the conventional (as elicited by magical spells and manipulations, or by artistic tropes), and those power relations that serve to elicit individual or unit identity, are both articulated through metaphoric innovations of this sort, *tadak* may be seen as a kind of general field for generating a broad range of individuative relations. All that is necessary to sustain the field are the two characteristics that, as we have seen, are traditionally attributed to *tadak*: that it maintain an independent existence as an entity in its own right, and that it enter into relations of rapport and correspondence with human beings and human groups.

We have seen that, in some respects, relating to pollution, intrusion, and direct affront, *tadak* will retain autonomy vis-à-vis their "own" human counterparts. Indeed, the *tadak* is never fully "known" in terms of its intentions and activities, and it is certainly never "controlled" by human agency. In fact, just as the Barok *taun* can be said to encompass the ancestors buried within its *balat*, or to contain the feasters at a ceremony (and even the ceremony itself), so the *tadak* "contains" persons and things in a kind of eternal suspension. It is said that when a *tadak* swallows a victim, the victim does not die, but lives forever "within" the *tadak*, doing its bidding. Informants recounted a catastrophic shipwreck that occurred several decades ago. Several Bakan residents, including a deaf-mute, were traveling by canoe to the offshore island of Lihir; one of the men, from Guogo, was jealous of the *mis* another passenger would receive for a pig he was taking to Lihir to exchange. The Guogo man had rubbed the stern of the canoe with sand taken from a *goron tadak* at the mouth of the Nambuto River, in order to induce the *tadak* to attack. When the canoe was halfway over to Lihir the *tadak* arose from the sea and swallowed all but the deaf-mute, who survived to tell the story in gestures. But it was deduced that the people had already been dead (killed in an angry quarrel in which the Guogo man flourished a bone) when the *masalai* swallowed them, for, many years after the event, their ghosts could still be seen walking out of the surf and into the "main camp" at Bakan. Now, when the *taubar* blows (as it did in December 1979, a few days before I recorded this account), only the *gagum*, the smell of decomposing flesh, fills the camp.[4]

The links between a *tadak* and its corresponding *bung marapun* can take any of a broad range of forms, from simple claims of association with and recognition of clan members by the *tadak* (members of the clan are all known to its *masalai*) to stories of clan origin via the impregnation of an an-

---

[4] Had the victims been alive when swallowed, they would have "entered the *masalai*" and not appeared as ghosts. The deaf-mute floated in the sea for a long time after the wreck, and was washed up near Kanabu, at Cape Lemeris. He was nursed back to health and finally returned to Bakan.

cestress by the spirit. Often, various kinds of links are claimed together, but never in a systematic or exhaustive fashion. Among the most common, and most significant, is an implied homological correspondence between "parts" (*masoso*, or divisions of them) of the *tadak*, and the *agana*, or else the individual human members, of the *bung marapun*. The first instance is well illustrated by Gunaun Clan at Kolonoboi. "Gunaun" means "base of the *Ficus* (*aun*) tree," and because the *Ficus* is a large, extensive tree, Gunaun connotes "wide, extensively branching line." The actual tree exists, at the *goron tadak*, and it has four main branches (*nit ma agana gunaun*, "four branches of the *Ficus* base") in addition to the trunk. Each of the branches of the tree, itself a *masoso*, corresponds to an actual *agana*, or lineage, of the clan, as does the trunk, and it is said that should any of the lineages die out, the corresponding limb would wither and break off. The *agana* are Gunaun Medalamo (*tadak* Mila at Bulu), Gunaun Kauwos (at Komalu, but nearly defunct), Gunaun Pagini Lamas (*tadak* Seluum at Kokola), and Gunaun Tumawin (*tadak* Tumawin at Belik Plantation). The trunk is Gunaun Tunu ("essential," or unmarked, Gunaun), whose *masalai* Rugawim, of the River Lumue near Belik Plantation, "bosses" the other Gunaun *tadak* and goes to stay at all of their *goron na tadak*. All Gunaun members may invoke the name of Rugawim, who lives at Tabunamawus ("where things do not rot"), on the Lumue River, and frequently travels overland to the Gunaun *goron tadak* at Kokola. Rugawim's most common appearance is that of a large python with a green belly and a red back, and with a *kabak* (lime powder) mark over the right eye and a charcoal streak over the left. Another Gunaun *masoso* is a large stone on the reef at Belik that has split into four parts, each corresponding to a Gunaun *agana*.

The characteristics ascribed to Rugawim and its *a goron tadak* are typical, and understandable in terms of the power that a *tadak* represents. It is claimed that organic material does not, in fact, decompose at Tabunamawus, and also that Rugawim (like many other *tadak*) possesses regenerative powers and is, indeed, indestructible. It is said that plantation workers at Belik Plantation have "killed" Rugawim many times, chopping up the snake form with their machetes, but each time the pieces rejoined and the snake was seen whole again shortly thereafter. Both immunity to decomposition and the capacity to regenerate are concomitant with the *tadak*'s power over form and appearance, for if a being has the power to assume or alter a form at will, the qualitative alterations of decomposition or dismemberment will present little challenge.

The second instance of *tadak*-human correspondence, that involving individual clan members, is actualized in personal naming. Barok names (*esem*) are given at the time of birth— generally by a maternal uncle or *orong*; sometimes by the father; or even, in a kind of complimentary sense, by visiting dignitaries representing a distant branch of the *bung marapun*. Names, with some exceptions, tend to follow matrilines, enlarging upon *orong* (human) and *masoso* (spirit) traits in their elicitation of personal identity, and it is quite common for a clan to retain certain "line names," often marking distinguished *orong*, and to transfer them from generation to generation. Events may also be commemorated in a name: a child might be called Ararum for the tabooing of a men's house. The idea of naming is approached by Barok with the intention of selecting an identity marker: *Arabo bulus-sik a lana ɠo esene barok* ("I shall put something to the name of the boy"). The term for namesake is *kip karaise* (*kip-kara-ese*, or "same name taken"), but the Laur-Patpatar word *maorang* has a wider currency. A certain diffuse relationship of mutual support is felt to exist between namesakes (*Maorang! A raot banga yo ɠo sogosogo a kabak*; "Namesake! Help me now to cut my lime bag"). A person may call the *orong* for whose characteristics he has been named "name-sake." The giver of a name *must* strengthen the name (*oro-ror-ese*) by making a small feast for the occasion, at which *mis* or a pig is given, or the name may be strengthened by a presentation at a feast held for some other purpose. When my name, Sogang, was strengthened at an Aun Gogorop feast, the head of the *a gana* slapped lime powder (*a kabak*) on my back as he announced the name.

Seventeen Usen Barok namings for which I could obtain glosses and/or information are shown in Table 6. Although the namings are listed for generally illustrative, rather than statistical, purposes, it is noteworthy that eight of the seventeen namings involve *masalai*. Two of these concern the same man: Kurus, named for a bird that flocks at a tree at Ta-bunamawus, the Gunaun *goron tadak*, also received the name Bokiu, from his father. He explained that he was named for his father's *masalai* only because he was a first-born child, though the name is seldom used. Of the remaining names, three (Mates, Metlie, and Mele) and possibly a fourth (Obin) seem to be what Andrew Strathern calls "met-onymical sorrow-names," or penthonyms, names that me-morialize sorrow for a deceased kinsman.[5] Two others com-memorate characteristics of particular *orong*; two comment on the holder's unique kin situation, a naming tradition that, like penthonyms, occurs elsewhere in Papua New Guinea;[6] and another seems to be based on personal characteristics of the bearer. Since all of the nameholders are living persons, the example indicates that *masoso* naming has not lost its currency among modern Barok.

Having a *tadak* for a *kip karaise* conflates power and iden-tity in somewhat the same way as having an *orong* as a name-

[5] Strathern, "Wiru Penthonyms."

[6] Both penthonyms and the naming of a person for the plight of his or her sibling group (including "only survivor" terms, as here) are common among the Daribi of Mount Karimui. See Wagner, *Habu*, p. 89.

TABLE 6. Some Usen Barok Names
and Their Sources

Barok Name	English Gloss	Source of Name
Pel Ges	"facial hair"	an *orong* named her for his beard
Mates	"MB drowned"	her maternal uncle died in this way
Selangasin	"stealing areca nut"	named for an *orong* who stole things
Talis	Talisa, a tree	a *masoso* tree of Guogo
Metlie	"never saw her MB"	her maternal uncle died before she saw him
Tabagase	"one alone"	he had no siblings
Turkie	"successor"	he is the only male heir to his *agana*
Bubulo	"flashing light"	named for a *masoso* that flashes light
Bikit	"shrunken, contracted"	possibly for his small stature
Obin	Ogobin, "deserted place"	?
Mele	"bitter, biting"	marks death of eater of bad substance
Masap	Masamasap, a snake	orange snake *tadak* of Gunaun
Ke	a sharp, cutting mollusk	lives in *masalai* water
Bolut	"shark"	*tadak* of Guogo
Bokiu	"porpoise"	his father's *tadak*
Kurus	"New Ireland drongo" (*Dicrurus magerynchus*)	these birds sleep at Gunaun *tadak* tree
Saganain	*Sagan na-en*, "bad fish"	name of fish from *tadak* at Pire

sake, and a somewhat diffuse and uncertain "power" emanating in the same way accrues to a *bung marapun* as a consequence of its being identified with and through a particular *tadak*. This power is invoked and communicated in a number of ways; the *tadak* will reach *orong* or ordinary clan members in dreams, or help the members to round up their quarry in hunting or fishing ventures. A *tadak* may also be invoked: one can call out, "Bemut, you sleep beneath our canoe, carry it to Lihir, and protect it from other *tadak*," or one can simply throw an areca nut into the *goron tadak* and ask, for instance, that it block off a *masalai* stream in which too many people have been bathing. Even members of other *bung marapun* may invoke a *tadak* in this way, though the act will likely be more effective if the invoker is "related"—through the father, for instance (he may then address the *masalai* as "father")—to the spirit.

It is difficult to determine whether the traditional anthropological notion of "totemism" applies here, particularly since *tadak* are incorporeal and identified with multiple "markers" in the form of *masoso*. In his thoroughgoing critique, delineated in his books *Totemism* and *The Savage Mind*, Lévi-Strauss has perhaps hastily dismissed the significance of analogical links between the human and totemic "marker" components, and resolved "totemism" into pure designation, in which the *differences* among a set of markers are in homologous correspondence with the differences among a set of human units. Although Usen *tadak* take on a variety of forms (python, human being, and shark being the most prevalent) and have, in addition, extensive fields of *masoso*, most of these forms are themselves named; and the *tadak* are also associated with a conventionalized "general" name and locality in such a way that there is no difficulty in accommodating them to the Lévi-Straussian notion of "denomination." A *bung marapun* is designated, in these terms, by the name and the most conventional form, or *masoso*, of its *tadak*, and also perhaps by its most distinctive *goron ta-dak*.

A *tadak* may also be "detotalized," in a somewhat more regular fashion, into *masoso* designating component *agana* and, beyond that, into *masoso* designating individual clan members. It is clear that, in all of these respects, *tadak* satisfies the concept of denomination as promoted by Lévi-Strauss, and I have no doubt that it sometimes operates in this way. On the other hand, the concept of *tadak* is also much richer than denomination alone requires; the notion of a *relation* of identity between human and *tadak* is a matter of *analogy* (like the kin relationship elicited by joking or respect relations) rather than of *homology*—it opens up a conceptual and behavioral "space" between designator and designated. And the field of relations opened up in this way becomes multiple and complex through the enlargement of the designator into an incorporeal "actualizer" and an extensive, indefinite field of *masoso*. The relation of power, or rapport, between human and *tadak*, a permutation of the identity relation, must also be articulated through an analogical link, and is likewise expanded and made recondite by the transcendent capacities of *tadak*. If this is denomination, or even "totemism," then it is a denomination or totemism caught at the point of its own self-transcendence.

If the power or influence of a *tadak* is a matter of analogical linkage, then an inauspicious alignment is, of course, as possible as an auspicious one. Such an unfortunate linkage is achieved in cases of intrusion into the *tadak*'s locality, when someone deliberately rubs substance from a *tadak* locality onto a canoe to provoke the spirit's reprisal, or inadvertently, as when Public Works men fastened the drums and pontoons of the Gogo Bridge at Kanapit with vines taken from a *goron tadak* and the *masalai* followed and killed them. Also, given the similarity of elicited kin and *tadak* relations, an inauspicious alignment may be provoked by an *ethical* misdemeanor. Among the *masoso* of Guogo Atare, or Otere (named for another *masoso*, the *atare* lizards that abound at the *goron tadak* at Pire), are a group of blue-eyed dogs that live at the Omara Wuluwun. If people treat them like human beings and give them human food, it is said, the dogs will stay with them; if they are given leavings, they will go off. The leader of these dogs, named Malom, once visited the local people when they had watermelons and, wanting to eat some, approached them. A woman of the place, named Ugom, reproached Malom and reproved him, saying that he was a dog and should eat rubbish. Malom went away, and returned later; he saw a piece of watermelon lying in front of the door, and then went and killed Ugom, because she had spoken ill of him.

A story that I collected among the Usen is significant not only for its commentary on the theme of ethical relations with the *tadak*, but also for the relevance of this theme for human kin relations, since the *tadak* here is also the *maruam*:

There was a man who spent his time hunting in the bush with his dogs. One day while hunting he came to the place of his *masalai*, a place that was full of snakes. The python there was his *maruum*; the snake's sister lived elsewhere, and her son was this man. The snake had made a little house there, like the house of a wild pig. The dogs cried when they came to the little house, and the man stalked up and drove his spear into the house, thinking to kill a pig. The snake said, "Oh, you shoot me, eh? You think I'm a pig. I am your *maruake*!" The snake moved off and, free of the spear, turned and began to coil around the man, starting with his feet. He tightened and tightened. The man had picked up a stick of green wood and held it against himself. As the snake tightened its coils, the stick snapped, and the snake thought it was the sound of his bones snapping. Then the snake put its nose against the man's nose, the man held his breath, and the snake thought he was dead. Then the snake loosened its coils and went off to get some friends to help eat the man. The snake's mother came and said, "Why did you kill him, don't you know he's your nephew?" "But mama, if he had any sympathy for me he wouldn't have speared me." "But he thought you were a pig." "Never mind, I am going to get my friends and eat him; he had no compassion for me, and I will have no mercy on him." Then the woman went to the nephew, after the snake had left, and said, "Alright now, you get up, go to your place, get a pig, cook it, get some green coconuts and areca nuts, and have a feast in your *taun* with the men. Later, when your *maruam* comes, try and give him some food, so that he will not eat you." The man went, told the other men, and they fastened a pig; the women cooked tubers, and all the men went to the *taun* and prepared for the feast. Then the snake's mother saw a long line of pythons coming, and she said, "Oh, you can't kill him; now you go look at what they've put at the *taun*." They got up and went, and those in the *taun* saw the line of snakes coming. They arrived, came up over the *olagabo*, lifted their heads to look around, and the snake saw his nephew sitting down and watching for him. The man got up, put his basket and lime bag down below, and sat down again. The snakes came forward, went past the food heaped up in the center, and came up to the man. "Aha, you killed me, then you pretended to be dead and ran away. I can't have mercy on you, because you had no sympathy for me." The python got up, coiled around the man, and squeezed. All the men just watched. The snake picked him up now, carried him to the bush, and all the snakes ate him. Afterward, the people held the mortuary feasts for the man.

This story has a relentless quality that evokes, for me, something of the Barok ethos and personality at large, as well as the specific themes of the action itself. A man hunting wild pigs is encouraged by his dogs and, as Barok hunters often do, attempts to spear his quarry in its shelter before it can escape. Alas, he spears the python that is also his maternal uncle, and the snake determines to kill him in revenge. He holds a green stick against his body, however, and the snake, hearing the snapping of the stick, believes it has killed him. As the python departs to bring "feasters," its mother suggests to the man that he present a formal feast to the *maruam* and, in effect, substitute a pig for his own body. He does so, but the snake, arriving with his line, chooses to feast upon his nephew instead. So the final "substitution" of pig for man is that of mortuary feasting, after the *tadak-maruam* has had his way. The man's *tadak* here is also his *orong*, and even that most sacrosanct of Barok occasions, the formal feast, is hopeless against ethos linked with power.

A Masoso

At once singular and plural, disembodied and manifest in many changing forms, like a saint in his miracles, *a taduk* is a remarkable Melanesian conception.[7] From a purely ethnographic standpoint it may be seen as a sort of repository, via a unifying notion of power over form, of the bewildering variety of local apparitions, curious and monstrous forms of life and landscape, and sometimes quite unsettling mysteries to be found in any part of New Guinea. An oddly shaped or colored rock formation, a tree with remarkable regenerative powers (such as the Guogo *masoso* tree that was cut down at Ralum and thrown into the sea; part of it sprouted in Ramat Bay, part floated to Lihir and grew in the sea there), or the birth of a hydrocephalic child—all of these are apt to be viewed or claimed as *masoso*, manifestations of *a tadak*.

The small size of most *agana*—a few families at most—coupled with historical or demographic incident and the splitting and assimilation of units, ensures that there will always be some distributional disparity between units and their *taduk* and *masoso*. Some clans live many miles from their *go-*

---

[7] Dr. Dan Jorgensen notes that the Telefol will confidentially ascribe all landslides and other *masalai*-related phenomena to manifestations of a single entity, Magalim, who is utterly unknowable. In these respects Magalim is roughly comparable in conception to *tadak*, though he belongs to an even more involute and complex conceptual world.

ron tadak. Such is the case with Nauntutu (in Barok, Buraun-tulo), now located in a Patpatar-speaking area, whose *masalai*, Labuang, lives in a hole in the reef on the southern edge of Bakan, manifesting itself as a *kwe* (Tokpisin *bikmaus*) fish, that leaves its hole every evening at twilight and flashes a blue light that can be seen beneath the surface of the sea. In other cases, *masoso* are known that belonged to totally defunct clans. On the beach at Kanapit I was shown a large, semiburied rock of sand-worn coral or limestone at the high-water mark. This was Musoli, a *masoso* of Tamrit Clan (no longer extant). Musoli is the "mother," and the other stones on the reef nearby, partially covered with water, are the "children." When there is a big sea, and waves have removed all the sand around Musoli, the bared rock has the power to calm the sea once more.

A clan may have a number of "characteristic" *tadak* forms and places (a shark, a python, a stream, and so forth), though even in its "completeness" it will doubtless represent a process of historical accretion. Wutom Clan, at Bakan, is a case in point. We have seen in Chapter 1 that Wutom, "Puntam Guogo," moved southward from Kolonoboi to found the first settlements at Bakan, and indeed its *goron tadak* and *masoso* are concentrated in the region between the two villages (see Map 3). "Wutom" ("Puntam" or "Wuntom") is the name of a place, a *goron tadak*, on the River Laumalaga, from which the clan takes its name, and which is said to be the true place of its *tadak*. The shark form of the *masalai*, its most commonly known manifestation, is that of a tailless shark that swims with its forefins alone, and is named Bemut. Bemut has a "house" at Luruto, in the Laumalaga estuary, which he leaves from time to time to swim out to the submarine rock formation (the rock "has colors") Torodege, located in the sea near Cape Bakan. It is said that Torodege moved down to its present location from an earlier site near Kolonoboi when Wutom relocated at Bakan. An isolated rock outcropping

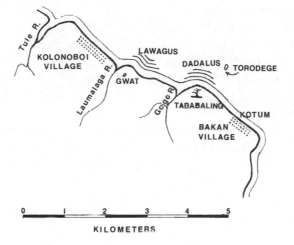

MAP 3. The *Masoso* of Wutom

along the highway just south of the Laumalaga, said to have
been shaped like a pig before it was partially leveled by road-
workers, is Gwat, the "pig" of Bemut. The cave Lamonagun,
which contains pictures of snakes, lizards, wallabies, sharks,
and so forth, is another *goron tadak*. The cave pictures are
themselves *masoso* and can be animated by the *tadak*, who
can then "go out" in the form of the depicted animal. Arala,
the wallaby *masoso* of Wutom, is one of the creatures pic-
tured (and animated) in this way.

The python form of the Wutom *tadak*, Barbarnao, was apparently earlier the *tadak* of the related clan Tamolmol, for
whose last survivors (it is now defunct) Wutom held the mortuary feasts. Barbarnao sleeps at the Gogo (its Tamolmol *goron tadak*) and Laumalaga rivers. If the water is held in the
estuary by stones, the *masalai* is sleeping there; if the current runs into the sea, he has left. The *momo*, or surf place,
of Wutom is Lawagus, between the Gogo and Laumalaga riv-

ers. An *urin* tree, Tababaling ("it falls down, hangs itself back up again"), at Dadalus, the "point" of Bakan, is the *masalai* tree of Wutom. In earlier times it had the power of killing those who tried to climb it, though now this capability has been weakened. The *uno no silie*, a line of little shore birds that run in single file along the beach at Kotum, are also Wutom *masoso*.

In addition to Barbarnao, Wutom also lays claim to the *tadak* Kawuluwun, the former *masalai* of Luage Clan, together with the extensive Luage grounds in the bush back of Bakan. Luage was a Tago clan that formerly shared *mis* with Nagira: the name Luage refers to the base of bamboo, and it is said that when the line was young the bamboo consisted of shoots; as it grew, the bamboo also grew; and when the line died out, the bamboo also withered and died. A childless Wutom man named Lewi went down to Punam, to the south, and purchased the last surviving Luage child, a boy, and brought him to Bakan. On the strength of its care for this child, and the promise of carrying out his mortuary rites, Wutom thus claims heirship of a clan of the opposite moiety.[8]

Kawuluwun lives at the small lake Tudamo, located in the bush inland of Bakan. Small ducks living on the lake are *masoso*, and it is understood that if anyone hunts or harms them, the *masalai* will not permit people to collect crayfish or eels at the lake. The origin myth of Luage, however, concerns another *tadak* (or rather *tadak* pair) and is regarded by the Usen as a marvelous bit of local folklore. It is worth repeating:

A man of Lulubo [Kolonoboi], back in the bush, took a net one day and went down to fish at the river Kelege. At the same time, the young woman Kelege [or Mene], daughter of the python Maluanga

---

[8] This is not in itself without precedent, insofar as a *taun* that passes from father to offspring must necessarily also pass from one moiety to the other. Apparently *tadak* and land may also, and succession is a separate consideration from the sharing of *mis*.

and the wallaby Luage [or Arala], left the cave that she shared with them and went down to the river to fetch water. As she replaced the folded-leaf stopper of the tube in which she carried water, she threw the old stopper out into the current. It floated downstream and lodged in the man's net. The man found it and said, "Oh, women use these to fasten their bamboo tubes—where could this woman be from?" The next afternoon he went down again and set out his net, and he caught another stopper. He went upstream to find out where it had come from, and found the woman sitting by the water. "Where are you from?" "My place is on top there with my mother and father; come with me and see them." When they came close to the cave, the woman said, "You wait here; I will go and tell my parents about you." At the cave there was a large limb of the *kala* tree that the python rested on; he would twist around it and rest his head in the fork at the top. The woman told her mother; her father was still ranging the bush in search of game. Her mother asked where the man was, and the daughter went and brought him to the cave. When they arrived, the girl told him not to be frightened if he heard the sound of a snake approaching, for it would be her father. Her father arrived, and wound around the limb, and the wallaby went and told him about the man their daughter had found. In the morning the python said, "Alright, our daughter has found a man and can marry him; now you [to his wife] can stay here, and I will go off and live in the bush—we will cease to be married." The snake went off to live in the bush; perhaps it is dead by now. The wallaby, which used to visit Belik, Kolonoboi, and Bakan, went to the lake called Tingamo [Tudamo], back of Bakan. Their daughter married the man and went to live at Lulubo. She bore the clan Luage. If someone of the line died, the wallaby would go to Bakan and stay there for the funerary feasts, and then go back after the banana feast [*a un gogorop*]. When the daughter and her husband left the cave, they carried with them the yam *a gaubo*, a large, round tuber, the yam of Luage, and all the people got it from there and planted it at their places.

If the woman is "Kelege," the river, then the man, in marrying her becomes, through a series of substitutions, the equivalent of her leaf stopper, fastening the flow of her fluid (as in Barok procreation ideology) and allowing her to conceive. This forging of a human bond supplants her nonhuman parentage, and her mother, at least, wanders off to become a *masoso*. Ultimately, human lineality (the Luage line) replaces the direct (and interspecific) generation of people by *tadak*. What is intriguing here is the possibility that this account may conceal the "charter" of an earlier assimilation of clans and their *tadak* (Arala, Maluanga), by Luage, just as Luage was later to be assimilated by Wutom. The myth is a statement of the clan's origin through the power of *tadak*, and this, as the final example demonstrates, is no mean consideration.

The *Masalai* That Drowned Namatanai

The regional center of Namatanai, with its police station, hospital, government offices, development bank, mission, and Chinese trade stores, is the product of a long colonial and postcolonial metamorphosis. Founded by the German administration in 1904 as a center for the pacification of the native population, it became, in the 1950s and 1960s, the model of an Australian subdistrict headquarters, with its exclusive club and its well-kept lawns (upon which indigenes were not encouraged to sit). By 1979, however, the expatriates' club was a shattered ruin, and informants recounted local history for me as we sat on the lawns of the once high and mighty. But the town is busier than ever, the retailing and copra-marketing hub of half of New Ireland; every day the town is inundated with colorful fleets of secondhand trucks and their occupants, and there is a furious exchange of money.[9] The pragmatic center of this life is "Father Joe" Gloexner's St. Martin's Parish workshop, where the trucks are kept run-

[9] The rustic facilities of the place (an informant once volunteered that "in a real town they cut the weeds") contrasts vividly with the sums of money that change hands there.

ning, and the bar of the Namatanai Hotel, nearby, where the drivers are serviced.

Down the center of the settlement, from the police station to the council chambers, runs a ravine, normally almost dry, which has made the town as vulnerable to the traditional powers of *tadak* as to the contemporary ones of economic development. I was made aware of this when, leaving a celebratory "singsing" sponsored by the Catholic Mission, I fell into step with a robust, white-haired old man. "This whole town, all of this ground, belongs to me," he proclaimed, gesticulating expansively as I privately pondered the likelihood of finding similar old men in, say, San Diego. My acquaintance was a Guogo man who had been born at Matatulet Hamlet in Bakan. During a later visit to Matatulet, he explained how he had "stopped the dozers" at a government construction site near a *masalai* place, and finally won the right to compensation for his connection with the place. The *tadak* concerned is named Urlaba; it is claimed by both moieties and associated with a spring and a small lake. The association with Namatanai is explained in the following story:

There were two boys [unnamed in the traditional version, identified now that there is litigation for the ground]; the elder was of Ririr Clan, Tago Moiety, and the younger was of Guogo, Malaba Moiety. One day their mothers went off to work, and the two boys played at chasing lizards. The Guogo boy chased a lizard, they both ran after it, and then the Ririr boy took after a second lizard. The Guogo boy chased the first lizard until it ran under a stone. He lifted up the stone to get at it, and water gushed out. He cried out, "This is my water," but the Ririr child responded, "No, it belongs to both of us." The Guogo child reasserted his claim. He took a sago midrib and marked out a course for the water to flow in with it, down what is now the ravine in the center of Namatanai, from the police station to the council chambers. The Ririr boy marked his course for the water to flow into the Nambuto River. The two boys fought, and the Ririr boy, because he was older, won. He dammed the water at the branching of the two inscribed courses, so that the water coming from the spring would flow down his course and into the Nambuto.

Eels from this stream may not be taken when only small ones are running, or when small and large ones are running together, but only when they run in pairs of equal size, in the Labur. When the eels are taken from the water, they may be killed only by striking them with the leaves of a red *tanket* (*geregere dadan*). If the eels are killed with a knife, or if people take them when large ones are running with small ones, the water in the spring will boil up and, instead of the present trickle, a flood will roll down the ravine and inundate central Namatanai. Once in the past someone cut an eel there, and central Namatanai was flooded in this way. When this happened, the old man took two shillings, some red ochre, and some *mis*, and placed them at the base of a *kwila* tree at the *goron tadak*; the water ceased to boil.

It is interesting to note that any compensation that representatives of the two moieties might receive would be for traditional land claims and land rights, whereas the boys in the story fought over the *water* and its direction. From the old man's point of view, however, it is more likely the awesome *power* of the spirit, capable of drowning the town at will, that holds Namatanai in fee.

Ultimately unknowable and unpredictable, *tadak* as power, as origin, or as the basis of identity, is analogical, an unglossed and unglossable metaphor. Like kin relationship, it is elicited rather than stated. And while the unglossable essence of either relationship or *tadak* is hardly proof against attempts to delimit, circumscribe, or control them, everyone knows what happens to the person who reveals his relationship and communication with his *tadak*. He loses them.

SIX

Pidik and Power

THE "WORLD" or "world view" of the Usen, as well as the generic facility of accomplishing things in the world, *a la lolos* (Tokpisin *paua ologeta*), is something of an unglossable expression or, at best, a realm of possibilities only partially encompassed by human convention. Yet it is understood as the broadest or most extensive field of relations within which human effort accomplishes its ends. Any human enterprise is a realization of *a lolos*, requires it, and may be hindered by an adversary's use of it. Marianne George, who undertook a study of the conceptualization of power at Kokola, reports the use of the expression *iri lolos* (Tokpisin *paua pinis*), "manifest" or "completed" power, in reference to the ordered ceremonial of Barok *kastam*. In this sense the realization of ethos, of proper customary form, is itself both testimonial to, and containment of, the power necessary in its accomplishment. The *taun*, which holds within its enclosure the bodies of ancestors, is quite literally "frozen," or solidified, power.

Kastam, what an anthropologist would wish to call "culture," and human enterprise in general are realizations of capability in this respect. But this capability, or power, ultimately a relative quantity, is itself vulnerable to the standards of convention. Power is no more and no less effective than its *application* to the world of human requirements, wishes, interests and efforts, and thus power may be seen as identical with its own application. This means that the form assumed by power may be that of some kind of trickery or deception, a technological or artistic innovation, a skill or talent, or any of a broad and diffuse range of spells, procedures, and techniques impinging upon the conventional order.

The problem of holding or fixing an unglossable mystery, a "power," within social or cultural forms is rather different from that of articulating a legitimate "closure" for elicited kin relationships. For, unlike the issues developed in relationship and inheritance, *lolos* itself cannot attain complete closure or resolution without losing its situation of advantage or "leverage" with respect to conventional forms. Thus, power must be retained socially in the form of a concealed "mystery" or cult, one that, as an "application" of power, stands in a contingent relation to social convention. The (Tolai or "Kuanua") term with which Barok identify socially retained mystery, *a pidik* (or *a widik*), quite significantly can be used either with reference to the mystery itself or with reference to the social aggregate (a "lodge," so to speak) in which it is contained. For both are effectively the same thing—a consensual *image* rather than a consensual symbol. An image is performative and self-contained; it is only to be witnessed or revealed. It is in this same sense that the complex of *kastam*, of feasting in the *taun*, can be described as *iri lolos*: it, too, for all the fact that it is the means of effecting social closure, *is* a consensual image. It amounts, as we shall later see, to a "picture" of containment itself.[1]

Pidik

What is in fact remarkable about *pidik* as the actual accommodation of cult within Barok life is its formal resemblance

---

[1] As collections of myths, rituals, and other self-contained forms, rather than texts, techniques, and "knowledge," Melanesian "cultures" on the whole tend to be constructs of consensual imagery rather than articulative symbol. Thus the comparative analogy afforded by our term "culture" is apt to be misleading in their case.

to *kastam*. Like *kastam* it is exclusively male; its activities are distinguished by esoteric terminologies and protocols and are centered on a special house, the *gunun a pidik* (in some cases, more specialized terms are used); and they culminate in a performance or presentation by a select few for the edification of a greater number. Likewise, not only the culmination of these undertakings, but every step in their preparation is marked by feasting (in most cases).

Beyond these resemblances, however, *pidik* is an optional, even incidental, part of Barok life. The word *pidik* is said to mean literally "breaking open," in the sense of "revealing," but it was glossed for me in Usen as *pet-sugu-me*, a work "in secret" or "done hidden." The work is undertaken usually for its own sake, for the pleasure of a somewhat conspiratorial participation, and often for the enhancement of the member's self-esteem and social standing. Some *pidik* (for example, *a tonoe*) provide the focus for the initiation or training of youths; others seem to draw in the young and statusless through the insinuation that membership will bring them arcane and useful powers. Although this motive may also persist in later life, a more common one is evidenced in the following reply by an informant, one of the more notorious "joiners" in the area, to my query as to why one would ever bother with a *pidik*:

Men try and see how many houses they can win. If I wish to raise the "cry" of the Taberan, and another man challenges my right to do so, I will ask him how many houses he has won. If he has won fewer than I, I will not have to pay him [a fine]. I have won five Taberan houses, three Talum Rokoi and two Talum Asa Sogopana. By seeing many houses, you can learn many details; different holders of the same *pidik* will use different techniques and materials. Raragot uses the rope of the *pidigut* vine for making the cry, Sangin uses a *tanket*, Aisak uses *worowos kulanga*, Bongal uses a kunai grass blade, and Misidoni uses rubber strings from an old [golf?] ball.

123

A number of general "kinds" of *pidik* have been known and performed in the Usen area, though the time and energy presently devoted to these activities probably fall far short of the effort committed in the past. *Pidik* that involve esoteric powers, such as the Gigip To, whose members drank the *maut*, or decomposition-juices of corpses in order to gain transcendental abilities, including the power of flight, and the Buai, much of whose terminology and imagery dominate Usen individual "power" usages, tend to be evanescent, possibly because of the rivalries and accusations that they inevitably provoke. The more widespread and popular *pidik*, the Taberan and Tubuan, amount to more-or-less institutionalized cults or "mysteries," a phenomenon that enjoyed a practically universal currency among traditional Melanesian cultures. Although initiation into the "order" figures prominently in the dynamic of these *pidik*, others, such as Tonoe and Kanut, seem to have been centered upon the initiation of youths. The former lodge (the latter will be described in another chapter) involves the dramatic revelation of an ingenious, self-releasing fish trap[2] to groups of youthful male initiates, who are kept in seclusion and taught to use the device, and who are also initiated into various kinds of fishing power.

The centrality of technological marvels in this *pidik* (as well as in virtually all others), and even in my informant's rationale for joining *pidik*s, is noteworthy,[3] and seems to be

[2] According to Dr. Philip Lewis (personal communication, 1980) such traps are known widely throughout central New Ireland. The youths are first told that they will have to dive deep into the sea and retrieve the traps, which have been sunk outside the reefs, and are then allowed to "discover" the released traps "magically" floating on the surface.

[3] The technological facility of New Ireland cultures, and perhaps also the degree to which technical "tricks" are incorporated into art and ceremonial, recalls the similar bent of the North American Northwest Coast peoples. A native of the west coast Mandak village of Dampet once described to me an indigenous local *malanggan* that ran on vine cables overhead and that took

the dominant motive in a final form, what I shall call the "culinary *pidik*." One of these, the Kalagorgor, is devoted to steam-cooking food in rock ovens in such a way that the food will not be disfigured in the process. Members of the *pidik* must first purify themselves through the *ololo* abstinence, and the food is then placed inside the leaf sheath of an unopened coconut frond for cooking. An even more ingenious culinary mystery is called Agon Ari Ararum ("Some Tabooed Water"). This is a *pidik* concerned with the serving of the juice of green coconuts in a decorative manner at a *taun* feast. First, a man climbs a tree to obtain *polo*, green (drinking) coconuts; these are not simply allowed to drop to the ground, as ordinarily, but must be carried down suspended from ropes worn on the sides of the body. The coconuts are then opened, and their juice is poured into the leaf sheath of the fruit-bearing stem of the coconut tree. Then a second sheath is pulled over the mouth of the first in such a way as to form an apparently seamless container. The container is decorated with a chain of white *gagus* (Tokpisin *gorgor*) flowers around the middle and a white chicken feather sticking up on top. Then each member of the *pidik* decorates himself as for a dance, places his *rat* on his left shoulder, and takes up a closed container in each arm. The men march in double file to the *taun*, where each man presents one container each to two of the assembled feasters. The feasters look in vain about the containers to find an opening from which to drink, until the leader of the *pidik* publicly demonstrates how to lift off the top sheath.

The highly organized and coordinated singing and dancing mimes that Barok call *a tinie* (Tokpisin *singsing*) are also prepared and rehearsed in a *pidik* format, until they are revealed,

---

the form of a human figure, the Liwiga La Malom. It paused from time to time in its traverse to disgorge ("defecate") tidbits to the waiting crowds below, but refused to move if anyone in the village had been guilty of a moral wrong.

like the *pidik* of *agon ari ararum*, to a wider audience. Specific *tinie* are named and are gender-specific (several are prepared and performed by women, others by men). Preparation is always a "secret work," integrally bound up with the prideful "face" and social standing of the performers and the community they represent. *Tinie* are rehearsed for weeks or months in advance of a performance, and preparation involves a "teaching" of the movements and details to performers, administering of power foods or manipulations, preparation of personal *bilas* (decorations),[4] and rehearsal (with the leader using a wand or baton to ensure coordination).[5] The sessions are held in a secluded area, one that is taboo to the sex not participating, and are managed and directed by an "owner" of the *tinie* (or of the associated *pidik*), someone who has purchased the knowledge and the right to perform it.

In September 1979, some men of Bakan and Kolonoboi invited me to take part in the rehearsal and presentation of two *tinie* for the *kaba* to be held at the northern Barok village of Lokon the following month. The *tinie* involved were the Pinpidik, a traditional piece whose association with a *pidik* (if it ever had one) has been lost, and the Ingas, the *singsing* that accompanies the Taberan. The sessions were directed by a young man of Kolonoboi, who was in process of purchasing the Taberan, under the tutelage of the older man from whom he was purchasing it. Rehearsals took place on several desig-

---

[4] The Tokpisin word *bilas* is often traced to the English term "flash," but my colleague, Professor H. L. Seneviratne, has pointed out to me that a Sanscrit term for "self-decoration" is *vilaśa*, pronounced *bilaśa* in modern Bengal.

[5] The leader of the *tinie* rehearses the percussion accompaniment by indicating rhythmic figures via the waving of his baton, and also by imitative vocal explosions, not unlike those used in rehearsal by a Western conductor. A leader whom I approached on the subject insisted that the use of the baton was traditional, and seemed never to have heard of the Western practice.

nated afternoons a week, in a small cleared area in the bush just above the beach at Biribiri, Kolonoboi. A small, half-pitch hut afforded shade and shelter for the performers, and for the delicate coronets that served as the major decorative element for the dancers. Every session was punctuated by a convivial gathering at the hut and a meal—at least rice and tinned fish, and, on one occasion, a feast of sea turtle.

But the *pidik* format was more than superficial. Although "membership" was open to all men of Bakan and Kolonoboi (they seemed to be largely younger men, in fact), the "rehearsal" might better be seen as a gradual and controlled revelation of the *tinie* both to and by the performers. This was evident from the manner in which the "teaching" was conducted. This was, except for practical details, entirely by example and imitation. Thus, as a performer of the *agono pit kundut*, the hourglass-drum accompaniment, I was instructed in how to hold the *kundut* (Tokpisin *kundu*), or drum, how to brace it against my knee, and how to hold my fingers in striking it. I was not, however, given any instruction in anything relating to the substantive "content" of the *tinie*, either in terms of rhythmic or melodic patterns, or in those of its "meaningful" verbal or mimetic intent, or even in the parsing of the whole into its *agana* ("branches"), or what we might call "movements." My task was simply to begin drumming along with the others in the *kundut* section, trying to keep their rhythm and figuration, stopping or changing when they did, and hoping not to be "caught out" when the whole barrage came to a halt. As a guide, I had the services of the director of the *tinie*, whose cues and signs may well have had a consistency to them, though their significance was never explained to me (or, as far as I can determine, to anyone else). The essence of the *tinie* is only to be experienced, and only through experience to be imitated, and only through imitation learned, in this procedure. Its relation to a world of verbalized concepts is entirely omitted.

127

Nor would this headlong venture into what in Tokpisin is called *mekim save* ("giving to understand," with an inflection of "Schadenfreude") have been very different had I elected to participate as a dancer, and learn the song line (*a sino ni tinie*), the choreography (*agono pigir nitini*), and the mimetic arm and body gestures (*agono winiwit*) of a full participant in the *tinie*. For these "lessons" were experienced in much the same way as those of the accompaniment. The power of the *tinie* was received as the power to perform it. In the case of the Ingas, the *tinie* of the Taberan, the power of the *pidik* itself is manifested in the performance. As a precaution against its effects, those of us who participated were assembled one day and whipped, one by one, across the backs of the calves with a plant stem that had been treated with ginger (*laie*; in Tokpisin, *kauwawar*) and bespelled. This would protect us from the consequences of invoking the power, and also render our legs generally immune to sores for a while.

The Taberan

The Taberan (in Tokpisin and in many indigenous languages the "b" is prenasalized: *tamberan*) and the Tubuan are widespread lodgelike cults or mysteries that are owned and performed in the Usen area. As *pidik* they are somewhat special and elaborate, and each is presided over by a spirit: the *barames* in the case of the Tubuan, the *taberan* in the *pidik* of the same name. The Tubuan, with its distinctive masked figures, is somewhat the better known of the two, though the Taberan, which I shall consider here, was more recent and active in the Usen area during my fieldwork.

The *gunun a pidik* of the Taberan is called a *kamnar*, and sometimes the entire *pidik*, or its two dichotomous manifestations, are known by this term (the corresponding term for the Tubuan is *taraiu*). The leader, or "owner," of the lodge is called *a unine* Taberan ("the base of the Taberan"); a qualified member is *ain pidik*; a novice or initiate is a *surumitik*; and a nonmember or "outsider" is a *moro*. The *unine* Taberan trains the *ain pidik*; when the best *ain pidik* has mastered it, the *unine* will sell it to him. The *surumitik* may make the "cry" of the Taberan, and the *ain pidik* may make the "cry" of the "mother of the Taberan." Should a *surumitik* attempt the latter, a *tanket* (cordyline or cordyline leaf) would be sent to him to let him know that he must pay the fine of a pig.

The central mystery of the Taberan is the power of miraculously joining or healing that which has been cut or rent asunder, and its social form is therefore dual, that of a scission. The respective "halves" belong to, and are composed of, members of the two moieties. The names of the divisions are in the Susurunga language, that of the area from which the Taberan was introduced: the name of the Malaba Moiety is the Talum Asa Sogopana, the "Wild Pigs of the Beach"; that of the Tago Moiety is the Talum Rokoi, the "Wild Pigs of the Bush." The Talum Asa Sogopana is said to be "female," and its initiation involves the making of many small cuts; the Talum Rokoi is "male," its initiation entailing large cuts. The Talum Rokoi at Kolonoboi was sold by Raragot, of Porabunbun, to Bikit for a *pram* of red *mis* worth about 20 *kina*; the Talum Asa Sogopana was bought by Aisak from Tuanela of Uris Village for one pram of red *mis*. When Aisak dies, his nephew will have possession of the cult.

The Taberan is "aroused" (an idiom for the "performance," which is at once a rite of constitution or affirmation and an initiation), at a *kamnar* secluded in the bush, by those in the *pidik*. At this time the cry of the Taberan may be heard in the distance, and there is a taboo or curfew on walking about on the road, lest noninitiates should happen upon any of the proceedings. The cry is made with a *tangalaop* bullroarer (taboo to the eyes of women) and with a *kio*, a reed placed in a frame and played with the mouth, something like

129

a kazoo. *Ain pidik* will come from the *kamnar*, sounding the cry, march to the village, circle the *surumitik*, and then bring him to the *kamnar*, where he may stay for a week or more. They may bring one of the pigs intended for the feast, seat the neophyte upon it, and carry him thus to the lodge. One *ain pidik* takes care of each *surumitik*; the latter is not allowed to speak, and must make gestures to indicate his needs. When the speaking taboo is to be lifted, one *ain pidik* will pluck a live fowl, put it into his carrying basket (*a rat*), and loose it among the *surumitik*. Their excited crying and jumping about effects a "spontaneous" end to the silence. The initiates eat pork for three days in the bush, after which the *ain pidik* go to the bush for the performance.

The Ingas *tinie* is performed as an integral part of the event, and is itself a public and dramatic enactment of the social juncture and integration of the two moieties. As an "entry" of the central *pidik*, or mystery, it has the effect of saturating the initiates, who are themselves prevented from any but the most rudimentary gestural communication, in a wealth of gestural, kinetic, and aural imagery. The dancers mime the confrontation and ultimate reconciliation of the moieties. The instruments used in the "cry" of the Taberan are employed, and dancers hold an ornament called *a balilai*. The *tinie* begins with two groups of dancers: the Talum Rokoi are the "men of anger," and enter, with their own *kundut* section, from the bush; the Talum Asa Sogopana, the "men of compassion," enter similarly from the direction of the beach. Each party is dressed in warrior's attire, and the dancers crouch and mime the whirling of a sling in the right hand. Each group enters the cleared area in a straight line, cutting diagonally across the open space so that the two parties come in like parallel slashes, each line facing the other. After menacing one another, the two are reconciled and dance together.

The verbal line of the *tinie*, in what appears to be a vernacular form of Tolai, seemingly cryptic, may actually comment on the interrelationship of the moieties. An *unine* Taberan glossed it for me as follows:

TINIE URUNO

[INTERPRETIVE COMMENT: Invokes the sorrow of the initiates' mothers for their sons, who must go off to the bush.]

Awe nago, tang balam
Oh mother, it cries my belly

To Malile, lumiai-i
Mr. Calm Sea, he's sorry about it,

O tang balam ten,
oh, it cries my belly again,

To Malile, lidori aie, lidori aie.
Mr. Calm Sea, it has a cause, it has a cause.

A-GANA MUMU

[INTERPRETIVE COMMENT: This is the talk of the father, who is at the end of his years; all the others garden, but he has no food.]

Gamuim, gamuim,
You all work, you all work,

maia wa tulu kis, ngodai nangoi
but I just sit down, what will come of me?

matu kamne balbal
there isn't anything,

yamude tare, yamade tari-a-o.
there's nothing, there's nothing now.

The two "movements" each constitute an appeal, or elicitation, to one of the two nurturing modes through which one relates to a moiety (and through which, as idioms, the moieties address and confront one another): that of maternal containment, and that of paternal inception and fosterage. Each initiate and member of the *pidik* will relate in one way or the

131

other to each of the respective moieties, or "sides," of the Taberan; and the invocation of the emotions that relate the
moieties serves to "present," as does the *tinie* as a whole, the
melding of these divisions into a social whole.

As they enter, the "men of anger" carry sticks (about 1 m
long and 3 cm in diameter); while the *tinie* is in progress, the
initiates come forward, bend over, and are struck on the back
with the sticks, as many times as the striker wishes. Then a
call is made for the cry to cease, it ceases, and the *tinie* is sung
more softly, for it is time to cut the initiates. Cutting was formerly done with an ax, but is now done with a razor. Either a
frame is made to hold the initiate while being cut, or, more
usually now, he lies face down. The *surumitik* is painted in
black, decorated with lime powder, and a leaf cape is put on
his back in such a way that he cannot sit down. Should the
cape fall down, and someone else touch it, the toucher would
be afflicted with terrible sores, for which a special cure must
be done. The initiates lie in a line. Two men are involved in
the cutting: one holds the razor; the other carries the special,
bespelled lime powder (*a kabak*), which is applied to the incisions. The man with the razor makes a diagonal incision
across the back of each *surumitik* (a second, for the Talum
Rokoi, will be made a week to a year later), and then his partner pours lime powder into the wound, mounding it up over
the slash so that some will spill out when it dries. The powder
holds the power to stop bleeding and heal the cut. After the
cutting, the *surumitik* lie down for about an hour, and the
leader of the cutting tells them when to get up. The excess
powder is cleaned off, and blood does not flow. After this the
initiates stay in seclusion for about a week. They cut a banana
tree, plant it in the bush, hunt wild pigs, fish for eels, and go
fishing by torchlight. Then they return to the village.

The lime powder is sung over with a spell known to the *unine* Taberan. Part of it is used for the initiates, and another
part is reserved to treat the women who cook food to send to

the *kamnar*, to keep them from getting sick. (The powder is put on the outer corners of their eyes.) The old *unine* Taberan who served as my chief informant regarding this *pidik* responded to my queries about the Taberan "spirit" with a patronizing smile. The "Taberan," he said, is a deception to frighten outsiders, and the power of the *pidik* resides in the bespelled lime powder. The cutting shows (*i mekim save*) or demonstrates the power of the cult, making the incisions heal quickly. Those who have the power of the Taberan will not be cut by thorns and vines in the bush.

The significance of this cult is that it concentrates a variety of imagistic means to manifest a single *pidik* mystery: that of the awesome force that welds or heals separated parts into a viable whole. That the same force acts socially, upon the two moieties, and physically, upon the human body, is central to its conception as a unitary power, and the knowledge and ability to use that power is the signal achievement of the Taberan, the "power" conferred upon its members. As with all *pidik*, this "principle" is revealed through a form of *giaman* (Tokpisin) or deception, that of the Taberan spirit, whose foreboding presence is dissolved for initiates by their witnessing of the instruments through which the "cry" is made, and ultimately by the demonstration of the lime powder.

The "deception" practiced here is a matter of considerable theoretical and ethnographic interest, for it pervades Barok culture as a basic approach to learning and knowledge, and is widespread elsewhere in Melanesia. As Barth's notion of the "epistemology of secrecy"[6] suggests, and Jorgensen's work among the Telefol[7] elucidates, it is a major preoccupation among the "Mountain Ok" peoples. In a sense, some of the most significant victims of the deception have been non-Melanesians (including, occasionally, ethnographers), for it is

---

[6] Barth, *Ritual and Knowledge among the Buktaman of New Guinea*, chap. 24.

[7] Jorgensen, "Taro and Arrows."

133

temptingly easy to regard the natives' own revelation of the techniques used in producing an effect as their tacit acknowledgment of a Western-style materialist "reality." There is, however, no evidence whatsoever that this is their intent. As serious Western practitioners of illusion and sleight of hand know,[8] the revelation (or the retention, as the case may be) of the "real" techniques "behind" the illusion represent not less, but more, power. As the illusion constitutes power over the noninitiate, so the revelation of its means amounts to power over the illusion. Those for whom technical gadgetry claims a more preeminent reality than the dynamics of learning and revelation might wish to separate these two "powers," but in terms of *a lolos* they amount to the same thing. The "gimmick" of a *pidik* is, however technological, real power, and so is the deception through which it is revealed. In the course of the Taberan performance a diffusely threatening spirit is transformed, for the *surumitik*, into the revelation of a powerful principle, or force, and into the means of its control. Knowledge is power here, and trickery the means to insight.

It is also, however, social power, for in bringing about a concerted effort on the part of many men and women for a considerable period, the instrumentive and educative intent of the *pidik* manages to compel and mobilize its own sociality. This is less appreciable in terms of the traditional Durkheimian notion of a society objectifying or integrating itself through its rites (for the "society" often represents but a motley selection of the available—younger—men) as it is in terms of "social power" for its own sake. An "expression," that is, of collective coalescence is elicited (in the evocation of the intermoiety motifs of motherhood and *nat* in the *tinie*) in

---

[8] My paternal grandfather, Robert Herrmann Wagner, who gave large public performances of stage magic and lightning-quick calculation, drew no professional distinction between illusionist techniques and the highly sophisticated algorithms he used in solving mathematical problems.

much the same way as kin relationship is elicited by joking and respect protocols. Something of the sort might also be seen in the lodges and fraternal orders of urban societies, though in Melanesia, where responsibility for the collective generally occurs only in a ritual context, the "magic" of compelling sociality might be understood to have a special appeal.

Power

Whether it is vested in *pidik* or held and transmitted individually, power (*a lolos*) is invariably esoteric among the Barok. While this is certainly the rule in Melanesia generally (and if power were not esoteric, the assumption seems to be, it would scarcely be worth bothering with), the claims, levels of public "confidence," and, therefore, accusations of fraud associated with it among the Usen are rather distinctively extravagant. Power is obviously, for them, involved in every successful venture or achievement, and it is also just as obviously involved when things go wrong. Even for the educated, to quote a rather subtle joke on the properties of the "supernatural," "these things work whether you believe in them or not."

Though it deals with every imaginable sort of contingency and problem, Usen power usage tends to focus upon occasions and interests that are central to traditional Usen life. Much of it concerns warfare, wealth, gardening and fishing, and sexual attraction (a power adept once assured me that "no one in New Ireland marries for love alone"). The staging of public feasts and *tinie* performances is conceived, on the practical level, to be a kind of wager, hanging in the balance between the positive power of those who organize them and the negative influences of the understandably jealous. Something of the same tension surrounds every circumstance of achievement or status quo, necessitating (and perhaps also stemming from) a broad range of "protective magic"—"watch" spirits and spells, as well as power to confuse judges so that they will drop a case. Beyond such "practically focused" power lies the realm of power as an end in itself—general procedures that are undertaken in order to enhance the efficacy of power, to obtain power or knowledge, or to nullify the power of others. It is in this area that the *pidik* concerned with transcendental capabilities, the Gigip To and the Buai, have at times dominated the scene.

Usen do not systematize or ideologize power and its sources. Like the *tadak*, power is sui generis; or it was put there by the creator(s) (Moroa, God, or possibly Silik and Kambadarai); or it is, like *kastam*, a legacy of the ancestors, communicated to present-day people through dreams and secret lore. In the end, the wellsprings of *a lolos* are coterminous with those of human life and usage themselves. One widespread technique of power is to capture the life force of the dead or dying, either by securing or treating bones and other relics, or by hiding a bit of ginger in the mouth of a dying man, and then retrieving it (or, failing that, a bit of froth from the mouth) upon burial.

Power is *a lolos* or *wewet* in Usen; an item of "magic," a spell and/or various abstinent or manipulative procedures, is *a mameng*, whereas the "talk" alone is *a kobo*. "Killing" sorcery is *a piot* or *a wiot*, or *piorin* (Tokpisin *posin*); "personal leavings" sorcery, wherein bodily exuviae or relics are treated in order to cause injury or death, is *songora maine*. Barok power usages make extensive use of ginger, *laie* (Tokpisin *kauwawar*), and of the *gagus* (Tokpisin *gorgor*) plant, with its profuse, small white flowers, used otherwise as a sign of taboo.

It would be difficult to estimate the number and kinds of *mameng* held and transmitted by the Usen; they are held secretly by individual persons or lineages, and are seldom talked about. Those that do come to light are not significantly different from similar usages found elsewhere in Melanesia:

they can be seen to construct an analogy between the actions and utterances of the *mameng* and the desired result. Thus Marianne George reports that an Usen *orong* seeks to amplify his wealth by reciting a spell as he sweeps up pig excrement in his pig enclosure; as he sweeps, he calls out the names of other *orong* and tells them to send him *mis*. An analogy can be seen here between the excrement, produced by the pigs in the course of raising them, and the *mis* produced through exchanging them, so that one objectified result of pig raising is identified with another in the verbal context of relations between *orong*. Another *mameng*, called *sumo gunun* ("shoving from the house"), utilizes analogical motion. A man, for instance, who wants a woman's husband to leave the house the next day can send him "north" to the *mara mangin* by going secretly to his house at night and shoving it in the desired direction while repeating this spell:

a bo, a bo, a bo,
the pig, the pig, the pig,

o kipla todi na oro te wosu
O fetch the man from his bed

(u)ri go mara mangin
north to the eye of the *mis*

The spell invokes spirit pigs to carry the husband away.

The analogy need not be verbal. When sardines (*tele*) come close to the shore at Cape Kono, just south of Bakan, the power *a bien i tele mogo wugis a tele* is done to hold them there. To work it, one goes to the bush and finds a kind of palm called *gele*, whose areca-nut-like seeds hang on a long vine. The ripe fruits are picked up from the ground and put in a *gagus* leaf until it is filled. A long, thin packet is made, fastened on the left side (*kubus ko lawa kes*), and carried back to the village. The man who wants to do the power must watch carefully to make sure that no people are out on the reef; if people are there, the packet is hidden for the time being. When the reef is empty of people the packet is buried in the sand near the cape, and stones are put over it. The power does not have a spell, though the analogy can be detected: a bush fruit that grows in long clusters, like schools of the gregarious *tele*, is gathered from the ground and fastened (from the left, *kes*, the side of "indirection") in the leaf of a *gagus*, a plant used for tabooing or "fastening." In the absence of any witnesses, it is secured and buried on the beach, a place medial (like the habitat of coconuts, the manifestation of Satele, "fisher of *tele*") between bush and sea. "Fastening" a wild bush fruit "on the left" and securing it between bush and sea can be seen to draw together the two "halves" of the food quest and to hold *tele* in the correct (e.g. "right") manner off the reef.

Weather magic does not have the salience among the Usen that it enjoys farther to the north, where it is treated somewhat like a *pidik*. Informants were able to list several rainmakers (*tene pet bara*) and sunmakers (*tene pet ʒaken*), and power is also known to call up winds and take away the heat of the sun. The local technique for rain involves a vine with "water inside" that grows in the bush. Many of these are cut and then tied up in a packet with wild bananas. The packet is put into the mud and allowed to rot. When it is rotten, black clouds begin to form and the rain issues forth. An enterprising *tene pet bara* at Kolonoboi simply keeps some of the vine and wild banana mixture in a small bottle in his *rat*; when he needs a bit of rain, he simply shakes up the bottle. A *tene pet ʒaken* of Belik uses a special stone for his craft; to ensure clearing weather, he paints the top of the stone with red ochre (*a tar*) and exposes it to the sun, "and the rain finishes." In Usen folklore the *kurus* (drongo) is a *tene pet bara*, calling out its characteristic *kurus lau lau* to invoke rain, whereas the *kalanga* (eclectus parrot) is the *tene pet ʒaken*, summoning the sunlight with its *ka ka ka*. People say that these birds compete, *du da i wewet bara, du da i wewet ʒaken* ("the two they conjure rain, the two they conjure sun") and that when patches of rain and clear sky appear in the morning, they are working out their differences.

Power, in its very conception, seems to have a competitive aspect for Usen, and much of the most prized power amounts to "antimagic." This is especially true of "watch" magic, intended to neutralize sorcery attacks and, like the Tolai *togal* planted by an adept (he was flown in from Rabaul) in front of my house, to "freeze" would-be thieves and intruders in their tracks until, questioned the next day, they make a full confession of their aims.[9] A power called *wat a bungin* is held by Liengmau Clan; it can be used to neutralize a large line in battle. The name of the power, used as a battle cry, weakens opponents "so that even women can kill them." A spell is recited upon meeting the enemy, who is then unable to respond. Another power involves a stone that can be thrown into a house so that when the inhabitants go to sleep, they will die completely instead.

Safeguards against pollution and contamination are essential in the practice of much Barok power, particularly the more demanding kind which involves transcendent capabilities. As a general rule, for instance, a menstruating woman or a man or woman who has walked about in polluted places should not enter a garden; nor should any person who has just eaten fish, sea turtle, octopus, or other sea creatures. A regimen of abstinence prior to the practice of power known as *ololo* works on the same general principles. *Ololo* is undertaken before serious ventures in hunting, fishing, shark snar-

---

[9] The *togal* was said to be human in form, the spirit of a dead man whose remains were somehow associated with the ginger plant (together with a cordyline plant) within the enclosure. No fish or remains of fish were to be taken near the fenced plot, and no one who had had recent contact with fish or fishing was to approach it, at the hazard of neutralizing its power. I was told not to be startled if I saw a human figure patrolling my house, and that it might also take the form of a firefly and make its rounds. Perhaps this explains the astonishingly rectilinear flight pattern of a firefly I noted on subsequent evenings, and perhaps it does not.

ing, planting gardens, doing love magic, performing a *tinie*, or entering upon any of the more demanding sorts of spirit communication and transformation.

Ololo may be practiced for as little as a day or for a considerably longer period. The seclusion for the leader of a *tinie* lasts a month or two; often it is done to prepare him for the *dedede*, the shaking or possession fit that coincides with communion with the spirit power of the performance. One leaves for the seclusion in the morning twilight, *kororo*, avoiding latrines or any other places befouled by refuse or excrement. The abstinent spends his time in and about a small secluded hut, like that which serves for *tinie* rehearsals. No contact with the other sex is permitted, and the use of any narcotics (such as areca nut or tobacco) or strong-smelling foods is strictly forbidden. Dogs should not be permitted in the area. Food sent to the hut may be prepared only by the abstinent's wife, and must be carried in a long basket. The abstinent may not eat seafood of any sort and should not consume much water. The only proper food is *ku*, the thickened grease of coconuts, together with bananas. Ripe coconuts, *manga*, are also permitted. *Iwis*, small cockroaches, must be kept away from the food. The skin of an abstinent becomes loose as a result of a long *ololo*, and his eyes sink in.

A more certain counteragency than pollution is the practice of *puso met ai ni todi*, "killing the skin" of a man. This is an arcane "neutralizing" technique, and it is said that there are people about with "dead skins," whose very presence in a house will negate the effectiveness of power paraphernalia through the killing power that remains on the skin of the victim.

Like *pidik*, usages that are concerned with power for its own sake are maintained as mysteries, though here the mystery is more of a deadly secret. Those who boast of such powers too openly are apt to be publicly connected with their effects, or to be challenged by ambitious or unscrupulous rivals. These adepts live in what Carlos Castaneda has called a "sorcerer's world," where the only conceivable interaction is that of challenge and response. Their self-sealing obscurity, using *giaman* as a shield and a weapon, is only deceptively different from that of the *pidik*, or indeed from the image-centered closure that perfuses all large conceptual forms.

The techniques of communion with powerful spiritual entities are generally linked with a tradition that is sometimes traced to the Rabaul area and the Duke of York Islands, and otherwise said to have originated in the Barok area and then reintroduced from the Tolai-speaking region. Whatever the truth of these claims, much of the terminology that accompanies the usages is Tolai, and seems to be connected with an at least partially defunct *pidik* known as Buai ("Areca Nut"). The *pidik* is said to consist of a series of mysteries, each conferring special powers upon the initiate. Secluded in the bush, the initiate is given a series of "plates" of *ku*, containing as a rule various abhorrent substances, each of which corresponds to one of the powers. After partaking of the plate, the initiate is able to communicate with an *ingal* spirit in his dreams, who provides him with a figurative "demonstration" of the mystery. Dreams (*wo pana bo*), which are "seen" (though not necessarily enacted, as in other parts of Melanesia) by the dreamer's soul, are in any case *the* principal means of spiritual communion and revelation for Barok. But dreams can only be helpful in this way if induced with the aid of a specific, (some bespelled ginger, perhaps) or a generic (*u la ni wo pana bo*), plant juices mixed with oil and spread on the face. Dreaming of this sort may be practiced independently of the Buai, and is accompanied by taboos and agents to neutralize pollution. The dreamer is said to acquire a "watch spirit," a sort of poltergeist[10] that makes its presence evident in his house to discourage intruders.

---

[10] I became fairly accustomed to the unending flurry of small rattling and ticking noises emanating from an informant's locked house whenever I passed it. Too persistent, loud, and varied to have been made by rats, these

A man (Buai power is said to be inaccessible to women) accomplished in Buai knowledge and facility is a *tene buo* (a Tolai term, as in *tene pet bara*), or, in Barok, an *unine buo* ("at the base of the Areca"). A man accomplished in the ultimate and most puissant degree of power, said to require years of training, is an *iniat* (Tolai), *isuo* (Barok) or *komkom* (Tokpisin). A term with connotations of shamanism and sorcery might perhaps be applicable to the *iniat*,[11] whose transformational capabilities are distinctive.

The nonhuman side of this practice, the *ingal*, is in its proper form a dream being, though it is otherwise explained as either the spirit of a deceased man or a bush spirit. *Ingal* have names, which are revealed to their communicants (that of a brother of my informant is named Uruga-bin). Another form of *ingal* is the *barames* (a term also for the spirit of the Tubuan *pidik*), which operates as a watch-spirit and manifests itself as a poltergeist. A *barames* may attach itself to a person as a result of dream communion with an *ingal* (though the precise relation between the two spirits is obscure); to hold the being, or otherwise attract one, it is necessary to keep *barames* substance about one's residence. This consists of hairs, fingernails, or other relics of a deceased person (often a relative) which are mixed with red ochre and lime powder and hidden in a container (a "tin bottle" according to my informant, but then the preparation he showed me was kept in merely a tough plastic bag). When this is secured, the *barames* will come in the form of a firefly and enter the house (the owner should greet him: *Domun!*—"Good evening!").

---

would continue all day long when he was absent; nor did I hear such noises from any other houses. On the other hand, I never saw the apparition (frequently reported by neighbors) of the absent owner smoking on his veranda.

[11] I suggest the Spanish "brujo," with the connotations of its use as a loanword by those involved in indigenous power practices in Mexico. Of all the Melanesian adepts I have heard of, the *iniat* seems most to evoke a Castanedan context.

142

The *barames* will create the impression of continued occupancy in the house when its owner leaves, making continuous small sounds and sometimes appearing to outsiders in the form of the owner. If the owner should set a pig trap, the *barames* will let him know, making a noise by striking something, when a pig is caught in it. When the owner goes to sleep, the *barames* may communicate this information directly.

Several techniques are used by people seeking the more powerful, or, as my informant put it, "bush" *ingal*. One that is often mentioned involves the catching of a short, light-colored snake called *bo*, which is killed and fastened within the fruiting sheath of the areca palm. When it has decomposed, the man seeking power drinks the *maut*, or juices (as the power adepts of the Gigip To *pidik* were said to do with human *maut*). The main task in acquiring an *ingal*, however, involves the obtaining of a *worowos*, the arboreal nest of a species of termite. The *worowos* "has a man inside," the *ingal*. A man who wishes to obtain one must first *ololo*; then, having found a *worowos* (a long nest is said to be the most auspicious), he approaches the tree in which it is situated (along its shadow, for the shadow is the manifestation of its spirit) and fetches the *worowos*. The nest should be kept and cared for; it should be "awakened" every morning with a command and a sharp blow. The wings of the *worowos* insects are mixed with red ochre and kept, as with *barames* relics.

The *ingal* appears to its communicant in dreams,[12] "bringing along many things that he shows as examples." He demonstrates things figuratively ("as in pictures"), and it is said that everything he explains will become a permanent feature

[12] In power dreams, the *ingal* "of the Buai" turns into a *moran* (python) and coils about the dreamer's body. It gives the dreamer power by slipping its tongue within his mouth and touching it to his (an act to which my informant rather startlingly referred as "kissing").

143

of one's memory. He will explain that certain leaves are used for love magic or for *tinie*, and he can teach the substance of *pidik*, such as the Tubuan. An *ingal* can warn a family of sorcery directed against them, and will coach and reassure its confidant in sorcery duals: "Put this leaf in your mouth and spit it at ——; it will kill him." It is vitally important to hold one's rapport with an *ingal* in secret, and also to make sure that one is not awakened during the revelatory dreams, for this will break the spell, and the dream may not be rejoined later.

The *ban, malagum,* or *langaron,* held by the leader of a *tinie,* is made under the advisement of the *ingal.* This is a wand made of the peeled stalk of a bush plant; the lower part is hollowed out, and magical substances (often bespelled ginger) are put inside. The wand has the power to draw people to come and witness the *tinie;* it can also weaken opponents and throw them down. To activate the power, one takes the wand to a secluded place, recites a spell, and "shoots the eye of the sun," aiming it at the rising sun and invoking the latter.

Another aspect of *ingal*-derived power involves *a tadak,* and some people in fact identify the *ingal* as the "spirit of a *tadak*" (whatever that might mean). The basis of an *iniat*'s power is a small stone enclosure called a *palawat,* which is planted with cordyline and with a plant called *bubu.* The trunk of this plant (some say the flower) can be prepared for magical use; it is stripped (in this form it is called a *bum*) and used to strike a *masalai* stone or tree. The *bum* is then brought home and put by the pillow or head-support of the *iniat* at night. In his dreams the *tadak,* or perhaps the *ingal* as "spirit of the *tadak,*" will come and "show him all the things that live within the *masalai*" as a kind of power-filled perception or insight.

An *iniat* cannot eat pork or any food prepared by a woman; he must prepare his own food. His transformational power is in fact something of a human equivalent of the *tadak*'s distinctive form-changing facility. Kialmat of Kolonoboi, an *iniat*, traditionally went about "inside" sharks and eagles. He slept on a palm frond near a *tinie* hut, and warned the men around there not to awaken him while he slept. Once he cried out at night and vomited a human liver. When he awoke he told everyone that he had killed a man of Siar who had spoken ill of him. Kialmat would often appear as a snake; once he appeared in this form among the banana leaves wrapped about some *ku*. He gained his power by striking the stone of the *tadak* Rugawim; his *ingal* came from a long *worowos* that was found in the top of a *Ficus* tree. Kialmat, together with others, received his *unine buo* powers from Kupkin of Siar.

The similarity in form of power between the most puissant sort of human adept, the *iniat*, and the most formidable non-human power source, the *tadak*, can scarcely be explained by apocryphal (and highly speculative) accounts of *tadak* metamorphosing into *ingal*, though this is as acceptable as a "native model" as any other. Possibly the *iniat* "learns his craft" by peering into the *masalai*. On the other hand, the power to change form—power *over* the image—can be seen as the ultimate realizable power in a society dominated by consensual (visual) image. Whatever its ethnographic value, this material demonstrates the centrality of image and the closure (whether formal or "internal"—compelled by the "mystery" of esoteric content) that image effects in individuative as well as collective aspects of Usen culture. It is to the definitive ethical and social form of image, the "public *pidik*," as we might call it, that we now turn.

SEVEN

The Icon of Containment

THE *taun* and the feast in the *taun* are two intrinsically related aspects of a single consensual image, which is the *constitutive* image of Usen Barok culture. The *taun* is essential
as the visual matrix of meaning for the feast—not only its
setting, but also its icon; not only its container, but also the
container of the previously interred dead (the "ancestors")
and of the pigs' jaws and other carefully preserved relics of
previous feasts that lend the weight of precedent and authority to the occasion. A valid feast cannot be held except in a
taun,[1] and the feast is the patent of validity itself. The *taun*,
however, is quite literally made of feasts, for every single labor of foundation, construction, maintenance, or cleaning relating to the *taun* or its site, and every day of preparation for
a forthcoming feast, *must* be consummated by a formal feast
in the *taun*, or in as much of the *taun* as has been completed.
It might be said that the *taun* is at once the template for, and
the artifact of, the feast, and that the feast is the *activation* of
this construct. Together they form a single image or realization, like the "demonstration" of a *pidik*, which is performative and verbally unglossable. The image is that of containment itself; its figuration, through the course of the
performance, reveals the interrelation of *malum* and *malili*,

---

[1] The only exception is the *kaba*, the large, ultimate mortuary feast,
whose iconography negates that of the *taun*, so that it must be held outside
the enclosure. Marianne George notes traditions from the west coast to the
effect that preparations for a large *kaba* eventuated in the construction of
ad hoc communities or hamlets in the past.

of the continence and mutual inception, or nurturance, of the moieties.

This image is *constitutive* of Usen Barok culture, acquiring its validating powers (and its self-validation) through re-creation of the culture's core relation. Its relation to authority and precedent is likewise complex and dialectical, for as much as the feast draws upon the accumulated power and authority contained in the *taun*, it also, in its very activation, gives life and validity to that power and authority. Present aspiration may root its claim in the past, but the past can live, and realize its power, only through the constitutive acts of the present. Thus the values of *kastam*, which I shall consider in more depth in the following chapter, involve successorship in an active, rather than a passive, way; for the giver of a feast, in his ability to provide for and to organize the event, creates the very thing to which he succeeds. The feast in the *taun* is in this sense neither the symbol nor the recapitulation of previous feasts, but quite importantly is their *realization*, in such a way that *taun* and feast (with their various antecedents and contingencies) become one.

Considered in these terms, Usen culture is not so much a reflection of Western ideals of order, structure, and collective enterprise as it is the expansion of a single image, valorized in kin relations and their inflections of ethos, and pluralized in the powers of *tadak* and *pidik*. The force of this image is oblivious to the (historical) particularist issues of when and where Barok men's houses and feasting acquired their present significance, or how they relate to similar usages among neighboring peoples. It is also evasive of glossing (whether Barok or European) or of "explanation" in any direct sense through combinations of words. Usen have no general explanations, practical or ideological, of why the *taun* is arranged as it is, or why the various stages of the feast occur when and as they do. They learn these things by participation, for the *taun* and the feast are their own image. Accordingly, my eth-

147

nographic approach here will be indirect, approaching *taun* and feast through a number of descriptive parameters, with the hope that a certain naiveté might serve to burnish, rather than eclipse, the ambiguities of the native image.

The *Taun*

The Barok *taun* (*a taun*, or *a gataun* in some west coast regions) is a highly distinctive, remarkably uniform, and carefully constructed and maintained edifice. It is immediately recognizable and is almost invariably the strategic and prideful center of a hamlet. The general (uncodified) conventions of structure and size (very roughly about ten meters across the *balat* enclosure and fifteen to twenty meters from front to back) are quite conservative. Indeed, the few extreme deviations, such as Pokpok's concrete, fiberboard, and corrugated metal *gunun* at Belik, or the archaic Komarabege *gunun* at Kanapit, with its semicylindrical "quonset" roof, are disparate enough to prove, rather than challenge, the rule. The rather more frequent spectacle of a *balat* without a *gunun*, or of a *gunun* with a makeshift bamboo enclosure, or no enclosure at all, is likewise less an exception to the conservatism of form than it is a concession to the majestic pace of *taun* reconstitution and refurbishment. Not only every foundation, erection, or act of refurbishment concerning the *taun*, but also every discarding or burning of old fencing or thatch, or of dried or rotten *bebe* (half-pitch shelters for feasters) requires a feast, and hence pigs. In November 1979, I attended a feast for the reopening of an Unakulis *taun* at Ramat, which was only then brought into viable form since its destruction by the Japanese during World War II![2]

[2] I should note here, as my lineage-mate did in a speech on that occasion, that the refurbishment of this *taun* was accomplished entirely by the efforts of two Unakulis women of Ramat. Despite this fact, they partook of the feast with the other women, *outside* the *taun* enclosure.

A *taun* is, in conception, free and accessible to all men: except during a feast (when the space is needed to accommodate feasters), any man who wishes may at any time lie down and sleep in a *taun*; food and refreshment, whether at a feast or at other times, are provided for all. Unknown people, *ause igo taun* ("strangers to the *taun*"), may remain and be assured of food and shelter, for as long a time as they wish, and their support is incumbent upon the *orong* of the *taun*. It is forbidden—on pain of quite respectable fines—to argue, speak crossly, be angry, or fight in a *taun*.

The visual image of the *taun* is framed by the *balat*, a regular and rectilinear dry-stone wall (usually about a meter tall and a meter across) forming a rectangular enclosure about the *taun* proper; by the *olagabo*, the distinctive, V-shaped "gate of the pig," a stile carved (and, before the days of modern tools, burned)[3] of the extremely strong *kana* tree; and by the *gunun*, the stylized "house" itself, generally set about two-thirds of the way back from the entrance. The *balat* is punctuated by *kus*, staves of wood anchored to the ground so as to stabilize the stones,[4] and often embellished with globular, glass fishing floats recovered from the sea. In the past, the *olagabo* was sometimes carved with representational figures.

Most conspicuous in the open area between the *olagabo* and the *gunun* is the *butam*, a display table for feasting, located roughly in the center of the space. This is a platform of polished bamboo poles (*ko*) lashed across stringers (*hugo-bugo*) supported by four forked poles (*okosan*). The *butam* is a focus of feasting, and is treated in a practice called *wowomas ko butam*. Shredded bark from an *irima* tree is put into a

---

[3] In 1979-80 the *olagabo* of an ancient *taun* still stood just back from the beach along the road between Matatulet and Karitis hamlets at Bakan The *balat* had been removed long ago, perhaps during World War II, but the gate itself, still erect, had been shaped by *burning* rather than cutting.

[4] Traditionally a Barok child who lost a tooth would find a hole in the *kus* or *olagabo* and place the tooth in it, to ensure that the incoming tooth would sprout quickly.

palm spathe and is poured into the postholes of the *okosan* as these are installed. Later, when a feast is served, a spell called *agonolingi* is recited; the power is to cause the feasters to be easily satiated, and thus make the feast appear more lavish.

Along the sides of the frontal "court," flanking the *butam* back to the *gunun*, and often extending along the front *balat* to the *olagabo*, are *ora*—long benches of polished bamboo, supported on horizontal lengths of coconut palm trunk, to serve the guests on feasting occasions. Over these benches the half-pitch, thatch-and-pole *bebe* are often constructed, to shelter feasters from the sun and rain. Erected for a specific occasion, they generally serve as semipermanent features of the *taun*. A feast, called *songot bebe*, must be held to allow them to be taken down. While they stand, they may be referred to metonymically to stand for the *taun* as a whole. An *orong* will call out, "Take this pig to the *bebe* at Giligin."

The centerpiece of the whole construction, the "men's house" proper, is the *gunun*. Although there is considerable variability in the construction and placing of the house within the *balat*, a stylized, gable-roofed design (Figure 2) is generally favored, low-slung, with an earthen floor. Several terms are in general usage for types of *gunun*. One that stands by itself, without the surrounding *a balat* and other concomitants, is a *bang*. Otherwise, *gunun* are distinguished according to whether the center post, *a gosong*, is present or not: a *gunun* with center post is called simply a *gosong*; one without is a *sigot*.

Of particular importance, corresponding to the *olagabo* within the enclosure, is the threshold log, *a bagot*, forming the foundation of the front of the *gunun*. An impressively large log is cut for this purpose, carried in by many men, stripped of its bark, and installed. The single doorway to the *taun gunun*, *a marami*, with the center of the *bagot* as its threshold, links the interior of the *gunun* with the feasting "court," *konono*, and is a focal point. It is the *marami* that is

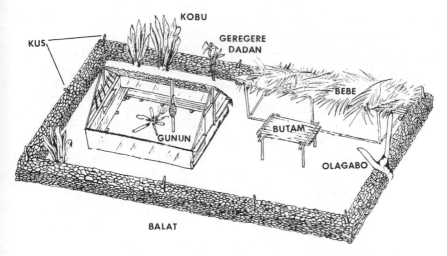

FIGURE 2. The *Taun* Enclosure

festooned with strings of *mis* when the *taun* is decorated, and the most honored seats at a feast are those within the *gunun*, flanking the *marami* on both sides. Just behind the entrance, about a quarter or a third of the way into the interior, is the single center post (*a gosong*) of the structure. Near the top of the post, facing the *marami*, is a small peg, *e noi*, from which the *teve*, or food basket, is hung. This feature is highly significant to the concept of the *taun*, for the presence of the basket (whether or not it is filled, as it should be, with cooked tubers) gives assurance of the constant availability of sustenance to all who should come to the *taun*. Between the center post and the *marami*, in the center of the earthen floor, is the *tauna*, or hearth fire, which should always be kept burning, but especially at night, to guide ancestral spirits (it is said) to the spot. The *tauna* may also be kindled in the rear-center area of the *gunun*, or one might be built in either location.

The sides and rear wall of the *gunun* are lined with *a ora*,

151

sleeping benches of polished, thick bamboo poles, generally somewhat wider than the sitting benches outside. A number of polished bamboo headrests (*lulungun*) are scattered about here for the convenience of anyone who may wish to nap during the day, and for the small group of men and boys who invariably, for one reason or another, spend their nights there. A low shelf, the *selaga*, is built into the rear of the *gunun*, atop the low rear wall just below the eaves. This is for the storage of food and ceremonial paraphernalia, including traditional weapons. One of the half- or side-ridge poles, midway between the center pole (*a pungun*) and the juncture of the sago-thatched roof with the side wall, is used as a repository for the pigs' jaws (and other remains of previous feasts) that form an important heirloom, or trophy assemblage, for the *taun*. The lower jawbones are hung over the *ana gunun* in an impressive row, and are carefully preserved and reinstalled in newer structures as the *gunun* is rebuilt. They manifest the temporal continuity of the *taun* as a feasting complex,[5] much as the interment of human remains within the enclosure serves to anchor the whole within the puissance of ancestral precedent.

The space between the rear of the *gunun* and the rear wall of the *balat* is the *ligu*, where human remains are interred (though in some cases, particularly those of infants or small children, the earthen floor of the *gunun* itself will be used for burial). This area, as well as the spaces between the *balat* and the sides of the *gunun* (*lawana gunun*), is ordinarily planted with a rich array of decorative foliage, especially red-leaved cordyline (*gere gere dadan*) and *kobu*, a bananalike plant with long, thin green leaves turning orange-red, whose leaves

---

[5] Similar assemblages of feasting "trophies," especially pigs' lower jaws, can be found virtually everywhere in Melanesia, though often there is no explicit rationale associated with them. This was certainly true of the Daribi and Polopa communities I visited. On the other hand, pigs' jaws seem to figure prominently in the important reliquaries of the Telefolmin area.

were used as a covering for human corpses before the general availability of cloth.

In all Usen hamlets the *taun* is paired with another structure, the *pan*, or women's cookhouse, which stands opposite the *olagabo*, about ten or twenty meters away. The *pan* is virtually the only building whose construction follows the aboriginal mode of horizontal bamboo poles lashed to an upright frame. The main feature of the *pan* is its capacious earthen-floored interior, upon which the women's large, vegetable-cooking *mumu*, or stone oven, may be constructed in inclement weather (otherwise it is made in the "doorway" of the *pan*, the *marami ni pan*). The special significance of cooked vegetable food (*a nien*) as a complement (*aginime*) to prepared meat or fish (*a sawi*) gives the *pan* an importance far beyond that of the merely practical. For *nien* is essential to the feast and to the normative provisioning of the *taun*, and its preparation makes the *pan* a point of ceremonial focus, though in a relatively less formal way than the *taun*. Here, in the *pan* itself or in its dooryard, the women have their feasts, concurrent with those of the men—and furnished with exactly equal portions of pig, areca nut, and green coconuts—but informal in their seating arrangements and always marked by an air of levity and buffoonery that contrasts with the sobriety of the male counterpart. The popularity of the *pan* as a casual socializing center for all villagers during the day is probably also attributable to its cooking fires.

As an icon, the *taun* is a perfect image of containment, a static tableau that is energized and given direction through the holding of feasts. In her discussion of the Mandak *eantuing*, or men's house, Clay notes conceptual associations linking the stone enclosure both with the womb and with the stone oven.[6] In a similar way, the Barok *taun* could be likened to a womb containing living feasters as well as the

---

[6] Clay, *Pinikindu*, p. 136.

dead—indeed, conjoining them in the mortuary feasts. It might also, following this sort of corporeal metaphor, be seen as a social "stomach," with the structure of the *taun*, and then the feasters themselves, enclosing the displayed food in the central place. But of course the *taun* is not a womb, because it is, among other things, a social stomach; and it is not a social stomach because it is, among other things, a womb; and it can be nothing like a womb or a stomach because it is not a human body, but an edifice; but it is no ordinary edifice, since it is intrinsically involved in the most significant acts of human containment and containment of humans—it is a "body" that holds bodies. As an image that is medial to the imagery of feasting, burial, the human body, and the social and spatial surroundings of the human body, it cannot be equivalent to any single one of the more specialized images it "contains." Nor, because of its very specificity, can it be adequately generalized. Like the proverbial picture that is worth ten thousand words, it *wastes* glosses or descriptions upon an object whose concise incongruity to any gloss or description inevitably demands further glossing. The force of what Freud called "condensation symbolism" is not simply that it contains many metaphors in one, or even that it serves as a "converter" among its constituent images, but that the image with these properties attains a synthetic singularity beyond the meanings of its constituent possibilities.

Beyond the obvious conformation of the *taun* as an enclosure (the *gunun*) within an enclosure (the *balat*), and its spatial encompassing of the feast, is the more subtle symbolism of directionality and centrality. The sides of the *gunun* (*lawana gunun*) and of the *balat* (*lawana balat*), as well as the spaces extending out from them, are relatively "neutral" or unmotivated. But the front and rear, the entrances (*marami*, *ola-gabo*), the feasting space (*konono*), the *ligu*, and the spaces radiating forward and backward from them (Figure 3), carry much of the significance of the structure and of the constitutive image of which it is part. By far the most distinctive

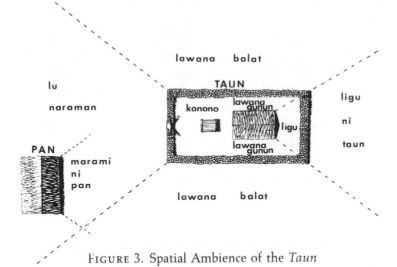

FIGURE 3. Spatial Ambience of the *Taun*

aspects of *taun* architecture are the entrances: the arresting high "V" of the *ologabo*, carved of the toughest wood, over which people must climb one by one, and the heavy *hagot* threshold grounding the *marami* of the *gunun* itself. It is these features that are embellished with *mis* when the structure is decorated, and it was from the *marami* that, in precontact times, the skeleton of a particularly obnoxious enemy, its tendons carefully left intact after cannibalism, was suspended (this usage is called *prr na giao*). The entrance is the architectural image of envelopment, the point at which the entrant submits himself, so to speak, to the structure and its space; it is this and also the "seal" placed on the act of containment, and these symbols of restricted, ceremonial entry and continence are significantly hewn of the toughest wood available, and celebrated as the mediators and "valves" between interior and exterior space.

As the forepart of the *taun*, the *konono* and the benches

flanking the *butam*, is the staging area for public feasting—the container, so to speak, of the feast—so is the rear of the enclosure, behind the *gunun*, the cemetery, or container of the dead. This *ligu* is normally as free of human traffic as the *konono* is busy with it; it is something of a sanctified preserve, in which the decorative plants flourish and grow tall. The rear wall of the *gunun*, which has no doorway, is surmounted by the *selaga*, the shelf on which ceremonial objects and the remnants of food are kept. Thus the rear of the *taun* stands in marked contrast to the forepart; instead of movement and the continual pulse of containment and disgorgement, it is the obverse of these, the place where honored and valued remains come to rest.

This contrast serves to explicate the place of the *gunun* as well as the image of the *taun* as a whole. For the *gunun* stands in the center, where the activities and influences of the forepart and the hindpart overlap. Feasting takes place in the *gunun*, and indeed it is the honored or valorized location for feasters; but the feast is staged, and the important transactions and speeches are made, in the *konono* area outside, between the *marami* and the *butam*. Likewise, the body of a deceased person prior to burial will be laid out in the *gunun*, and in some (relatively rare) cases the body will be interred beneath the floor of the building. Thus the *gunun* is the centerpoint that holds together and mediates life and death, feasting and mortuary concerns, which are brought together at the archetypal feasting occasion: the mortuary feast. The *gunun* is an enclosure within an enclosure. Approached from the front, it presents the same aspect as the *taun* as a whole: just as one enters the *olagabo* to be immediately confronted with the *butam* loaded with food, so does one enter the *marami* facing the *teve* of cooked tubers, hanging from its peg on the center post. The difference is significant, though, for the *teve* is to provide sustenance for those *living* in the *taun*, clan members and their guests, whereas the food on the *butam* is for all feasters. The *gunun*, then, marks the distinction between those who "live" there, the clan members as successors of the buried ancestors and as "containers" of the feast, and the feasters, whom the clan "envelops" for the occasion. The preeminence of the *gunun* is the preeminence of the clan (and of its honored guests, the *orong*) whose members, through their simultaneous assimilation of the living and the dead, ground the mediation of precedent and authority (and the activation accomplished by the feast).

The valances of the forepart and the hindpart of the *taun*, extended respectively outward from the structure itself, provide a further demonstration of the *taun* image. The *lu naraman*, generally spoken of as the "door" or "doorway" of the *taun* (Figure 3), extends for some distance in front of the *balat*[7] and includes both the space of the *pan* and its "doorway," the *marami ni pan*. This is a "respected" space with a somewhat diffuse ethical "charge"; the women's feasts and activities (such as preparing structural members or stitching the sago-leaf thatch) connected with the refurbishment of the *taun* take place here, and the area is suffused with something of the *malum* associated with the *taun* itself. The corresponding area radiating out from the rear of the *taun*, the *ligu ni taun* (Figure 3), marks a region of avoidance and intermittent pollution. Like the *lu naraman*, the outer limits of the *ligu* are arbitrated by members of the *taun*. When someone has been buried within the *taun* enclosure, the decomposition products from the corpse are said to flow outward beneath the ground into the *ligu ni taun*, and to enter all the trees and plants growing there. There is a taboo, sanctioned by a stiff fine, on taking any fruits or other products from here until

---

[7] According to my informants, the demarcation of these spaces follows diagonals traced outward from the corners of the *balat*. Where the *lu naraman* or *ligu* of defunct *taun* appear at present as rectilinear blocks, as for instance at Koinigogo in Bakan, this is the result of subsequent arbitration or simplification.

the *a-un gogorop* feast has been held to complete the mourning for a particular deceased person.

The *taun* is not purposely oriented to face a particular cosmological direction or feature, such as the sea; many nowadays are built simply to face the road. This is not so much the result of a defect or oversight on the part of the Barok as it is an indication of the centrality of the *taun*, which is itself a spiritual "center of gravity" and orientational focus. Nevertheless, it sometimes happens that *taun* on separate tracts are situated back-to-back, as with the Guogo Balitas *taun* at Giligin, and the Gunaun Tunu *taun* at Malalai, in Kolonoboi. In such cases a doubly bounded space is generated through the overlapping of *ligu*, and this space, associated with a taboo called *mok*, is considered to be permanently affected by the condition of the *ligu*. No one may cry out, sing, or behave obstreperously in the *mok* area; nor may a woman carry a *kis* (the reinforced produce basket) there; nor may people fish, or search for shells or shellfish, on the adjoining beach and reef. The penalty for breach of the taboo is payment of a pig, called *ogawuk*, to members of all the *taun*.

All of the distinctions of structure and usage concerning the *taun* and its surrounding spaces, when considered together, call to mind G. Spencer Brown's initial definition: "distinction is perfect continence."[8] The *taun*, as the objectified half of a coordinate image, offers a *pidik*-like picture of containment, a dual encompassing of feast and ancestral power that, in the name of the host lineage, elicits a relation of legitimated successorship to the dead, much as the taboos and protocols of Usen kin usage elicit the significant relationships of daily life. In this sense, the modern merger of kin usage and the ceremonial feasting complex in the Tokpisin word *kastam* makes perfect sense, for the constitutive im-

[8] Brown, *Laws of Form*, p. 1.

agery of *taun* and feast amounts to the root evocation of *malum*, and of ethos in general.

The Feast in the *Taun*

The other half of the coordinate image—the ceremonial feast—is, for all the variations of scale and elaboration that attend upon its various occasions, as exacting and formal in conception as the icon of the *taun*. It is here, nevertheless, in the activating "event," that the formal distinctions are introduced—as matters of protocol—which serve to articulate the "intent" or "meaning" of the image and its occasion. The nature of these inflections will be the concern of later discussion; for the present, let us consider what we might call the "basic feast." For, whatever details have been introduced or altered to mark the occasion, Usen feasts conform quite rigidly to a standard format.

The common metonyms for ceremonial feasting, and indeed for *kastam* itself, are *bet lulut* and *kurubo*, "cutting pig." The expression *il nor aranga buo*, "first giving areca nut," is used more specifically for the formal feast in the *taun*, and refers to the "diachrony" of the first "refresher" (areca nut, betel pepper, and green drinking coconuts), distributed prior to the purchase and cutting of the pigs, and the serving of the main course.[9] This two-course structure is characteristic of even the most perfunctory of *taun* meals, for even a small repast of rice and fish, or of pork received from a larger feast elsewhere, will inevitably be preceded by the passing out of a few springs of areca.

The preparations for a large feast may take weeks or months, involving vast expenditures of time, effort, and wealth on the part of many people. For most significant

[9] An informant who had once worked as an assistant to a Chinese cook likened Barok ceremonial feasting to the Western meal in its succession of courses, in contrast to the "synchrony" of Chinese meals.

feasts, however, a few immediate preparatory steps are worth noting. To announce a feast, an outer fiber is torn off of a coconut husk for each *taun* in the area. This *sibi-gini lamas* is then sent to the *taun*, and is properly reciprocated with one "rope" of green drinking coconuts (*polo*), one bunch of areca nuts (*a bung buo*), and a *timin sie* (a leaf packet of betel pepper), which are brought along by the members as an acceptance gift.

On the morning of the feast day (a feast generally gets underway at 1:00 P.M. or so), the vegetable food (*a nien*) and meat (*a sawi*) are prepared and set to cook on stone ovens by the women and men, respectively. The women's bake, *da go baliklik*, takes place in the *marami ni pan* or, failing that, in the *pan* itself. The cooking stones are piled atop a stack of firewood, which is then kindled to heat them. Meanwhile the women sit about "shelling" (i.e. peeling) the tubers and "marking" them with distinctive signs for identification. When the firewood has burned down, the peeled tubers are laid on the heated stones to dry out (*omari nien*); then the stones are spread out (*i-wat*) and arranged (*las da*) for the *mumu*. The tubers are put into packets and placed among the stones (*ara-su*); then they are covered with stones (*ridimit*), and the whole pile is sealed with leaves (*bus da*). It will be uncovered (*sog da*) several hours later, when the feast begins.

Pigs for the feast will have been caught ("thrown," sat upon, and trussed up) or delivered (nowadays by truck) the night before the feast. In the morning, they are killed, always by suffocation: leaf plugs are inserted in the nostrils, the snout is securely tied, and generally someone sits atop the bucking, trussed up animal until it expires.

The *da ni koro*, the men's bake, is made on the beach, or on a piece of land just inland of the sand or coral. Butchering (in this case merely gutting) is done on a bamboo platform, covered with banana leaves, called a *bie*. Chopped greens are scattered over the top of the *bie*, to absorb the blood and juices of the pork, and are later cooked and eaten. Internal organs are discarded by throwing them into the sea, and a lively sport is had casting with an entrail-baited hook for the congregating reef sharks. Some tidbits, notably the liver and lungs, are cut up to be steamed in packets with the greens from the *bie*. The whole, gutted pig is then sewn into an envelope made of tough, pandanus-like *obo* leaves with bark thongs (*owa*). When the firewood has burned down, as with the women's oven, the whole, covered pigs and the packets of meat and leaves are placed on the stones, and the entire affair is covered with leaves and then with ashes (sometimes earth).

Early in the day of the feast, young men of the host lineage as well as those of guest groups will gather quantities of areca nut, betel pepper, and green drinking coconuts. The gathering and conveying of *polo* is known as *pis polo*. Youths or young boys shinny up the palms to gather the fruit, which is then husked on a pointed stake set in the ground. The husked *polo* (each with a strip of husk left on for the purpose) are tied together, two by two, and the pairs are nested crosswise one atop the other to hang in a long column beneath the pole on which they will be carried to the *taun*. A special, decorative form of *pis polo*, called *balus*, is sometimes undertaken as a sort of flourish. The coconuts are gathered from the plantations of different owners; all go to one stand of trees, make a small basket of woven coconut fronds, fill it with *polo*, and then go on to another grove. A sprig from the *kongo* plant is placed in the bottom of each basket for its pleasant aroma, and the baskets are then stacked on the *butam* prior to distribution.

About an hour after noon, visitors will begin to arrive at the *taun*, propping their "ropes" of *polo* outside, along the *balat*, before they enter. As distinguished visitors, particularly those from far away, enter the *olagabo*, their names are called out by the older men assembled there as a sign of respect; this is called *sili bebe*. The "host" lineage will already be assembled, its younger men prepared to serve and to perform cleaning duties in the crisp and attentive manner characteristic of such occasions.

The order of events in the holding of a feast is so well known to every participant that those who wish to argue or debate some point of protocol will simply appeal to the experience of their audience. By the same token, this order is never objectified outside of its performative context—through the use of mnemonics or ideological accounts, for instance. The following order of events was collected from a single informant, who reconstructed it by imagining the progression of a feast. Each stage is identified here by its conventional Usen designation. The sequence given here is that of the "basic" feast:

Sele bana sie. Areca nut and betel pepper are purchased for distribution at the feast. The hosts will publicly make the purchase, in the center of the *konono*. When this is done (and it is by no means always a feature of the feast) the areca nut and betel pepper of the men is purchased together with that of the women; then the women's portion is separated out and carried out to the *pan.*

A inia oronga buo. Areca nut and betel pepper are distributed. Large sprigs of areca, still on the stem, together with two to four or more *sie* (betel peppers), are handed smartly to each participant in the feast. (The feasters are by now seated quietly on the *ora*, making quiet and polite conversation.)

Eraba ma polo. Green coconuts, which have been removed from the husk in a stylized manner (with the nub at the top and a section of husk remaining to facilitate peeling off the outer fiber and "cleaning" before drinking), are distributed. At first, one or possibly two *polo* are presented to each feaster; if a sufficient number remain after this, a third may be given. In serving, the distributor fills his arms with *polo* and scurries down the bench of feasters, handing the requisite number to each. If the distributor's supply is exhausted before he

162

reaches the end of the feasters, the last man to receive a *polo* should hold it up to remind the distributor where to begin when he returns with a fresh supply. (To slight anyone in the distribution is considered to be extremely shameful.) At mortuary feasts or on other important occasions, it is customary to cut or break the *polo* cleanly across the middle for drinking purposes. This is a mark of respect for the deceased, "who is not yet decomposed," and "if you play with the end of the coconut, you play with the deceased." The *polo* is then drunk from, by squeezing open the cut above the open mouth so that a stream of liquid falls directly into the mouth. The *polo* is used in the manner of a Spanish "bota," or wine skin: one retains a quantity of liquid in the mouth by constricting the throat, then swallows while still drinking. The shell is then split fully in half, and the meat is worked out of it either with the thumbs or with a special shell scraper (*a kinis*) that most men carry in their *rat*.

Sog a da. The pigs are taken out of the stone oven.

Ko bus anu gip. The pigs, in their wrappings, are tied beneath poles for carrying by (younger) men.

Bulus a labana. Coconut fronds are put down between the *butam* and the *gunun* for display, purchase, and cutting of the pigs.

Mo kip a langa (or, plural, *a bung*) *bo ra.* The cooked, wrapped pigs are carried over the *olagabo* into the *taun.* All pigs must be brought in this way—"before the sitting down of the *orong*"—to be purchased. Half of them will be carried out, still in wrappings, to the women, and the others will be cut in the *taun.*

Mo luok oga a nien ko butam. The vegetable food, having been taken from its oven, is brought to the *olagubo* in *teve* by the women, and handed to the men over the gate. The men bring the *teve* to the *butam* and place the tubers there.

Ma palas a bo. The wrappings are removed from the pigs, now situated properly on the coconut fronds (*labana lamas*).

163

Ma sevi bo. The pigs are purchased. This is a matter of public show: the owner of the pig goes up to the pig and slaps it, calling out the name of the buyer. The purchaser then takes the purchase money (in bills) and *mangin* and, flourishing it in the sight of all (or, in the case of *mangin*, giving it to others who hold it end-to-end down the length of the *taun*), gives it to the seller and then slaps the pig to acknowledge having bought it. (The pig, bought in this way, is by no means his possession: it is understood to be given to those holding the feast, who will cut and distribute the animal, and who will even present special parts such as the forepart and legs for later reciprocation, without any responsibility to the purchaser.) The price paid for the pig is announced by the buyer or someone else immediately before purchase, and the purchaser will announce his reasons for providing the pig ("buying the shame of ———") at this time.

Sele a bung bo. A speech—"calling out before the bunch of pigs"—is made by the *winawu* (Tokpisin *maus man*) or *a todi na tinange* ("a man of speech"). This speech announces the reason for the feast, and may include any side comments that the speaker feels are appropriate. Following this speech, any other adult men (generally the more eminent ones attending) may rise and add comments. Although these may also be in the nature of "side comments," they are often enough observations or severe criticisms concerning the protocol or other details of the particular occasion.

Duang mogo use, morakora a bung bo. Next comes the calling out for knives with which to cut the pigs. The cutter of the pig slaps his hands down on top of the animal, lying on its stomach, and rolls it outward onto its side. Then he proceeds to cut the pig in half just below the rib cage: the forepart is the "head" (*ogono*), and the hindpart the "back" (*sabonu*). Cutting the pig is called *kurubo*. The pork intended for distribution to the feasters is then cut for this purpose.

Nangadi mogo iriraba, moro bulus ao-wa. They put down

164

the leaves—i.e. the leaf plates, or *bala*—in settings of six to ten or more large, fresh leaves. The plates are placed on the ground at regular intervals in front of the *ora* on which the feasters are sitting, both within the *gunun* and in the *konono*. Plates are put down at the discretion of the server, generally to serve four or so feasters, who, randomly placed as they may be, share the food among themselves (including the portions to be taken home afterward). They cooperatively cut the portions into smaller servings, and show a general air of good-fellowship.

Ma bulus e nien, ka o. The vegetable food, hot from the oven, is brought by servers at a run, and one or more tubers of each variety (yam, sweet potato, taro, *mami*, etc.) is put down hurriedly on each leaf plate.

Mo teve bo. Pieces of cooked, cut pork are put on the leaf plates, generally to be cut further into small pieces and, held in the hand, eaten together with cooked tuber.

Misinari ora pira lotu. Someone with mission experience is asked to stand up and give a brief prayer, either in Tokpisin or in Barok, during which time the feasters, who may not yet eat, bow their heads and offer a brief, muttered "Amen" at the end.

Yope—a nien im ("Enough—eat the food"). Feasters eat with their hands from the common assortment, taking as they wish in a spirit of mutual good-fellowship.

Karange bo. Parts of the pig are distributed; the head, legs, and other special parts of the cut pig are reserved for important men. Names are called out, designating certain men or *taun*, and the parts or packages are presented. Frequently an individual man will be given pork on behalf of his *taun*; it is taken back and eaten communally by the standard protocol a day or so later.

Bo kobus mo kubus ao ogono bo. The "head" (forepart) of a particularly large pig, traditionally a *tunan* (worth twenty *pram* of *mis*), is offered to the feasters, beginning with the

165

most important, in the hope that one of them may accept it for later reciprocation. Most people refuse, but eventually someone is found to accept. Acceptance constitutes a pledge for an equivalent return at a later time.

Gaien bang ("Good evening now"). The feasters leave, taking their wrapped portions of food with them, usually after cleaning their hands in the sea (though sometimes a bucket of seawater is brought up to the *taun* for this purpose).

Omalanim a taun. The *taun* is cleaned up. This is done by the younger men of the host lineage, often young boys (who will usually have made the rounds earlier, picking up discarded green coconut shells and areca nut stems).

Food will often be sent from a feast to significant local people who were not able to attend. People who have not been present at a feast and want some food will put a leaf plate next to the road where others will be returning from the feast, carrying the remains of their repast. Then those who have put down the plate hide in the bush or on the beach nearby. As the feasters pass, each will put some food on the plate, until a generous portion can be found there.

The situation of the feasters in this scenario, as well as the spirit in which the feast is presented, provides a means of coming to terms with the feast as image. For the guests are obliged to take a passive role: sitting quietly on the *ora*, witnessing the staging of the event, and receiving the bounty of the feast. Any tendency toward self-assertion or unseemly action is constrained by the *malum* they should exhibit toward the *taun* and its ancestors. The elaborate solicitude embodied in the formal succession of courses, the generous quantities of euphoria-producing areca nut, the cool, invigorating drinking coconuts, the bounty of rich foods—all of this serves as their reward. It is an invocation of *malili*, the "calm sea" of contentment, bestowed equally, in an atmosphere of conviviality, upon all comers. As the guests are compelled to a kind of self-abnegating spectatorship, a deference to *taun*, hosts, and occasion, so are the hosts obliged to provide the utmost in scrupulously fair hospitality as proof of their ability to contain feast and feasters.

The feast is coordinate with the image of the *taun* because the provision of a feast is a complementary demonstration of containment to the *taun*: instead of the static picture of the container—the stone wall holding living and dead—the feast offers a savory and ornate display of the contained, and of its orderly and leisured assimilation. The festive meal is provided for the guests—and in a social sense this means the opposite moiety—to contain within their bodies; it is, so to speak, a foil for the containment of the *taun* itself. For the ability to satisfy, to *suffice* the guests in this way, is a measure of the worthiness of the host lineage (and clan, and moiety), and the power that is made at the *butam* is directed toward this end. To satisfy the hunger, thirst, weariness, and need for fellowship of those who come to the feast (all men are free to do so) is to contain these needs—needs that the exacting egalitarianism of feasting protocol encodes as a de facto definition of man. Containment is "shown" to the guests in the most appetizing way possible.

In marked contrast to the *taun*, with its sedate transcendence of human lifetimes (it transcends them, moreover, by means of *feasts*), the food served at the feast, the substance, as it were, of containment, is eminently perishable. The "containment" proffered as an inducement (the "bait") for the guests to submit themselves to the more emphatic containment of the *taun* is transitory in relation to the structure itself. In a sense, the pigs given for the feast are "sacrificed" for the gain of containing feasters, a foil of impermanent encompassing to enhance and activate the eternal containment of the *taun*. And in this respect the feast, with its provision of refreshment, food, and consideration, enacts the Usen concept of fatherhood, *nat*, which is viable for a single generation

167

only, but comprehensive in its solicitude. The *taun*, by contrast, enacts (and in fact constitutes) the containment of the *bung marapun* and hence enacts the other of the two claims of the Barok moiety—that of the absolute encompassment of its own (and, of course, whatever else it can get).

Containment is manifest in the plan of the feast. For the food, prior to distribution and consumption, is arrayed for *display* in the central space of the *konono* and is, in its purchase, publicly *secured* on behalf of the feasters. Like all formal transactions and dispositions of wealth among the Barok, this act of purchase must be open and its details shown and announced to all.[10] The otherwise cumbersome (and, for Melanesia, somewhat anomalous) custom of purchasing one's pig after it has already been cooked can be explained in terms of the need for closure in encompassing the food prior to its distribution. It is at this point, when the elements of the feast have been emphatically contained in the *taun*, that the feast, and the reasons for the feast, may be announced by the *winawu*. This is the moment of bestowal. The speech marks the centerpoint of the feast, as the display of purchased pigs at the prestigious focus of the *konono*, between *butam* and *gunun* (between the "center" of the feast and the *orong*) lies at the cynosure of authority. The speaker heralds his message by holding up a sprig of areca over a green coconut (the "refreshers" whose initial distribution metonymizes the protocol of the formal feast) or at least by grasping them in one hand while speaking.[11] It is apposite, at this juncture, for any criticism of the arrangements or procedure followed at the feast to be aired, and although the taboos and constraints of

[10] The implications of this tendency for modern politics are rather refreshing, and it is not surprising that the native of Bakan who served as provincial finance officer during my fieldwork enjoyed a reputation for exemplary uprightness and honesty.

[11] A deputy speaker in Kavieng told me in 1979 that this ritual usage had been adopted in the Provincial Government for occasions of public speaking.

the *taun* are in force to inhibit unseemly outbursts, the discussion can be quite acrimonious.

The distribution and subsequent consumption of food amounts to a festive transference of containment from the open display in the *taun* to the bellies of the feasters, themselves of course contained for the occasion within the *taun*. If we understand "encompassing" in Louis Dumont's sense— as a statement of hierarchical precedence—then the precedence of the *taun* and its members is sealed in this act of transference, for the encompassment of a feast is the "encompassing of encompassment": the image contains its own demonstration. As a constitutive image, it enacts the moiety's claims to containment of its *nat* (e.g. the opposite moiety) via the encompassed act of feasting them, as well as its containment of its own members, conceived and nurtured as the *nat* of the opposite moiety. (As we shall see, these two modes of encompassment serve to distinguish the two major types of feast.)

It is notable that the two principal comestibles distributed at the feast, green drinking coconuts and pigs, must each be split or cut cleanly in half along the transverse axis prior to consumption. In each case, this is done within the *taun*, and the pigs in fact will have been gutted, cooked, and brought whole into the *taun* in anticipation of this metonymically important "cutting of the pig." In the instance of coconuts, which are cut individually rather than collectively, there is the oft-repeated warning that "playing with the end of the coconut is like playing with the deceased," that it shows disrespect for the dead. It is not difficult to imagine imagistic rationales for this: one would, in puncturing the "eyes" or "mouth" at the end of the fruit, abuse the countenance of Satele, or one might, in "suckling" the tip, give the impression of taking the proffered "refresher" as maternal nurture (a bold and unseemly claim for those of the opposite moiety). The Usen, however, do not offer these or any other interpretations, and both feature what may be misleading analogies to the human anatomy. The treatment of the pigs offers a more clear-cut parallel, and in this case there is a significant distinction, as with the *taun*, between forepart and hindpart: *ogono* and *sabonu*. These halves are handled in markedly different ways in the distribution of pork: the *sabonu* is generally cut up for distribution to the feasters, whereas the *ogono* is often reserved for presentation whole (in anticipation of later reciprocation) to feasters from *outside* the *taun*. As with the *taun* itself, the forepart of the pig is its relatively "external" or "public" face—that which is given over to the ends and purposes of feasting. The hindpart becomes the "nurturance," or the "stuff" of the lineage that is used to sustain the feast itself, just as the *ligu* of the *taun* is the "proper" basis of the lineage.

Cutting the pig, then, enacts the all-important distinction, and separation, between the "public" and the "proper" aspects of the image, lest these be confounded. As a sacramental act, it "pictures" holographically the division of the feast (into the "forepart"—the "refresher" course of areca nut and coconut—and the "hindpart," the nurturant "main" course) as well as that of the *taun*—its "public" *konono* and "private" *ligu*. And the clean bisection of the *polo*, the "pig" (carried trussed up on a pole) of the first course, can be understood to foreshadow this. For the *polo* is bisected "out of respect for the dead," and this constitutes a personal acknowledgment, on the feaster's part, of the sanctity of the *taun*'s (and lineage's) containment of the dead.

Ararum

The Barok custom of *ararum*, the "tabooing" of a *taun*, carries the coordinate image of *taun* and feast to its ultimate realization, and sheds further light on the symbolic correspondences we have examined in this analysis. The term *ararum*[12] was explained to me as being the most general Barok term for "taboo," in contrast to other terms, such as *tamtam* or *tami*, which generally denote food proscriptions.[13] Although *ararum* has a fairly broad usage, it is most commonly used with reference to the tabooing of *taun* or of male children. This honor is generally reserved for the first-born son (*marina barok, barok sila*) of an *orong*, and is conferred on an occasion called *vi vi ga barok re*, when the father puts *tar* (red ochre) on his son's skin. The child will be *ararum* for life; as a child, only members of his own or his father's clan may carry him about, and so long as he lives no woman may walk behind him or put a *kis* on his head. When the boy is perhaps a year old, the father should hold an *oli lewi* feast for him, in which pigs, *mis*, food, and personal items of various kinds are presented to the child. The expectation is that when the *ararum* child reaches puberty, his father will hold an *una ya* (large) *kaba*, at which the son, officiating as *winawu*, accedes to the successorship of the dead and the status of *orong*.

A *taun* that is tabooed is divided laterally into two sections, either by planting a row of cordyline as a divider or, more commonly, by the erection of a partitioning *balat*. One section (the left, facing the *taun* from the front; or the right, facing outward from within the *taun*) becomes the *ararum* half, and is treated honorifically. Food may never be taken out of this section (a condition that applies to the ordinary *taun* only during certain kinds of feasts), which is called "the part where food is finished" (*agono mogo nien kirip*) in contradistinction to the ordinary *taun* (*agono mogo ginigip su*). Should a

---

[12] My colleague, Mr. Frederick H. Damon, reports a similarly important, and apparently cognate, equivalent term for Muyuw (Woodlark Island): *bwutatum*.

[13] Obviously cognate with Tokpisin *tambu* ("taboo"), these Barok terms are thus related to the Tongan *tabu*, source of the English loanword "taboo."

171

feaster leave the *ararum* section with food still in his mouth, or in his hand, he is subject to a fine (*oro kun a taun*) to the amount of a *mangin a tus*. The *ararum* section is traditionally restricted to older men (men with *salup*, or long beards), who would, according to most accounts, consume human flesh there in secret. The two sections of the *taun* each have their own *ola-gabo*, and when pigs are purchased, each half has its own pigs and its own transactions. There is an additional fine for touching the areca nut or green coconut of a man sitting in the *ararum* section, which is to provide a pig for those associated with that section.

A *taun* may be tabooed because it contains too many burials, and hence should be reserved for more serious purposes, or simply in order to do honor to the *taun* itself, the lineage, or to a particular person. Mareo, an *orong* of Wutom, divided his *taun* by making *ararum*; when he died, the *ararum* section was reserved solely as a burial place in his honor. *Gunun* may be constructed within an ordinary *ararum* section, but must be built far to the rear, behind the burial area.

The feasts for the establishment of the *ararum* section represent exaggerated versions (in terms of cost and preparation) of their ordinary counterparts. A pig must be killed and cooked for each step: viz. when stones are gathered from the seashore for the *balat*, when the stones are piled for the *balat*, when a new *ola-gabo* is installed. The consecratory feast for the completed *ararum* is distinctive in its form, and amounts to the most lavish and closely constrained feast known to the Usen. (The establishment of an *ararum* entails the construction of a new "orthodox" *taun* section adjoining the tabooed enclosure, or at least the walling off or separation of the latter.)

As the guests enter the new *taun*, the head of each *a-gana* of the opposite moiety must make a payment of one *pram* of *mangin tunu*. This payment is called *nat* (the same term that is used for a man's offspring). Another, similar payment is made when the areca nuts and *polo* are brought in; another when they are placed on the *butam*; and another when they are distributed. When the coconuts have been distributed (only one may be given to each feaster), one man must cut all of them with a single knife, and each may be cut only once. All the coconuts must be fresh and soft; if a hard one is found, its contributor must pay one *pram* of *mangin tunu*. Another *mangin tunu* is given by each *agana* head after the *polo* have been drunk.

Preparation of the pig has also been financed by the *agana* heads of the opposite moiety; *mangin tunu* are due from each on the occasions of killing the pigs, singeing off their bristles, gutting them, covering them with leaves, placing them in the stone oven, lighting the fire, and (later) removing the food from the ovens. At the feast, further payments must be given when the food is put on the *butam*, when the pigs are cut, when the leaf plates are set down, when the food is set out on the plates, and when the feasters are ready to begin. When the feasting commences, those who take the payments go to the *olagabo* and block the exit, exhorting the guests to eat and eat. Only upon additional payment may the feasters leave the *taun* to wash their hands in the sea. After this they must all sit quietly without chewing areca nut unless yet another payment is made.

The "throwing away" of *mis* in this way (*rurawe*) is intended to provide a "profit" (*ogagawa*) for those making the *ararum*. In addition to the *mangin* given by *agana* heads, individual feasters (of the opposite moiety) often contribute smaller amounts (nowadays Papua New Guinea *toea*). All gifts must be recorded, and gifts of *mangin* must be reciprocated later with large pigs. This reciprocation, known as *omamat*, occurs at a "finishing" feast (*gogorop*) for the *ararum*, which can go on for many days.

Food may not be taken out of the *taun* at any of the *ararum* feasts and must be cooked within the *taun* itself. All trash and food leavings accumulated during the *ararum* feasts must be kept beneath the *butam* (*ene butam*) and may not be carried outside. Afterward, a "bed" will be made behind the *balat* (in the *ligu*), and the trash will be placed upon it. When the trash is to be burned, the line that made the *ararum* must provide a pig and cook it to provide a feast for the guests.

Whether it applies to a firstborn son or to a *taun*, *ararum* amounts to the invocation of exaggerated protocols of respect and avoidance in order to elicit relationship, as in affinal kin usages. In these instances, however, the relationship is that of ceremonial hierarchy. Both the *ararum* child (or nascent *orong*) and the *ararum taun* are shown deference in a number of explicit and highly visible ways; and the child as well as the *taun* membership are provided, via the consecratory feasts (*vi vi ga barok re, taun ararum*), with a means of acquiring, through general contribution, the wealth that is indispensable to exalted position or precedence.

The *ararum* of a *taun* may be regarded as an inflection of the coordinate image of *taun* and feast: both aspects of the image are affected, and in the same way. To put it most succinctly, *ararum* extends the image to the point of complete containment—"perfect continence." The "closed" feast, from which even the trash may not be removed without a special, separate feast, is strongly reminiscent of the *tabanat* described in Chapter 3; in both cases, the opposite moiety is obliged to provide "profit" for the hosts. In the *tabanat*, contributions are given by (or in behalf of) the *nat*, the "blood" of the host clan's male members; in the *ararum* feast, the contributions themselves are called *nat*, so that the host clan effectively assimilates its "*nat*." The entire preparation and disposition of the feast, as well as ingress to and egress from the *taun*, is controlled (and "sealed") by repeated payments of the nature and amount of fines.

The spatial inflection of the *taun* image in *ararum* is most intriguing, and is likewise enactive of continence. For the *ar-*

arum basically extends and establishes the hindpart of the *taun*, the *ligu*, as a parallel entity to the *taun* itself. The restrictive and honorific qualities that normally distinguish the *ligu*; its association with the dead and the elderly; its sanctified air; its absolute containment—all are characteristic also of the *ararum* section, where the *gunun* must be constructed *behind* the burial area, thus in effect merging the *konono* with the *ligu*, and the feast with the space of the ancestors on whose behalf the feast is held. The result is a *taun* that represents the complementary significances of forepart and hindpart, successor and ancestor, *malili* and *malum*, through a reduplication of itself.

The coordinate image of feast and *taun* is not conceptualized as a means or instrument for the accomplishment of social, political, or economic ends. It is an image, like the *tadak* or the mystery of the *pidik*, and like them its force and effect cannot be explicated by verbal glosses. As a component element in the definition of the *bung marapun*, the *taun* and its image of containment serves to assert ceremonial precedence and validation; yet, that legitimation is an effect of the image itself, and not a "collectivizing" function of the group of people who comprise a *bung marapun*. The *taun*, as we have learned, may pass from one clan, and one moiety, to another without impairment to its significance or effectiveness. It is not that feasting and protocol serve as an "idiom" of social power or group cohesion, but rather that the image of containment has become the conclusive realization of validity and precedence. Rather, it is our terms—"social," "political," and "economic"—that are "idioms."

The constitutive force of this condensed image for Usen life cannot be fully understood or appreciated simply from a presentation or description of the image itself. It must be seen and lived in the relation of the image to the course of human existence, and to the values which infuse that relation.

EIGHT

Asiwinarong: Preemptive Successorship

As a basic focus of human culture, ethos may be approached theoretically from a number of viewpoints. It was introduced in Chapter 3 as the object of creative elicitation along the lines of Bateson's "This is play" to emphasize that the most elemental relations of culture may be cogently understood as being continually invented or synthesized out of one another. This is the perspective of "innovation," of the dialectic creation of iconic symbolizations out of one another that I have explored elsewhere,[1] and that provides a foil for the modern folk tenet of the a priori imposition of order, structure, or system as a "contrat social," a social sacrament, or an evolutionary achievement.

An image, like a *tadak*, a *pidik*, or the coordinate one of feast and *taun*, is elicitational or innovative in this respect, constitutive of its own relations and its own effect. Such a constitutive image can be seen as generative of order, quite as much as order is often comprehended as the germ of a culture's meaningful production, or reproduction, of itself. For production, as Marx clearly understood, is ultimately contingent upon an ethical substrate of human relationships; it emphasizes a collective or integrative perspective in which responsibility is assumed for the tasks and replenishment of society at large. It is thus an essentially conservative concept,

[1] See Wagner: *Habu*; *Lethal Speech*; and *The Invention of Culture*.

176

ultimately opposed (as all forms of reproduction must be) to death, and to the consumption and extinction of relationships. Human beings, their tasks, ideas, predilections, and social forms, are produced and reproduced in anticipation of an inevitable end.

Death is the hinge, the alter ego of production; it does not, in the individual form in which it is pragmatically encountered, negate the significance of the life morality of human continuance and replenishment, but merely confers upon it a different center of gravity. Like power and the other insoluble and unglossable mysteries, that of death is "held" and enacted by the Usen Barok; but here, in the "social" *pidik*, the force of the mystery is not ancillary knowledge or power, but closure, resolution, and legitimation. A death, by this shift of emphasis, elicits a value or potential that we might call "successorship," that of human replacement within an apparently limited set of properties and privileges. Death is the summative point, the completion of life that objectifies the person, and the Usen mortuary cycle amounts to the control of that objectification and its values via the image of containment. Successorship is the core value of the Usen Barok, radiating on one hand an image of "the ancestors," replete with exaggerated moral authority and precedent, and on the other that of the *orong*, the preemptive heir of that authority and precedent.

Without the concept of *orong*, the whole ethical and "public-oriented" world of Barok *kastam* would lack a "face." *Orong* is an ideal, never fully realized and yet never treated lightly. The ideal was confused, in traditional usage, with that of Moroa, the creator of New Ireland, and the name by which Christian pastors made reference to the Divinity throughout most of the colonial period. An important man might be called *orong* or Moroa in respectful (or flattering) allusion to his attainment of a commanding hierarchical ascendancy. In this sense the formulaic announcement at the culmination of the *kaba*—*asiwinarong* (*a-siwin-a-orong*, "the need of an *orong*")—and the idea of the people as *barok*, "boys" or "children," can be understood as expressions (however formalized) of a single, basic contingency of Barok life. The people are children, strong only in their leaders, waiting to be encompassed by the worthy and the powerful. An old man of Kolonoboi couched this need in terms of the passing of the traditional life:

Nowadays there are too many leaders. There is the council, the church, the courts, and the government. No one knows who to follow. In the past we had one *orong*; he told you what to do, and anyone who wanted to know what to do next came to him. I told this to an Australian anthropologist in the year 1935; we sat down there under that tree, by the beach.

The collective relations of Barok life—the submission demanded by its arcane convolutions of taboo, self-restraint, and the "purchase" of shame—are not so much celebrations of collectivity as they are power relations. And the whole public theater of submission and *malum* would be faceless and in vain if there were no one forthcoming to assume the ascendancy. "The need of an *orong*" is thus real, and must be so if the relations of Barok public life are to be realized.

Death and Divination

From the moment a death is known in any of its villages, the whole of the Usen area goes under the *lebe*, a general taboo that amounts to an extension of *malum* beyond the confines of the *taun* to encompass the whole of the people and their life space. The *lebe* is a taboo on any sort of work, such as gardening or housebuilding; also, calling out, talking loudly, exhibitions of anger, laughing, and the building of large fires are prohibited (on pain of a stiff fine). Usen also say that no cry of mourning may be uttered until the squeals of the pig(s), caught to be killed for the first of the feasts, are heard, or until the pig goes into the bake. The *lebe* remains in force until the *gogorop*, the feast that "finishes the sitting down" of the mortuary cycle, or some temporary or ad hoc equivalent, has been held. The corpse (*mi nit*) is wrapped from head to foot, with the face showing (nowadays in bedsheets), and placed on display at the rear of the *taun gunun*. This is done regardless of age or sex. In earlier times a special platform, or "bed," called *sesebe*, was made for the body, but this is no longer done. A "wake" is held in the *taun* until burial, generally on the day following that of the death, and mourners come to cry and view the body.

Burial today is in the *ligu* of the *taun* of a person's own lineage, or in that of a spouse or other relative. Earlier, the bodies (or, in some cases, bones) were deposited in certain caves, or were weighted and sunk in special deep "burial places" in the sea off the reef (or out toward Lihir), or, in the most honorific instances, allowed to decompose in an old canoe propped up in the *taun*, either with the idea of drying (mummifying) the corpse or of recovering the bones.[2]

Traditionally, a warrior or famous or influential man would be *seated* in the *taun* after death; lime powder (*a kabak*) was put on the face, the body was rubbed with red ochre (*a tar*), and spears were put in its hand. (Spears might also be grounded around it.) An appointed government official, a *waitpus* or *luluai*, would be seated with his cap on. In traditional times the belly of a pig, *li ni bo*, was laid on the breast of the deceased as he lay in the *taun*, and the arms, legs, and body were decorated with attractive leaves. For burial at sea,

---

[2] It is said that in the (south) Mandak village of Kanabu, at Cape Lemeris, an *ararum* woman of Barlu Clan died, and was mummified in a canoe. After this she was interred beneath a sheet of glass at the point of Suma Plantation. Feasts were held every time people went to view the preserved remains and cry, but those of other clans were excluded.

a platform or raft of bamboo was commonly prepared,[3] and the body placed on it. The legs were tied together, and a stone was attached to each. A hole was made in the *ti ni bo*, and the deceased's arm was inserted into it, up to the shoulder. Then the body was floated out on the bed to the burial site; when the party arrived there, one man would take the body under each arm and escort it beneath the water until it reached the bottom, or the maximum bearable depth.[4] Then the escorts surfaced, and all members of the party would strike the surface of the sea with paddles, beating it to a froth all around the place where the body went down. Then they came ashore and built a big fire on the beach just inshore of the burial site. This usage is called *odedek a tongon*, "drying out the shade." The men would all hide in the nearby undergrowth after building the fire, and wait to see the *tongon* of all people buried at that site troop out of the sea and warm themselves in a circle around the fire. *Odedek a tongon* would be done for three days following a burial.

An *ararum* person would not be buried at sea, but would be treated in a manner called *a ugis ko sim*. The corpse would be placed in an old canoe (*a sim*), upended and supported on bamboo poles within the *taun*. Coconut fronds were fastened around the *taun* enclosure, and the penalty for anyone who broke the taboo was death. A tube inserted in the bottom of the *sim* allowed the decompositional juices to flow out into a hole in the ground. Some young boys were selected as *kanut*, to be confined in the tabooed *taun* with the corpse. Their bod-

[3] Another method of sea burial involved the dismemberment of the corpse. The parts of the body were each placed in a woven coconut-leaf basket together with a section of pig and a stone (the head was put with the head of the pig, and so on). The baskets were taken in a canoe far out to sea ("halfway to Lihir") and dropped over the side.

[4] Informants from Kolonoboi recalled that when bodies were taken out for sea burial, the escorts could see the immense fish called *bikmaus* (Tokpisin), or *kwe* (Barok), waiting for their meal. The reported size of the creature makes it difficult to identify.

ies were covered with charcoal (*a kung*), and their task was to watch and listen at the *sim*. When an arm or leg parted from the corpse and rolled to the lower end, the *kanut* would send word to the men, and a pig was baked. When the *kanut* heard the head roll down, the last feast was done, and many pigs were killed. It is said that *kanut* grew well while watching the body, because of the festive food that people brought for them. When the last feast was finished, the taboo on the *taun* was concluded, and the *kanut* were washed.

The surviving spirit of the deceased is properly called *a tunu ni minet* (*tanu* is also a term for the soul of a living person) if the death has been nonviolent, and *a yuo* (*birua*[5] in Tokpisin) if the death resulted from *birua*, 'violence," including murder or a violent accident, such as drowning or fatal injury. The term *a tongon* is frequently confused with *tanu* by Usen, but is properly applicable to the apparition of a person, whether living or dead, when separated from the body. We might gloss it as "shade" or "body soul."

Ghosts and apparitions of the dead are not infrequently encountered among the Usen, and there are reported cases of possession. In earlier times the outer shell of a *galep* nut was often hollowed out to be used as a noisemaker by flicking the thumb or finger against it. These *kaliko* were placed in the hands of dead bodies, and the sound of the *kaliko* at night was taken as evidence that a ghost was abroad. Certain birds are known as "birds of the dead," including those sorcerers the *kurus* (drongo) and *kalanga* (eclectus parrot), as well as the *kamkum* (coucal), *tutut* (a fruit dove), and *dudu* (a Tyto owl). The bat (*a bege*) is also in this category. Startled in the bush, a ghost will quickly turn into a *kamkum*, a *kurus*, or perhaps an owl. When a ghost comes to the garden, its birds precede

---

[5] The Tokpisin term *birua*, which can be glossed as "enemy" in its generalized usage, has a more specialized denotation in New Ireland, and perhaps in adjacent areas. Here it means "violence," or "a victim of violence," and hence the ghosts of the violently slain.

it; and when someone is breathing his or her last, the death birds will come up to anyone who ventures into the bush and cry out to celebrate the new ghost that is coming to join them.

A yuo are altogether more sinister. They fish the sea, and sometimes hunt over the land, in waterspouts (*a marailu*) or whirlwinds, victimizing whatever they can draw in. A smell of decomposition blown in from the sea (*a ga-gum*), or a brisk wind that fetches spray from the whitecaps inshore, signals the presence of *yuo*, and careful mothers will bring their children indoors then. People see *yuo* up in the trees during thunderstorms; fire flashes from their eyes and armpits. Falling stars are also identified as *yuo*, and *yuo* can also turn into bats—the smaller, fruit-eating kind the Barok call *mangini*. For this reason, those who eat fruit partially consumed by bats are in danger of *gugong*, or possession, by *yuo*.

Several divinatory procedures are known to the Usen for use when the cause of a death or deadly illness is obscure, or suspicious. A sorcery divination, known as *a udu*, works on a time-honored principle. A rope of areca nut is hung from a pole, and the *bung marapun* of the sick man will gather around it and call out the names of different lines, and then different people. The pole and the areca nut will not move, but the guilty party will not want to come near them, and so implicates himself, whereupon others will speak with him about any secret practices he may have been carrying on. A murder divination resembles *odedek a tongon*; if the deceased died in the sea, the diviners will bring some fresh water to the beach above the place of death and say, "———, here is some water for you." Then they light a big fire, and watch for the ghost of the deceased to come up from the sea, bringing the *tongon* of his killer along with him.

The most ambitious procedure, however, is that called *ris-ras*, or *kip sinibo*, the "long bamboo," since the two techniques are frequently done in series. When the deceased has been buried, one man from each of the *bung marapun* represented in a village will be selected as diviners, so that the findings can be made public without shame. The men *ololo*, and rub leaves on their bodies to "cool" their skin. A long bamboo pole is cut, and a pig bone from the *songot kalu* feast is mounted on the end of it, together with some ginger, and *kapuan* leaves are fastened behind it. The pole is laid atop the mound of earth on the grave. Then, at sunset, the time of sorrow and longing for home that Barok call *melsur*, the diviners go up to the garden of the deceased and ruin it, breaking down the fence, uprooting tubers, smashing the yam house, and breaking off bananas. Then they conceal themselves at the *to no bus* (the "back" of the garden, outside the fence) and wait. A man who was a good friend of the deceased goes to the grave at dusk and tells him that his garden has been ruined; the ghost will then follow the bamboo pole, which is brought to the garden. The ghost, appearing in visible form, is angry at the sight of his garden, but his anger turns to his killer: "Hey, ———, you poisoned me, and now the men have ruined my garden." He shouts this at the *tongon* of the murderer, who appears on the path but will not enter the garden.

If the killer's *tongon* does not appear, the diviners will call out to the deceased man, "———, now all your children have been killed at the village," hoping to provoke an angry outburst, and a naming of the killer. If this does not work, the men will carry the pole back to the village on their shoulders, with the bone and leaves at the end, behind the last man. As they walk, the ghost of the deceased, in the form of a bat, may be heard nibbling at the bone. When they come to the house of the deceased (or, in some cases, to his *taun*), the end of the pole that bears the bone will be inserted into the door or into a small hole in the wall. A crowd, often people from many places, will have gathered to "support" the divination. Then one of the diviners calls out the names of villages: if the village is not the correct one, the pole will move from side to side (or "turn"); if it is correct, the pole will move in and out (or "shake"). Then the names of clans are called, with the same response. As the inquiry approaches closer to the identity of the culprit, the pull will be greater. They call names, and when the correct name is called, the ghost will try to pull the pole into the house; a tug of war ensues. The diviners give a mighty tug and pull the ghost, together with the apparition of his killer, out of the house.

Frequently only part of this composite procedure will be undertaken, though the whole (or a part of it) may be varied to fit the circumstances. Those who described the procedure to me claimed that they had seen it successfully performed many times, and that the apparitions were witnessed by the crowds present (though "their features were blurry"). An attempted *kip sinibo* that I attended at Belik Village in October 1979, however, failed, and it was noted that the young men who acted as diviners included no knowledgeable adepts at the practice. Divination is now resorted to only in cases of considerable suspicion, but its "burning issue" has given a name to the first division of mortuary feasts: *ꞡoꞡorop a wiot*, the "poison *ꞡoꞡorop*."

The Mortuary Cycle

Death is the single point at which Usen public life takes a person inevitably into account; everyone in the area is constrained by the *lebe* that follows upon a death, and anyone with any sort of affiliation to any lineage can expect ultimately to be honored by the full mortuary sequence. I was told that if I should die during my fieldwork I would surely be buried in the *ligu* of my *taun* with full funereal panoply.[6] In its universality and inevitability, as well as its centrality to

---

[6] This would be, but for the Schopenhauerian demurral of consciousness, the ultimate act of participant observation.

the coordinate image and the value of successorship, the mortuary feast is the archetypal Barok feast.

As many as six separate, named feasts, one or more of which may be recapitulated on successive days, may ultimately be held to honor a specific death. This total, however, includes the 'temporary" *gogorop* usually held nowadays to terminate the *lebe*, so that the "true," and more lavish *a un gogorop* may be held at a later time, when resources will be more plentiful. It also includes the elaborate *kaba*, something of an exception because it is not held within the *taun*, which is so expensive that a single event is usually (though not always) held to honor the memories of a number of recently deceased persons.

Usen know of several terminological sets for designating or differentiating mortuary feasts. In the most commonly used (and the one I became familiar with), the first, or "wake," feast (*ge woso*) is held on the day of death and before burial; this is followed on the second day, or after burial, by *songot kalu* (which may be repeated one or more times on subsequent days); a temporary "finishing" feast, called *korop kinis*, is generally held after this, at present, to terminte the *lebe* and the initial set of feasts. The "true" *goro-gorop* (or *gogorop*), i.e. the *a un* or "banana" *gogorop*, which originally concluded the *lebe* and the initial series, is now held as much as a year or so afterward. At some time after this, a relatively minor feast called *songot bebe* ("scorching the *bebe*"), which is not often mentioned in discussions of the mortuary sequence, may be held. This is to legitimize the tearing down of the *bebe* and other paraphernalia erected in the *taun* for the feasts. The *kaba* is not properly a part of the cycle, as it is divorced in time and space from the rhythm and sequence of the other feasts; but it is indeed devoted to the memorializing of the death, and is the ultimate patent of successorship.

Another set contrasts the two prior feasts—i.e. the *gogorop a wiot*, or "poison *gogorop*"—with the *gogorop* proper,

185

and speaks of *ge woso* as one of the five "pigs" to be killed in this part of the feast.[7] The first feast may also be called *a segen gamut* ("beating the *garamut*," or slit-gong), for the traditional manner of announcing a death. Neither of the terminological sets, however, achieves more than a cursory description of the feasts and their differences; *garamut* are scarcely important and are hardly ever used anymore, and divination and poison accusations are something of a rarity. *Ge woso* refers to the crying at the "wake"; *songot kalu* ("scorching the greens") registers the fact that greens must be cooked atop a fire (and not in a stone oven); *korop kinis* means simply to finish the "sitting down," or sustained feasting, that is consequent upon the death and the imposition of the *lebe*. *Gorogorop*, generally shortened to *gogorop*, refers to a cutting in half, and is said to indicate the cutting or halving of the *matmat*, the grave or cemetery. The repetition of the term in the phrase *gogorop a wiot* is clearly derivative, an attempt to pair the "finishing" feast with a division of like moment. And although we shall see that this attempt, as well as the term *gogorop* itself, is not without significance, it is clear that such descriptive epithets can scarcely afford more than the most cryptic indication of the sense of the feasts, either singularly or as a sequence.

This should hardly surprise the reader, for we encountered much the same reticence in the description of the stages of a typical feast in the *taun*, and met with the same intransigence to glossing or verbal explication in considering the mysteries of *tadak*, *pidik*, and power. Like the names of *tadak* or *pidik*, the terms used to designate feasts are nomenclature rather than imagery; for, in a culture as clearly committed to (and constituted by) image as that of the Usen Barok, the imagery

[7] According to Marianne George, the first "pig" may also be called *a bo na gagaraorut*, the "pig for when the man goes into the ground"; the second is called *a galunagaso*, "bring everything [which is mine] to me." The final three pigs are unnamed.

itself is identical with its power and its revelation. The mortuary feasts are best approached, and understood, through their character as images.

Considered from this perspective, from the way in which the icon of the *taun* and its activation through the feast are implemented, there are in fact only two kinds of feasts. One, in which the holding and containing aspect of the image is emphasized, I shall call the "closed" feast; this form is characteristic of the *tabanat*, and reaches its culmination in the *ararum* consecration for a *taun*. The other kind of feast, emphasizing the provident and nurturant aspect of the image, is what I shall call the "open" feast; in addition to its mortuary forms, this format characterizes the *maranien* feasts, held to celebrate the abundance of seasonal foods, as well as other "incidental" repasts.

The closed feast is an assertive enactment of the *taun*'s containment of its ancestral authority and power, and of its own inception and nurturance. Through the *taun*'s association with a moiety, and with a *bung marapun* and an *agana*, this enactment becomes the constitution and definition of that moiety, clan, and lineage as against the opposite moiety and its constituents, which are conceived of as the "fathers," the begetters and nurturers of its membership. As the *taun* contains the ancestors, so it contains this latest deceased; as it contains its objectified membership, the *nat* of the opposite moiety, so the *taun* encompasses the proffered nutriment (or its analogue) of the opposite moiety. The closed feast enacts this relation. But if it is to be a true constitutive act, and not the mere statement or token of such an act, then it is essential that the feast encompass nurturance actually provided by the other moiety, or by some acceptable substitute. Accordingly, the food partaken at a closed mortuary feast is always provided by the opposite moiety—sometimes in alternation, so that one feast will be provided by the deceased's affines, another by his or her father's line, and so on. At the *tabanat*, the *nat* bring wealth (*mis* or money) as contributions to the "profit" of the lineage; at the consecratory feast for an *ararum taun*, as we have noted, the contributions of wealth given by the opposite moiety are themselves significantly called *nat*. It is also noteworthy that, in the strictest reading of traditional custom, the closed mortuary feast is taboo to those married to the sisters of the deceased—the actual fathers, that is, of his closest lineage.

The closed mortuary feasts are those done immediately after a death, just before and just after burial: the *ge woso* and the *songot kalu*. At these feasts the food, provided by the opposite moiety, is brought *into* the *taun*; the pig, at least, must be singed, butchered, cooked, and eaten wholly within the *taun* enclosure. (In some instances all the "rubbish," the debris of butchering, cooking, and feasting, is retained within the *taun* as well, but this is criticized by some as an unnecessary imitation of the *ararum* feast.) The greens (*kalu*) used to absorb the juices of butchering, which are later cooked together with the viscera, must be broiled (*songot*) atop the fire. *There is a stringent taboo on taking any food outside the taun;* even those who inadvertently leave the enclosure with unchewed food in their mouths are obliged to pay a fine. Thus the flow of food (Figure 4) at these feasts is *into* the *taun*, where it is contained; the only outward flow is that of the *maut*, the decompositional juices of the deceased, which, after burial, are thought to penetrate underground into the *ligu ni taun*. The imagistic movement of the closed feast is constitutive, from the "contemporary" front to the "ancestral" rear, as indeed the deceased has shifted, in the act of dying, to a quasi-ancestral status.

This enactive movement is sustained in the protocols for displaying the cooked pigs and distributing the "refreshers" and food to the feasters. The pigs, as they are brought in and laid out between *butam* and *gunun* for display, must be positioned with their heads facing *inward*, toward the rear of

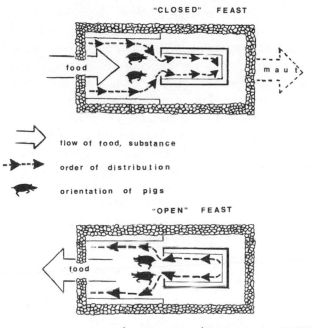

FIGURE 4. The Imagery of Feasting

the *taun*; and the courses of refreshers, drink, and food must be distributed in a sequence commencing at the front of the *taun* (i.e. those feasters nearest the *ola gabo*) and moving toward its conclusion at the rear of the *gunun* (Figure 4). Thus it is the feast, the activating mode of the coordinate image, that serves to focus this image in terms of the appropriate ethos for the occasion.

The ethic that is most emphatically elicited at a closed feast is that of *malum*, the posture of forbearance and enhanced respect and solicitude toward the deceased, his line, and his moiety. To be sure, *malum* is evoked and expected throughout the mortuary sequence; but here, at its inception, it is given its strongest emphasis. Until the *a un ɣoɣorop*, the widow or widower of the deceased must not wash or do anything to enhance her or his bodily appearance; dressing up, decorating the body, and dancing are expressly forbidden. Other members of the opposite moiety are subjected to *inio ges*, the smearing of lime powder and ashes on their faces (and sometimes bodies) to ruin their appearance. (This must, needless to say, be taken with good grace.) The sense of this evocation was given in a woman's comment: "You are the children of our moiety, your father gave you meat and good food; and now we may disfigure you by rubbing lime and ashes on your faces, we may sit on your shoulders when you dance." The evocation of *malum* sometimes extends to *palik*, or outrageous joking. This can include various forms of humiliation: taking property; emptying out men's *rat*, or carrying baskets, and humorously analyzing the contents; women dancing close to a man or even sitting on his face. At a Belik *songot kalu* in 1979, some Tago people drew lime powder "license plates" (circular designs with radii extending) on the backs of a group of Malaba young men. Those of the "father's moiety (and clan) have, for their part, the right to place a *tamtam* (a special food taboo) on members of the deceased's lineage. The penalty for breach is a fine of *mis* payable to the opposite moiety; the *tamtam* itself is made known by hanging up a specimen of the tabooed food—a pig's bone, a yam skin, or a taro leaf—in plain sight of all. A *tamtam* on foods especially associated with the deceased may also be assumed voluntarily by a close relative.

Tamtam remain in force until the *a un ɣoɣorop*, although the *lebe* is generally removed a few days after the death at a *korop kinis*, or "temporary" *ɣoɣorop*. Another funerary taboo, the *a bino*, which is placed on the use of the deceased's possessions, may remain in force until the disposition of those possessions is settled. It is often claimed that in traditional or precontact times, when the bananas necessary for its celebration were more readily available, the *a un gogorop* was held immediately after the *songot kalu* feast. On the other hand, it is also said that a true "finishing" feast like the *gogorop* should not be held until the body of the deceased is fully decomposed, something that would surely not obtain a mere three or four days after the death.

Difficult as it may be to reconcile these two statements, each can be seen to have a certain logic to it. For the *gogorop*, as an "open" (and an "opening") feast, must necessarily occur so as to reverse the flow into the containment of the *taun*, with its constraining regimen of taboo and *malum*. But a final or definitive reversal of this flow before the complete decomposition of the corpse would compromise the distinction between closed and open feasts; it would initiate a double flow of foodstuffs out the front of the *taun* and decompositional fluids out the rear. Thus the present system of "temporary" and "final" *gogorop*, whatever the exigencies that may have prompted it, furnishes a viable solution to an otherwise difficult dilemma.

The notion of a "halving," or subdivision, of the *taun* occurs wherever (as in the *ararum*) the burial part of the edifice is to be distinguished from the section devoted to feasting. Since the "grave" or "cemetery" is the *taun* enclosure itself, then, it is possible that its "cutting," or *gurogorop*, refers to the shift in emphasis from the burial to the feasting part of the *taun* (or aspect of the image) that is effected in the transition from a closed to an open mode of feasting.

Whether or not this is the case, the open feast enacts the image of a replete and fully constituted *taun*, extending its bounty outward for the nurturance of its *nat*, those of the companion moiety. As an act of the associated moiety, clan, and lineage, this enactment becomes the substance of their fosterage of—and their claims upon—the opposite moiety, considered as their "children." In this sense it is the living, rather than the dead, that are encompassed, for it is the *nat*

191

(and all those of the opposite moiety are *nat* of one's own, yet to be sealed within the containment of their own lineages) whose needs and desires are satisfied by the feast. As the *taun* sustains its own members, so it sustains its guests; and as it nurtures the latter, so it provides for its *nat* wherever they may be. As an earnest of this enacted relation, the food for an open feast is provided by the host unit—and is provided in sufficient quantity that everyone will have some left after his own needs have been satisfied, so that food may be taken home afterward. Food is often sent out to those who are not able to attend an open feast, and baskets of a seasonal delicacy featured at a *maranien* feast are often made up and sent to each of the nearby *taun*.

The flow of food at an open feast is outward from the *taun* (Figure 4), and the imagistic movement of the feast is nurturant and providential, from the authoritative and "ancestral" rear to the "public" front, just as gifts from the *orong* (or the ancestors themselves) might proceed. This image is completed, again, by the protocols for displaying the pigs and distributing the food. These are, of course, opposite to those of the closed feast: the pigs in the open feast are positioned with their heads toward the *ola-gabo*, and the courses of the feast are distributed in an order beginning at the rear of the *gunun*, moving progressively toward the front, as in Figure 4.

Although it may begin with an expression of *malum* (specifically early in the morning of the feast itself), the *go-gorop*, as the definitive open feast, enacts the transformation and reorientation of the coordinate image from a figure appropriate to *malum* to one appropriate to *malili*. (Both of these ethical postures are, of course, present to some degree or other at every feast, just as the hindpart and forepart of the *taun* are always present. And it is for just this reason that the additional figuration of closed and open feasting is necessary—in order to focus selectively on hindpart and *malum*, then forepart and *malili*.) The *go-gorop*, then, is a "finishing" feast precisely because of its directionality—its figurative transformation and "cutting" of the *taun*. For in its reversal of the flow, it complements the closed feast and completes the composite image: the *taun* has encompassed the deceased and the foods proffered on his or her behalf, and the *ligu* has absorbed the products of decomposition; having thus contained death, the image must demonstrate its power by sustaining life. The systole and diastole of the mortuary cycle enacts and therefore constitutes the basic relations of Usen culture: *malum* and *malili*, the containment of the *bung marapun*, and the nurturance of *nat*. It aligns moieties and fixes between them the exigencies and responsibilities of life and death.

It is clear, then, that the coherence of the mortuary cycle lies not in the arbitration of classificatory distinctions, or even in the programmatic exhaustion of a set of arbitrary rules, but in the elicitation and completion of the appropriate image. It is essential that the paired sequence of closed and open feasts be enacted, and in that order. And because mortuary feasting is the archetypal legitimating form in Barok culture, this sequence is recognized (though not always realized) as the ideal order for all formal feasting. The feast for the consecration of an ordinary *taun*, for instance, should have a *songot kalu* and a *gogorop*, because the base of the *olagabo* is buried, in its installation, as a human being is buried.

As enactment, a Barok mortuary feast (or cycle of feasts) is an accomplishment, a kind of coup. Although it perhaps "says something," it can hardly be summed up as a "message" or "conveying of information"; and although its sponsors may be conceded to win "successorship" by demonstrating their worthiness, it is a "game" only in a very trivial sense. A major feast is constitutive not only in its imagery, but also in its organization of those who are most intensively involved in it. It is an episode, a part of life with a life of its own. Perhaps the best example of this would be a summary description of an *a un gogorop* which I observed, and in whose preparation and performance I participated, in November 1979.

The *gogorop* was planned for a time when gardens would be producing and bananas would be ripe. For more than two weeks before the selected date (November 17 was originally designated by the lineage head, though the feast was actually held on the sixteenth), work progressed on the building of a new *pan* and the completion of the *taun konono*. As soon as the *pan* was completed (about October 27) a group of women and children from the lineage of the husband of the deceased moved into the structure, where they would live until the feast, clearing the ground and providing daily ovens of vegetable food. From this time on, as the work (readying of *bebe* and benches, constructing the *butam*, gathering firewood and stones for the ovens) advanced, daily feasts were held in the *pan* and the *taun* for those participating. The meals were preceded by a formal distribution of areca nut and green coconuts, and included some kind of meat or relish as well as rice. Work crews included members of Unakulis, the sponsoring clan, as well as people of the Malaba moiety, who worked as "affines" and "father's people."

Beginning on November 6, the Unakulis truck was used to collect bananas, for an *a un gogorop* takes its name from the large quantities of artificially ripened and softened bananas that are served with the main course. On the sixth and seventh, bananas were purchased at all surrounding villages by Tago men, and on the eighth they were purchased by Malaba men. Bundles of taro were also obtained. On the ninth, men began cutting tree bark with which to cover the bananas for the ripening process; and *kun*, or ripening beds, were begun to hold them. On the night of the twelfth, men began gathering in the *taun*, and women in the *pan*, for the singing of *a gogo* (Tokpisin *goigoi*), short, commiserating songs concerning casualties or misfortunes, sung in a distinctive manner

194

with an arresting, two-beat rhythm to honor the deceased. *A gogo* is sung nightly from this point until the night before the feast.

Bananas were formally presented to Unakulis by the Malaba lines of Bakan on November 11; they called out for the lineage head and told him they were giving the bananas to help with the feast. Malaba people contributed at least eighty bunches of bananas, Tago people at least seventy-five. Areca nuts, green coconuts, and taro baked in coconut grease can also be formally presented in this way. Four *kun* "beds" were made: one large one apiece for the men and women at the main feast, and one small one each for the men's and women's ceremonial "breakfast" following the final night of *gogo* singing. There is an *ololo*, or set of avoidances for those who work with the bananas: those who did not touch bananas when they were children, or men who are currently having sex, may not come into contact with the fruit. Those who carry the bananas must avoid *pasaba* trees and old vines (the kinds used for fencing); they must not touch the bananas, nor may the people who come into contact with them. If these avoidances are not respected, it is said, the bananas will not ripen. The *kun* are supported on three coconut logs with crosspieces of bamboo, and have sides built up of bamboo. They are lined with sheets of tree bark, and when the bananas have been stripped off their stalks and loaded into the "bed," they are covered with sheets of bark, and then with *pagum* leaves. Banana stalks are piled on top of this and tied up whole.

On November 13, at about 2:00 P.M., the men of Kanapit Village arrived, bringing firewood for the pig ovens at the *gogorop*. They were treated to a feast in the *taun* and, that evening, led the *gogo* singing there, in order to make a better showing than the previous night, when the women had outsung and outlasted the men, and had tied a bunch of sweet-

195

smelling *kongo* leaves to a *tawan* tree near the *taun* as a triumphal flourish.

On the fifteenth, preparations were made for a large *da*, or stone oven, of *olos*, taro slices steamed in coconut grease. A scraper as well as bags for expressing the grease were borrowed from Kanapit. Parallel poles were laid out on the ground, with strips of tree bark going crosswise, and leaves were put over them to form a mold in which the taro disks and coconut grease were arranged. Then the bark strips were folded over and tied into packets. A large stone oven (about five meters in diameter) was set up by placing stone atop firewood; when the wood burned down, the *olos* packets were arranged on the hot stones, followed by leaves and earth. The bake was kept closed all night.

As the large pigs for the feast were brought into Bakan, several old women began to cry publicly—a kind of funeral wailing. They were crying for the deceased, because she could no longer take part in such feasts. The *gogo* that night included sets of men and women grouped in the *taun* enclosure according to village. The north and south sides competed in singing, as the "Kavieng" and "Namatanai" sides respectively; the singing developed into an answering of songs (picking up on the last words of the previous song by the other group, and singing them over in response).

Early on the morning of the sixteenth, the Tago *gogo* singers filled buckets with cold water and poured them on the Malaba people, and also rubbed lime and ashes on their faces (traditionally they threw them into the sea, or took them into the bush for sex). Then the *olos* bake was opened, and a pig was killed especially for the morning feast of the *gogo* singers. The smaller *kun* of bananas (reserved respectively for the men and the women) were opened, and a lavish "breakfast" of pork, bananas, and *olos* was served in the *taun*. At about 1:00 P.M. the *gogorop* was prepared and the large *kun* opened. Fourteen pigs were killed: six "for the feast," the remainder (also for general distribution) on other pretexts. The "heads" of the pigs and packets of *olos* were distributed in a long session after the feasting, in which Unakulis men stood before the *butam* and called out the names of men and lines as recipients. Woven coconut-leaf baskets of bananas were sent to various *taun* as gifts, bringing the "open" feast to an appropriate conclusion.

The costly and elaborate production of an *a un gogorop* as a "last feast" provides a memorial counterbalance to the sustained effort immediately after the death. The image, as production, commands and receives a huge investment of human effort and attention, commensurate with its cultural significance. This is true on an even grander scale for the culminating effort in the Barok mortuary sequence, the *kaba*.

The *Kaba*

An image like that of containment has the prepossessing advantage, denied to referential symbolism, of embodying its own referent. The *taun* becomes an image of containment by enacting containment. By the same token, however, the image has the inarguable disadvantage of inflexibility. If it cannot be glossed or paraphrased adequately in words, it also lacks the facility, which words possess, of articulative recombination and qualitative inflection. The image of containment, in the mortuary feasts, is thus limited to its own application and relaxation—the "closing" and "opening" of the mortuary cycle. The *taun* encloses (perhaps "digests") the body of the deceased, and this containment literally "incorporates" the deceased within its continuity. But this enactment of successorship, powerful though it may be, is also limited by the special qualities—the moiety and clan affiliations, the "collective" anonymity—of the *taun*. Successorship implies more than containment alone, and for these additional implications a different image is required.

197

The great final mortuary feast, the *kaba* or *kabai* (*gabai* on the west coast)[8] is made, as the Usen say, to "suffice" the dead, to "finish all thought of them." The feast is sometimes spoken of as *songot a tanu*, "scorching[9] the souls," in the way, perhaps, that the *bebe* also require a feast before they may be dismantled and burned (*songot bebe*). Not a part of the mortuary cycle as I have analyzed it here, the *kaba* is nevertheless essential to proper treatment of the dead; if it is not performed, their ghosts can be expected to trouble the living. A large and expensive undertaking, the *kaba* is not ordinarily done to honor the memory of a single person, unless that person is worthy of special recognition.[10] Most often, it is done for all of those who have died since the community's prior performance of the feast, and most often there are other reasons as well. Like the feast in the *taun*, the *kaba* is two-sided: it honors the dead through the worthiness of the living, and through the ritual propriety of the *winawu*, but it also legitimates the successorship of the living through their honoring of the dead, most especially that of the *winawu*, who is often a candidate for *orong*ship.

The *kaba* proper is a cleaned, cut, and prepared section of a tree, set up in a cleared area (often a *lu naraman*) as the centerpiece of the feast, which bears its name. Barok distinguish two basic kinds of *kaba* feasts: the more elaborate *un na ya*

---

[8] The word is pronounced with a fairly even stress on both syllables, slightly favoring the last, but *not* with the flourish of emphasis on the second syllable that English speakers use to mark foreign or exotic words.

[9] *Songot* is used by Barok for processes involving direct contact with fire, such as broiling or burning; thus the resonant Tokpisin ambiguity of *kukim* ("cooking"), used both for heating food (in any manner) and burning, is a bit imprecise, and I have chosen "scorching."

[10] An *una ya kaba* was held for my namesake Sogang, of Ramat, at the Unakulis grounds in the Sokirik village of Pire. Sogang was a *waitpus* (from the German "Weissputz"?—for the white hatband that designated his rank), or paramount native chief of the Barok region. It is significant that the current Unakulis *orong*, who showed me that *una ya*, asked to be photographed standing atop it.

("base of the tree"), which centers about the inverted root-stock of a tree, and the less ambitious *agana ya* ("branch of the tree"), which makes use of an upright section or trunk (with larger limbs) or a major branch. Informants at the northern Barok village of Lokon identified yet another sub-variety of *kaba* feast, the *kaba musmus*, performed in response to provocative language (*tok bilas*) or a challenge such as, "Many people have been dead now for a long time; when, then, will you make the *kaba*?" The *kaba musmus* is performed to "finish" the onus of such talk as well as to "finish" the dead. In it, two *kaba* trees are carried in, one by the perpetrator of the verbal affront, and the other by the affronted line.

As the largest and most elaborate of Barok feasts, the *kaba* entails extensive preparation and forethought in terms of provisioning and social prearrangement. The first step is a solicitory gift called the *kuruse*. This takes the form of a *pram* of *mis* given, by the *orong* who intends to give a *kaba* for that person, at the *gogorop* of a deceased person to anyone of the *orong's* own moiety who attends the *gogorop*. A prudent *orong* will give *kuruse* to wealthy and trustworthy men who are likely to honor the expectations of the gift. The offer of a *kuruse* may be refused with good grace, or the original *mis* may be returned to the giver if the recipient has been unsuccessful. But the ideal is that the recipient will use the *mis* to buy a small pig, which he will raise and bring to the *kaba* when it is full-grown. He should also garden so that he may bring taro as well. He may, if all else fails, simply purchase a pig at the last moment, making supplemental use of the *kuruse*. The sense of the transaction, however, is that the recipient of the *kuruse* becomes a helper in the production of the *kaba*. He is allowed the use of the *sabonu*, or rear, of the pig he has brought; the "head," *ogono*, goes to the *orong* for the *kaba*. The *orong* will also inform the people of his own place that he intends to hold a *kaba* in the future, and will tell them, too, to buy small pigs and raise them for the feast. When the pigs are of ample size (worth ten or twenty *pram* of *mis*), the *orong* will say, "Now go and prepare some big gardens." Extensive reserves of pork and vegetable food are necessary, given the amount of feasting involved.

When the gardens have grown, the *orong* calls out for people to go to the bush with axes and knives in order to cut the tree. The tree selected is either the *kana* or *kanao* (also used for the *olagabo* of a *taun*) or another tree called the *osa*. The *agana ya*, or "branch of the tree," is comparatively easy to obtain; I shall describe here the preparations for the more difficult and elaborate *un na ya*, "base of the tree." To begin with, the axman stands against the trunk and marks it by reaching up with his hand; the tree above this mark is cut off and felled. This event, and all subsequent major steps in the preparation of the *kaba*, necessitates a formal feast in the *taun*, with at least a cooked pig apiece for the men and the women.

Then the ground is broken, and the roots of the tree are dug out with sticks, and cut out at a certain limit (generally about two meters) radially about the trunk. The completion of this event is marked by a feast with pigs, and another is held when the great taproot is cut, down below. After this, the trunk is laid over on its side. On another day, poles and vines are cut, and poles are shoved under the base of the trunk and lashed into place to form a supporting framework. Then a road is cut through the bush from the tree to the site of the *kaba* feast. After this, the host community harvests taro and bananas, and a cordyline (*tanket*) is sent to all places, inviting people to come and help carry the tree. When they have assembled, the man who is to serve as *winawu* is adorned; he climbs atop the trunk, where he stands, calling out, *asiwina-rong! aswininarong!* while the tree is carried to the feasting site. The large feast of *kip kaba* ("fetching the *kaba*") is held then, with pigs and the first harvesting of taro from the gar-

200

dens planted for the *kaba*. After this the *winawu* says, *Pinisie kaba* ("Clean the *kaba*"), and all the irregularities and epiphytic growths are removed from the tree trunk. The tree base is then inverted, its roots pointing skyward, and planted in the ground (*sula kaba*). A "bed" is made, threading poles through the roots, with ripe coconuts interspersed as a filler to make a level platform (about two meters above the ground—though sometimes there are several "tiers") for the display of pigs. For this work (*asing kaba*) as well as, earlier, for the "planting," a pig feast is held.

A *bang*, or unenclosed *taun*, and a *pan* are often built at the base of the *kaba* to hold the men and women participating in the feasting. After the tree is in place, and the bed has been prepared, bananas will be cut and fastened in *kun* for the forced-ripening process, and more food will be harvested. People from everywhere are invited to come and carve the *kaba*; they cut figures of human beings, sharks, lizards, etc. on the trunk and are then given a large feast, with newly harvested tubers, force-ripened bananas, and pigs provided by the Tago moiety. This is the *abung go tago*,[11] the small feast of the Tago people. It is followed by the *abung go malaba*, with pigs provided by the Malaba moiety, held in order to announce the time at which the *kaba* will be held. A cordyline is sent out to all places, announcing the date of the feast, so that those communities planning to perform *tinie* may commence their preparations. (It is a point of pride that the men, or women, or both, of a village be represented by some sort of *tinie*.) At some time after the announcement (at Lokon in 1979 it occurred roughly one month before the *kaba* proper), at a feast called *musabet*, "beds" (platforms) are set up, one for each moiety, to hold taro and other tubers contributed to the feast.

[11] This is assuming that the host clan is Malaba. The first *abung* is given by the guest moiety; the second one, announcing the date of the *kaba*, is provided by the host moiety.

201

Just before the main feast is to be held, bananas are cut and ripened again, food is harvested, and pigs are cooked for another preliminary feast, called *a inim kaba* ("decorating the *kaba*"). The clans of the host community, grouped according to moiety, compete to decorate the tree; each takes a side, and hangs strings of *mis* from the upended roots, to see which moiety possesses the most *mis* and can completely cover its side. (The moieties alternate in hanging their decorations.) After this, the feast is held.

On the night before the *gisawot*, or culminating feast of the *kaba*, the slit-gong, or *garamut* (Barok *gamut*), is beaten; the practice of *a ben* (Tokpisin *bot*), a nightly promenade about the sounding *garamut* by radial lines of slow-stepping singers, is a common occurrence in many communities once the feasting for the *kaba* gets underway. (At the Lokon *kaba* in 1979, pigs' jaws from the feasting were hung on the *a-gana ya* in tribute to the men who beat the *garamut* at night.)

For a day or two before the *kaba* feast itself, *tinie* are performed by various participating communities to help celebrate the cause of the feasting. These may be done by male or female groups, each performing, in brilliant attire, some recognized *tinie* proper to its respective sex. The order of presentation is determined by the officiating *winawu*,[12] and the atmosphere is highly charged, both by the intensely focused consciousness of pride or shame contingent upon the quality of performance, and by the expectation that those who are able will bring powerful resources of negative and preventive *a lolos* to bear upon the performances.[13]

---

[12] Mr. Nicholas Brokam, the noted statesman and traditional leader who served as *winawu* at the 1979 *kaba* at Lokon, wrote out the schedule in Tokpisin on a large blackboard and hung it up at the *kaba* site.

[13] Power gestures and power-related incidents abound in the charged atmosphere; at Lokon in 1979, a woman experienced a sudden rush of menstrual bleeding after stepping over a taboo mark. That same morning, a young *tinie* leader fell into so obvious a power-related shaking fit that the

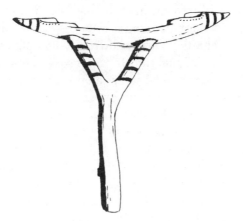

FIGURE 5. A *Dawan* Chair (from
an example at Bakan)

The *kaba* feast itself marks the culmination of the whole ceremony. The pigs for the main feast, eviscerated and with their bristles singed off, are put up on the beds over the tree roots; the *winawu* will stand atop them to play his part. Young boys—including especially those who are *ararum* and are expected one day to take the role of *winawu*—also mount the platform, and sit behind him. These boys, called *igisinbo*, are decorated with *mis*. At the base of the *kaba* are favored young girls, called *dawan*, their hair and bodies covered with red ochre and decorated with *mis*. They sit on carved, painted seats, called *dawan* chairs (see Figure 5), which are thrust into the ground; each *dawan* holds areca nut, betel pepper, and a pouch of lime powder in her hands, and rests her feet on a wrapped, uncooked, taro corm.

The *winawu*, ideally a "new man" who has been coached

audience went wild, and the *tinie* was inaudible owing to the screams and laughter of the onlookers.

203

and carefully prepared for his role, has been fed special betel
pepper (*sie*) and plant and tree substances to make him speak
well (and, incidentally, to cause others to buy pig from him).
He carries the traditional fighting ax (*asok*) in one hand, and
a spear in the other; and he wears a *bun*, a hanging egg-cow-
rie with dependent dog's-tooth ornaments, as well as special
mis, about his neck. (A traditional "sunburst" pearl-shell
medallion, if available, may also be worn on the breast.) A
man stands at the base of the *kaba*; he is called the *un na winawu*, and he is the man ("at the base of the *winawu*") who
coached the *winawu* in his speech, and who gave him special
preparations to eat. First the *winawu* stands up, and the *un
na winawu* takes some lime powder (*a kabak*) and slaps it on
the base of his neck. The *un na winawu* says to him, *Tago,
oro lek wongon* ("Hawk, now you will spill yourself"), and
the *winawu* shrugs, causing the lime to fly up in powder
smoke. Then the *winawu* stands up ready. The *un na winawu* says, *Gam, nongon tenginini* ("Go ahead; you talk"),
and the *winawu* begins, in falsetto:

   *Saaaa, asiwinarong, asiwinarong, asiwinarong, asiwina-
rong!*

He calls out the names, then, of all the places from which people have come to the *kaba*:

   Ramat; Ba-gan; Kanawit; Lulubo; Belik; Loloba; Karu;
      Kanam; *aaaaaaaaaa!*

Then he intones the *winawu*'s traditional address:

   E mumongan nana magasi ne muma'
   E mumoro tadangi, evi anine a oronga,
   Aie bak madak.
   Era tenge, -go ya wina.
   Ire tenge -go maramuna, -go ya wina,
   O-gono wiriwit tobut.

(The sense of this, which my informants had difficulty ren-
dering exactly, goes something like: "All of you have come
to rejoice with us; there are no *orong* here, only small boys."

204

Ogono wiriwit tobut means "the head of the hawk.") After this, the *winawu* may add any additional announcements he wishes to make, especially relating to the event and the reasons for celebrating it. He then announces publicly the sum of the wealth expended in organizing the *kaba* (at Lokon in 1979 it was 8,000 *kina* and forty *pram* of *mis*), and calls out for a count of the pigs on display.[14] A man designated for this task then counts the pigs publicly, slapping them one by one with his hand; he calls out the names of the deceased to be honored, and says that the pig is to be cooked "upon them." Then he shouts the total number of pigs to the *winawu*, who announces it to those at the feast. (At Lokon there were sixty-six pigs on display.)

The pigs are then thrown down and placed on leaves preparatory to cutting. Before they are cut, a sprouted coconut is thrown (or merely rolled)[15] by the contributor of a large pig, who is seeking someone to "eat the coconut" (i.e. the *ogono* of the pig). He throws the coconut to one likely recipient after another, calling out, *Tadi oren a bobo ne lamas sere.* Should Tadi not wish to accept, he throws the coconut back. When someone is found who is willing, he breaks the coconut on the ground, and all clap and cry out in surprise. The recipient is obliged to return the head of a similar pig later. When the *ogono* have been disposed of in this way, the pigs are cut up and cooked, and the feast is carefully distributed among the large throng that has collected for the culminating rite. Every man and woman receives a plentiful supply of taro and pork, and since this is in no conceivable way a "closed" feast, there is always food to take home. The *kaba* is concluded

---

[14] Numbers up to a hundred can easily be accommodated within the Barok quinary-decimal system; adoption of the Tolai terms *mar* (hundred) and *arip* (thousand) extends its compass considerably. At Lokon, however, the pigs were counted in English.

[15] Barok tend to roll them; but at a large feast (the equivalent of an *agana ya*) at Pinikindu in 1979, the coconuts were hurled, occasionally landing amid the crowds of onlookers.

205

rather abruptly with a loud shout, the beating of *garamut*, and the striking of sticks and bamboo against trees, "beds," tables, and so forth—"to chase away the visitors."

Barok distinguish the *kaba* as against *taun* feasts by noting that the former is a *pablik* ("public") event, open to all, and not enveloped within the *iri lolos* of a particular moiety, clan, and lineage. It is, like the *taun* feasts, a staged spectacle and a conventional image of great legitimating power. But it is also strikingly and contrastingly different from the *taun* feasts, and it is worth our while to consider the differences.

First of all, the "tree" for which the feast is named, and around which the spectacle is enacted, is often enough the same variety which is used in fashioning the *olagabo* of the *taun*. Both the *kaba* tree (either form) and the *olagabo* are the object of painstaking preparation, brought to the feasting site with ceremony and installed with a substantial feast. Both are frequently embellished with carving, and both are draped with *mis* on important occasions. Barok compare the installation of the *olagabo* to the burial of a human being, and mark it with a *songot kalu*, but it is the *digging out* of the tree (in the case of the *kaba*) that is likened to the interment of a corpse. Most important, the *olagabo* amounts to the use of the tree as a vital part of the image of containment—it is the "valve" of the *taun*'s envelopment, whereas the *kaba* tree is central and free-standing, contained by the displayed pigs rather than containing them.

Second, although a *bang* (an *un*enclosed *taun*) and a *pan* may be built at the base of the *kaba*, they do not represent the type of venerated, containing edifice that a *taun* does. They are peripheral and ancillary to the tree itself; whereas the *taun* enclosure contains the pigs and the feast at a *taun* function, the displayed pigs (on their platform) and the feast itself surround the tree at the *kaba*.

Third, although the *kaba* is hosted by one moiety, it is not contained by that moiety and its ancestral *lolos* as in the case of a *taun* feast. The moieties at a *kaba* stand in an openly competitive relationship, providing their respective *abung* and decorating the tree in conspicuous rivalry. The *kaba* has a collective aspect, and the *tinie* that introduce it are presented and promoted by communities per se, rather than by clan or moiety units.

Fourth, the significance of the *orong*, and the role of the *orong* as *winawu*, always a feature of the formal feast in the *taun*, becomes the dominant emphasis of the *kaba*. The *winawu* speaks at the central, focal point of the *taun* feast, enclosed by the *taun* and its ancestral authority; but the *winawu* speaks *on top of the pigs*, which are then cooked "on top of the deceased," at the *kaba*. In a significant sense, the *kaba* is *about orong*, and the need of *orong*, rather than about the containment of the dead and their power.

In all of the above respects, the image presented in the *kaba* would seem to embody a canceling or negating transformation of the *taun* mortuary feasts. The imagery of this transformation is not that of reversal—the "opening" of the *gogorop* that cancels the "closing" of the *songot kalu*—nor could it be, for with the conclusion of the *a un gogorop* the sequential significance of the *taun's* containment is exhausted. Instead, the image of containment itself is annulled via a composite of inversions: the tree as contained centerpiece rather than containing gateway, the men's house as peripheral adjunct rather than all-encompassing frame, the symmetrical rivalry of moieties as opposed to their complementary roles in nurturance, and the transformation of the contained *winawu* into the "head" of the feast.

These contrasts help us to understand the place of the *kaba* in a succession of images. But it is also necessary to come to terms with it as an enactment in its own right—as an image of succession. Its aspect as a large, public feast with vivid, day-long entertainment and plenteous food for all places it in diametrical opposition to the *lebe* and the constraints on eating and personal adornment imposed at the time of death and during the mourning period. In this sense the *kaba* enacts a kind of renascent *malili*, a celebration of life. But the central image of the *kaba* is the tree, removed from the forest with painstaking care and much feasting, carried to the site with ceremony, erected and decorated, and then surmounted by the *winawu* and his youthful accomplices for the oration. The tree adds a new dimension, that of vertical transcendence, to the imagery of mortuary feasting; it raises *winawu* and pigs over the throng.

The *agana ya kaba* makes use of a large, forked branch or trunk of the tree (reminiscent, again, of the *olagabo*), around the base of which a platform for the pigs will be erected. The tree is often hung with small gifts or "favors"—areca nut, and nowadays candy and cigarettes—on the occasion of its erection; and small boys, decorated with *mis* and red ochre, will perch in it as a kind of anticipation of the *kaba*. (This seems to be an example of the decorated, festive tree—a motif that enjoys a wide distribution in world folklore.)[16]

It is the *un na ya*, the full, or complete form of the *kaba*, of which the *agana ya* may be regarded as a token, that carries the vertical image of the tree to its final significance. For the *un na ya* is a perfect enactment of the "overturning" of an old order. It is not merely a "supplanting," as we might say of the *agana ya*—vertical ascendancy captured by human effort and brought from the forest to serve as the centerpiece of the feast—but rather a supplanting used as the articulation

---

[16] Boards or poles for the display of bride wealth, like the Chimbu *minge-ende*, are known from many parts of the highlands; the Yagaria speakers of Legaiu described one to me in 1964. In parts of the Huon Peninsula, an actual tree is used. Many examples of decorated trees (like the European Christmas tree) can be found in world ethnography. Typical is the *parchem*, the decorated wedding tree of the Komachi, nomadic pastoralists of Iran described by Professor Daniel Bradburd. The *parchem* is painted and embellished with the names of Shiite martyrs, and small gifts are hung from it.

of a relationship. For if we consider that Barok regard the grounding of an *olagabo* or the digging out of the *un na ya* rootstock as imaging the interment of the dead, then the inversion of the *un na ya* enacts the displacement of the deceased. The roots image the ambience of the dead, and perhaps their basal relation to the living; to upturn them is to provide a new base.

This may become more obvious if we return for a moment to the significance of the *kaba* as the successor image to that of the *taun* feasts. For the meaningful dimension of the *taun*, which forms the basis for the transformation from "closed" to "open" feasts, is that of *ligu* and *konono*: the private rear that contains the dead, and the public forepart that contains the feasting. Given the displacement of the *taun*, one may move from one of these to the other—toward closure or openness, as the case may be. But one may not confute this spatial and procedural order without damaging the *taun* itself as an image of clan continuity and authority. Yet the *kaba*, as a vertical surrogate or translation of the burial-feasting order, is not subject to this limitation. The *un na ya kaba* enacts the final obviation of the order, and of the distinction between burial and feasting; for it merges the two by "cooking the pigs on top of the deceased," literally a *songot a tanu*.

The rootstock of the tree, corresponding originally to the *ligu* (burial) portion of the *taun*, is upended to form a platform for the display of pigs, whereas the upper trunk, corresponding to the *olagabo* and feasting portion of the *taun*, is buried in the earth. The dead, the ancestors are based upon the feast (as indeed there are no honorable dead without a feast), whereas the feast is made upon the dead (as there would be no feasts without the bounty of the ancestors): the dialectical relation of the present and past, of event and authority, is fully realized. At the "new" base of the image, young girls, who are the source of lineal continuity, are seated, their feet resting on uncooked taro corms; at the top, surmounting the pigs that cover the "ancestors," stands the *winawu*, with his escort of future *winawu*: the ancestors support the *winawu* as the feast supports the ancestors.

The contingency, or necessity for human action, that this condensed realization of the interdependence of feasting and ancestral legacy evokes is precisely that which the *winawu* intones in his oration: *asiwinarong*, the "need of an *orong*." For the dead are already there, and since the dead are supported and "made" by feasts, what is needed is a worthy successor, an *orong* who can honor them by giving lavish feasts, and who can thus prove himself the legitimate heir to their power and prestige. The contingency is the more socially significant for the fact that successorship and *orong*ship are in no sense lineal or hereditary, but preemptive. One becomes an *orong* by giving feasts, and one becomes a successor by preempting the succession—by showing oneself worthy.

Succession is the final step in the honoring of the dead; by furnishing their replacement, if only in a formal or titular sense, the *kaba* "finishes all thought of them." Precisely because it resolves and obviates the values of the *taun* to reveal a transcendent idea of feasting, the *kaba* becomes the ceremonial investiture of the *orong*, and the means to the reinforcement and reinstatement of social leadership. Without the capability of the *orong* (as well, perhaps, as the revelation of his investiture), the Barok would truly be "children" (*aie bak madak*), or heirs without heritage.

The Succession of Images

The revelation of the *kaba*, that burial and feasting are completely interdependent, a revelation that constitutes *orong*ship as the *taun* feasting constitutes ethos and moiety relations, is achieved through the collapse, or obviation, of the tension between burial and feasting. This tension is set up in the first, or "closed," mortuary feasts, where *malum* and the containment of the *taun* forbid any removal of food from the enclosure. It is relaxed somewhat by the "opening" and exhaustion of the *taun* space in the *a un goborop*, following the decomposition of the corpse. The deceased are then *tanu*, mere spirits who may trouble the living if they are not "finished" or "scorched." The act of "cooking the pigs on top of the dead," which "finishes" the latter, also concludes the mortuary process and dispels its imagery. The mortuary sequence is at once a social process and a knowledge process.

The three major evolutions of image that constitute the sequence may be seen as a succession of collective or social acts to contain and objectify the existential stages of the deceased. Death and burial are followed by the "closed" feasts; decomposition, with its "contamination" of the *ligu ni taun*, is concluded by the principal "open" feast, the *a un goborop*; finally, the disembodied *tanu* are "cooked" under the pigs of the *kaba* and "finished." The successorship evoked in the *kaba* represents the culmination of the process, the transformation of death into an act of succession, a relationship between living and dead.

But the *kaba* shows the dialectical relation between death, in its stages, and feasting. The phases of death, differentiated by the ceremonial, are also images—so that the moral force of feasting can be seen to enter into a dialectic with the factual changes of death. The dialectic, moreover, is of the self-closing kind that I have elsewhere[17] introduced as "obviation": i.e. a sequence of dialectically related images that returns to, and negates, its own beginning point.

A dialectic that closes upon itself is ternary (consisting of a thesis, an antithesis, and a resolving synthesis), and this Hegelian form, providing a "middle" or mediating term to resolve the opposition, furnishes the basic image, or framework, for the analysis of obviation. Thus the closed feast, the

[17] Wagner, *Lethal Speech*.

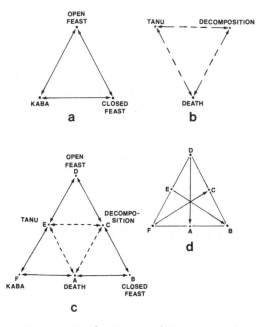

FIGURE 6. The Stages of Feasting and
Death as a Closed Dialectic

open feast, and the *kaba* stand in this relation; for the "the-sis" of the closed feast is opposed by the "antithesis" of the open feast, whereas the *kaba* resolves the two by cooking its pigs "on top of the dead" (Figure 6*a*). The stages of death are apportioned by this sequence into three: death itself, decomposition, and the freed *tanu*, or spirits, and may be shown to form a mediational series similar to that of the feasts (Figure 6*b*). When these two series are interdigitated in their sequential order, so that the respective stages of each are seen to mediate those of the other, they generate three interlocked mediative series set holographically within the larger mediation (Figure 6*c*). Finally, the antithesis of each successive triangle

212

has the effect of directly complementing or completing the thesis of the previous one, so that the *gogorop* (*D*) releases the *lebe* and other taboos imposed at death (*A*), the release of the *tanu* (*E*) resolves the "sealing" of the body in the closed *taun* (*B*), and the *kaba* "finishes" the *tanu* to complement the bodily dissolution of the deceased (*C*). The (social-factual-social) series *DEF* thus supplants the (factual-social-factual) series *ABC*, as the social series *BDF* supplants the factual *ACE*.

What we have constructed in Figure 6 is an explanatory image that is simultaneously sequential, or temporal, and synchronic. If we follow the outer edge of the triangle counterclockwise from *A* to *F*, and note the "obviating" successorship between *F* and *A*, we will "map" the Barok mortuary sequence in its temporal order. But if we consider the dialectical relations that we traced in the preceding paragraph, it becomes apparent that *every point in the sequence is connected directly to every other point* through one sort of relation or another. The meaning of the whole is implicit in each of the stages, and this meaning is not so much "stated" as it is realized, in the fulfillment of the sequence. To borrow a phrase from Victor Zuckerkandl,[18] it grows "in a dimension perpendicular to time." The complex image of Barok mortuary rite, which is coterminous with that meaning, is so involute that it may be explicated only through another image. Figure 6d has been provided to that purpose; but for Barok it is the *kaba*, as the final image in the sequence (that which exhausts its meaning, or obviates it) that reveals its core. For in creating an *orong*, and a need for an *orong*, it makes them *barok*.

[18] Zuckerkandl, *Man the Musician*, p. 191.

NINE

Conclusion

THE ANALYSIS of cultural meaning, of the interpretive constructions and perceptions that are collectively known and acted upon by the people under study, has become a fairly well-known and accepted anthropological approach. It contrasts in method and theory with other explanatory approaches (such as functionalism) which are concerned to show how indigenous usages operate to fulfill basic human or social needs, constitute a native realization of "enlightened self-interest," and so forth. In its primitive stages, the study of indigenous meaning did in fact borrow an explanatory rhetoric from functionalism, attempting to show how certain meaningful constructions helped to integrate the group, to get people to do "what they have to," or allowed them to measure up to our own standards for a moral, well-run culture, a businesslike clan system, and the like.

A reasonably consistent regime of cultural meaning, of course, can be expected to define and delimit its own ends. These may or may not be reconcilable with what we might expect of a society or a culture; they may or may not correspond to what an anthropologist or an educated person in general considers to be rational or logical (for "rational" in its common usage may mean anything from "the pursuit of economic advantage" to "a well-integrated system of linear logic"). Because of this, a conscientious analysis of cultural meanings should be exploratory; it should inquire into the ends, the motives, and the means of indigenous usages, rather than simply assume them from the outset.

What has emerged from this study is not an account of a native "system" motivated to close itself into a set, linear pattern, or of an organization of juro-economic "institutions" straining toward the efficiency of a single, societal institution. Although the Barok seem, even by contrast with their New Ireland neighbors, to be obsessed with boundaries, limits, and taboos, these concerns need not be equated with an interest in integrating "society" or creating an efficient institutional base. Consider that the tutelary clan spirit, the formless *tadak*, likes to amuse itself by tricking and fouling male clan members and seducing their women; that a man can (and often one does) deed over thousands of man-hours of clan labor, and considerable clan wealth, to another clan (and moiety) by bequeathing his *taun* to his children, that the *kaba* ritual overthrows not only the significance of the ancestors, but also the symbology of moiety interaction embodied in the *taun*. Whose expectations are compromised here? Certainly not those of the Barok, for these usages are part of their expectations.

I have suggested that the core of Usen Barok *kastam* is an ethos, a "collectively held and collectively felt motivation and code for the conduct, expression, and experience of social and ritual life." This ethos is elicited by the dialectical interaction of the moieties, through a set of relational protocols involving avoidance, respect, and joking, and through a range of (iconic, nonverbal) images concerning nurturance, containment, and successorship, and centered on the *taun* and the *kaba*. "Elicitation" implies a seemingly indirect and reactive, or competitive, inducement to action, analogous perhaps to Bateson's notion of schismogenesis; instead of literally commanding or explaining what the actor is to do, the actor is confronted with the contingency in which he is to act. Whether the confrontation takes the form of an intended joke, a circumstance calling for avoidance, or a nonverbal image that requires comprehension and "dealing with," the actor is put on his mettle, thrown back on his own resources, in providing a response. (In all fairness it should be added that whereas elicitation is *literally* indirect, it presents the contingency for acting directly, whereas a more literally direct approach—injunctions, instructions—often merely implies the contingency.)

Ethos, then, is a style of improvisatory action in response to demonstrated contingencies. As the object of elicitation, it draws together the kin relationships discussed in Chapters 3 and 4 and the iconic symbology by which the interaction of the moieties is resolved and completed (Chapters 7 and 8). *How* it does so is perhaps best approached through the discussion of *pidik* and power in Chapter 6, for Usen feel that all significant or worthwhile things are grounded in power. The meanings of the *taun*, the feast in the *taun*, and the *kaba* are all an aspect of their power. That power is the power they hold and compel as images, as *iri lolos*, or "manifest power," contained in the ritual forms. A true image, like a metaphor (and a metaphor is a verbal image—an iconic use of language), can never be adequately glossed. It must be experienced in order to be understood, and the experience of its effect is at once its meaning and its power. To achieve such an experience is to attain power, but since the perception of the experience as meaning is largely a work of personal interpretation, we can say that the images of Barok ritual elicit meaning in much the same way as the taboos of kin behavior elicit relationship.

Meaning is elicited via a kind of joking or avoidance relationship of image, as metaphor, with language; on this plane, that of relationship within the realm of symbolic reference, ethos undergoes a metamorphosis into meaning, or into the social power which that meaning manifests. But the substitution is at least consistent, and reversible, for if the images of social and ritual form are "manifest power," then the skill and tact needed, and developed, to respond appropriately to

216

the challenges of kin taboo are perhaps "kinetic power," power in motion. The ability that grows (or is inculcated— elicited) in the small child to respond appropriately to the seeming violations, demurrals, and exaggerations of kin pro- tocol, and thus attain for itself participation in a relationship, is the germ of social power as the Barok understand it, as well as of social meaning. Its transformation into a *lolos*, or power, and the *iri lolos* of social power coincides also with the transition from novice to adept, from youth or young adult to *orong*.

The *pidik* is the institutionalization of this transition. Largely made up of young men, and often used, as in the cases of Kanut and Tonoe, as lodges for their initiation, the *pidik* is organized around the revelation of power. The *kind* of power in question might vary from the trivial to the tran- scendental; the social standing conferred is rarely, if ever, un- ambiguous. But neither of these considerations is perhaps as important to these young men as the fascination of realizing the possibilities of ethos as power, turning relational compe- tence into practical "leverage" or effect.

It makes sense, in this respect, to approach the imagery of feasting and the mortuary cycle as a kind of social *pidik*, for in the feasting rituals organized and enacted by *orong*, the power acquired is a revelation of social meaning itself. And it is most significant that this revelation is not simply an iconic representation or analysis of the social dynamic—showing the moieties, for example, locked into their mutually suppor- tive and ongoing dialectic—but a *resolution* of the social dy- namic. For, in an ultimate sense, having power over some- thing amounts to having the power to nullify it, and the revelation of social power must necessarily involve the nul- lification, or obviation, of conventional social meanings. This is accomplished in the definitive form of the *kaba*, where feasting and burial are conflated, and where the distinction between the nurturant and encompassing functions of the

217

moiety, upon which all kin relationships are based, is nullified. It is no accident that this form of the *kaba* effects the successorship of a new *orong*, for *orong*ship is created by this nullification, and by the social power it releases.

It is no accident, either, that Usen social meaning resolves inevitably in its own negation, and that this negation is a source of power. The transcendence of such meaning by adepts, particularly elders accomplished in ritual, has been noted again and again in studies of indigenous Australian and Melanesian peoples, notably in Barth's account of Baktaman ritual,[1] and, most comprehensively, in Jorgensen's analysis of the Telefol "Mother House" and its secret knowledge at Telefolip.[2] In the latter work, it is the (secret) nullification of the conventional Telefol "taro and arrows" (nurturance as against killing) opposition that releases power and autonomy to the elders who partake of it.

A point raised earlier, in the discussion of *pidik* (Chapter 6), might help the reader come to terms with this effect of the Barok "social *pidik*." It will be recalled that when the secret of a *pidik* is revealed to be nothing more than the mere operation of a technological "trick," or device, this is not taken either as an invalidation of supernatural power generally, or as a demystification of the *pidik* itself. Rather, it is simply the legitimate power of the *pidik*, and *additional* power for those to whom it has been revealed. Similarly, the effect of the *kaba*'s "cooking of the dead" is a power over and above the special meanings of nurturance and containment, and of the feast in the *taun*; it is the legitimation of legitimation, the containment of feasting iconography by the larger process of which that iconography is a part.

That process—the transmutation of ethos (the moral force, we might say, by which society runs) into social meaning (the

---

[1] Barth, *Ritual and Knowledge among the Baktaman of New Guinea.*
[2] Jorgensen, *Taro and Arrows.*

ideological resolution of ethos)—is necessarily social as well as symbolic. But the reader should be reminded that this transmutation is a matter for adepts; its social and moral manifestation is hierarchy—the successorship of the *orong*. Significantly, it is the mortuary cycle that serves as the "social *pidik*," the revelation, through images, of the meaning of the human life course via its social symbols, and, finally, of the power and precedence of the *orong* via their obviation.

As an image—a single, composite image of conflated feasts and states of the deceased—the social *pidik* is so completely condensed as to beggar verbal description. It is "for witnessing." Symbolically, its result is obviation: beginning with individual death, it moves, through a series of transformations and dialectical cross-implications, to a point of resolving (i.e. "killing") social meanings and of actually "cooking" or killing the dead in an act which is neither really an affirmation nor a denial of its beginning point—what Richard Schechner would call the "not-not" of the death. Pragmatically it achieves the point of obviation by inserting the *kaba*—the feast that contains, rather than being contained; the tree that inverts feasting and burial—as a "thirdness" to resolve the tension of the moieties.

This thirdness, the point beyond life and death and the mutual nurturance and production of the moieties, serves as a point of contrastive definition, *external* to its "content" and stated concerns, for Barok ethos and culture. It is precisely *because* Usen life is "about" blood, food, nurture, respect, and *malum* for the dead that power over Usen life must come from a point beyond these things, and beyond the moieties that generate them. One thinks of the traditional *Kabaka* of Uganda, and his power to kill his subjects. Death is the seal of power, and the death of meanings is the seal of power over them.

Images, such as those through which Usen social meaning is elicited and resolved, can enter only into analogical, or transformational, relations with one another. Thus the focal point of a *pidik* is a revelation, a transformation of thought, not a structure, and the point of definition achieved in the *kaba* is an *obviation* of social meanings, rather than a paradigm of them. Given the role of the social *pidik*, with its succession of images, in the transmutation of ethos into social meaning, and the obviation of this meaning to produce social power, we might inquire as to the relation between this "manifest" social power and power as it exists "in the world."

The most formidable phenomenal occurrences of power in the Barok world are the *tadak*, the clan-spirits described in Chapter 5. These beings are immortal and powerful for the same reason: they have power over appearance, and possess the capability of changing form at will. They maintain, in other words, the same sort of power over images that the social *pidik* holds over meanings—that of negating them. This power is the more awesome, and the more capricious, for the fact that it controls particulars: specific locations, living creatures, occasions, victims, destinies—in a word, specific appearances.

But the *tadak* is identified in an elemental way with a particular clan, with its origin and place of origin and (at least ideally) with its *orong* through a kind of rapport. It is, as Barok say, the "strength" of the clan even as the *kaba* is the "strength" of the *orong*. *Tadak* is a kind of spontaneous, willful (but uncontrolled) manifestation of clan strength and identity in the world of phenomenal appearances; it is clan identity manifested as self-efficient image. In this respect, however, it is the analogical inverse of the social *pidik* and its succession of images; for the latter exhausts a series of images to bring about a negation of the generic meanings of clan and moiety, whereas *tadak* manifests itself through the production of concrete images that serve to specify the identity of a particular clan. It is as if *tadak* were a kind of essentialist backlash of the *orong*, representing as disembodied force the loyalties he has had to renounce in the negation that grants him social power.

The transformational relation between *tadak* and the social *pidik* provides a key to the esoteric world of power and meaning that both vivifies and mystifies the Barok. It is a world of image, in which the verbal capability, however ultimately necessary, is ancillary; the manifestation or production of unusual (or provocative) images evidences uncanny power, and power in the world is apprehended through the presence of such manifestations or appearances. The images can be those of the celestial bodies and their movements, as in the archaic and little-remembered calendric system; those of unusual natural objects or events; or those of the coordinate spectacle of a "singsing" performance. Meaning, and ultimately power, comes from the successful penetration—experiencing and exhausting—of images, a process that (as in the *pidik*, which is the container and effector of power) can be accomplished only by confrontation and "seeing for yourself."

System and structure—the projection of institutional, functional, categorical, or mathematical relations onto this world—are both peculiarly alien and peculiarly familiar in its epistemological environment. For, on one hand, the systematic approach is overly precise and literal when dealing with substantives—it projects laws, institutions, rights, and explicit functions where there are intentions and tendencies—and, on the other, it misses and fails to specify the ambiguities of conception and interpretation that fuel human motivation and understanding with contingencies. But the systematic and structural approaches of anthropology are also *pidik*—"schools" that, regardless of their sharply delineated logics and other explanatory virtues, must be experienced and penetrated firsthand by those learning anthropology. No structural, functional, ecological, or other program or methodology is a direct recipe for success; all must be learned and applied with insight, and their innermost relations must be "seen for oneself."

New Ireland is known to the world through its images, largely the splendid, aggressive, and often quite sophisticated *malanggan* carvings. Behind this superb iconography is a peculiar reticence: the items we usually see displayed or depicted are poor in glosses or explanations, and one generally has to experience them for oneself. The people will generally explain that the meanings are lost, or were known only to the ancestors (those folks who are so methodically "finished" at final death feasts), and so the characteristic silence remains. The Usen Barok did not originally make *malanggan* (though they may have flirted with the practice), but if this study of their *kastam* can help in some way to interpret a world of reticent images, a small step will have been taken in understanding a remarkable island.

APPENDIX

Reciprocity and
the *Orong*

THE BAROK *orong* represents a remarkable conflation of the widespread Melanesian stereotype of the "big man" with the roles of ritual expert, definer of public propriety, and clan or community leader. An *orong* who served as the head of a clan (or of a large and autonomous *agana*) was the holder and dispenser of the clan's treasury of *mis*, and was obliged to remain in rapport with the clan's *a tadak*, or tutelary spirit. Although it is clear that not all men identified as *orong* meet all of these qualifications, the use of the term in any instance can be understood to evoke a sense of cultural mastery and authoritarian preeminence.

In more pragmatic terms, an *orong* is someone who arranges and stages successful feasts according to a rigid protocol. When they point this out, Barok also say or imply that the *orong* must be adept in the "power" necessary to bring off a successful feast, and to counteract the negative powers exercised by rivals. It is also understood that an *orong* must sponsor and build a *taun* at his own expense. Whatever else this might imply in terms of the politics of inheritance and interpersonal interaction, it means that an *orong* must also "prove himself" through his mastery of exchange and reciprocity.

Although this book is not primarily concerned with the sociology of Barok life, or with the question "Given a particular culture, how does one pick one's way through it?" it may still be useful to examine at least the *orong's* role in manipulating cultural resources. In this regard, the symbolism and the practical exigencies and capabilities of the *orong* come together. For in all matters in which the hospitality of the *taun* is extended outward, to guests, as in feasting and general accommodation, its recipients are treated and defined as being exactly equal. All adult men are welcome to a feast; any adult man may claim accommodation (and meals) in a *taun*. Each is entitled to an equal (and generous) portion, to the satisfaction (and pleasure) of life. But the *orong* is conceived as one who is "equal," in his resources and capabilities, to the *sum* of these appetites: he satisfies, and thus encompasses them, through the *taun* and through the feasts that he sponsors. Each is equal to the other; but, in the role of provider, the *orong* is equal to all.

Where do his resources come from? Beyond the extent of his personal holdings—pigs, vegetable gardens, areca groves, access to producing coconut trees—an *orong* relies on redistribution. The difficult, and admired, part of his job involves calling in obligations for labor, service, and foodstuffs from a range of clanmates, affines, friends and supporters in the village, and trade partners. Some degree of support in this regard would be available to anyone; to the extent that he has cultivated ties widely, is prominent in his clan, and shows a likelihood to reciprocate, the *orong* is able to expand his support base to the point where significant pools of labor and foodstuffs are ensured. (At a true mortuary feast, much of the support would be forthcoming through the obligations of relatives to the dead, but even at a *taun* consecration, clanmates of related lineages are obliged to give *some* support.)

The amount of "refreshers" (areca nut, green drinking coconut) and foodstuffs (pork and tubers) necessary for a given feast can never be precisely determined beforehand, an uncertainty that is evident in the varying size of individual portions from one feast to another. As he is unable to control, or even anticipate, the number of feasters who will show up, the *orong* can only prepare by maximizing his resources. (He will also do "power" to reduce the appetites of his guests.) In practical terms, the only sure course in maximizing a redistributive function is to extend one's network of relationships and obligations, so that there will be more to redistribute.

The positive side of this chancy venture with many variables is that a *taun* will hold only so many men, and a man can consume (and take home afterward, an important consideration) only so much food. When the limiting condition of *orong*ship, a redistributive potential "equal" to the collective appetite, has been met, the remainder is pure profit. Pork in particular, but also prepared vegetable foods such as *olos*, may be presented publicly at the end of the feast, in order to discharge obligations, establish additional obligations in others, and generally advance the *orong* in his circle of relationships. The "excess," in fact, is often built into the scheme of the feast itself. Pigs presented to "buy the shame" of lineage members are simply added to the feast's resources; the "heads" (*ogono*: forepart, from the back of the ribcage to the head) are offered to guests for eventual reciprocation. Special portions of the pigs are cooked separately in packets for presentation. When conducted properly, a feast can be managed as something of an "investment."

Like his counterparts in the Kula of the Massim and the Moka of Mount Hagen, the *orong* depends ultimately on the good will of those with whom he has made arrangements. Certainly some will default, but the significance of the defaults will be diminished as the *orong*'s range of relationships increases, and their likelihood may well diminish as the *orong*'s prestige grows. Thus, a successful feast is an investment in other regards than that of "trading stock" alone; the folk adage that an *orong* is someone who brings off feasts is a shrewd penetration of tactics as well as an accurate description.

Nevertheless, it is possible here to misunderstand profoundly, by considering the *orong* as an entrepreneurial individual working to maximize his interests via manipulation within the "rules of society." The depth of alienation implied by the ("developed") Western ideas of "individual" and "enterprise" is simply not a feature of the traditional Barok ambience. In pursuing his tactics, the *orong* energizes social relationships; in holding feasts according to strict protocol, he embodies the interests of his society and achieves its ends. If there were no *orong*, there would be no one "equal" to the sum of the social appetites, no containment of the social, and therefore no containment of power—ultimately, no society at all.

GLOSSARY

THE WORDS listed below belong to the Usen dialect of Barok except where qualified as follows: TP = Tokpisin, or Melanesian Pidgin; T = the Tolai, or Kuanua, language of the Rabaul area; L = Laur, a lingua franca based on Patpatar. All Barok nouns have an obligatory prefix *a*, which has been disregarded in alphabetizing.

agana: ("branch," "limb"), lineage
ain pidik: adept of the Taberan *pidik*
ararum: tabooed person or object
asiwinarong: ("the need of an *orong*"), invocation of the *kaba*
awat: season, "year"; transit of the Pleiades

bagot: threshold log of a *taun*
bak arige: children sharing the same (clan) paternity
balat: the stone wall surrounding a *taun*
bang: a men's house without enclosure
barames: watch-spirit, poltergeist
barok: children
bebe: half-pitch shelter roof in *taun*
bet lulut: ("cutting pig"), ceremonial feasting
birua (TP): vindictive spirits of the violently slain
buai (TP): areca nut
bun: an "heirloom" shell ornament
bung marapun: clan
bungli: the Pleiades
buo: areca nut
butam: display table for feast in *taun*

da: "oven" of heated stones
dawan: favored young girls at a *kaba*
de: blood (also a euphemism for "semen")

esem: name

garamut (TP): a large, wooden slit-gong (Barok *gamut*)
ge woso: "wake," or preburial, feast
giaman (TP): deception
gilam: hairy, monstrous bush-spirit

227

gogo: nocturnally sung mourning songs
gunun: house

gaken: the sun; noon
Gigip To: former *pidik* whose members drank effluvia of the dead
gogorop: the "open" mortuary feast
gogup: a cross-cousin of the opposite sex
goron tadak: hallowed site of a *tadak* spirit

ingal (T): a power-spirit familiar
ingas: the *tinie* of the Taberan cult
iniat (T): a shaman, "brujo"
iri lolos: "finished," or "immanent," power
isuo: a shaman, "brujo"

kaba, kabai: the cumulative, ultimate mortuary feast
kamnar (T): *pidik* seclusion lodge
Kanut: a *pidik* of youths who watch over exposure coffins
kastam (TP): traditional culture
kauwawar (TP): ginger
kina (TP): "dollar" unit of Papua New Guinea currency
kip karaise: namesake
kip sinibo: bamboo-pole divination for murderer
konono: forepart of *taun* enclosure
kun: enclosure "bed" for force-ripening of bananas
kunu mingenge: "buying the shame"
kurubo: ("cutting pig"), ceremonial feasting

la gunun: (generic "house"), village, hamlet
La Marana: Namatanai town
labur: the northwesterly monsoon
laie: ginger
Laur (L): a Patpatar lingua franca
lawana: the side of the *taun*
lawuke: same-sex cross-cousin
lebe: state of taboo following a death
leges: breach of moiety exogamy; one guilty of such a breach
ligu: the rear of the *taun*
lolos: power, in the general sense
lu naraman: the "doorway" of, or space before, a *taun*

lua: the "first," or small, garden

Malaba: the "Sea Eagle" moiety

malagan, malanggan: mortuary sculpture of northern New
    Ireland

malili: the ethic of conviviality

malum: the ethic of forbearance

mamat: dead calm

mameng: magic spell

mangin: traditional shell-disk wealth

    mangin dek: "fine" (high-grade) *mangin*

    mangin tunu: "essential" (ordinary) *mangin*

maorang (L): namesake

mara: eye, focal point, epicenter

    mara bo: ("eye of the pig"), southeast direction

    mara mangin: ("eye of the money"), northwest direction

marami: door or doorway of *taun gunun* or *pan*

maruak-gogoup: mother's male cross-cousin, "mother's brother"

masalai (TP): place-spirit

masoso (L): a habitual manifestation of a *tadak*

maut: decompositional fluids

mile nien: ("throwing out food"), compensation for parent's
    nurturance

minenge: shaming self-consciousness, "shame"

mis (TP): traditional shell-disk wealth

Moroa: traditional creator deity of New Ireland

Nabo: the (north)western, or "sunset," Barok dialect

nat: paternal offspring

    nat arige: children sharing the same (clan) paternity

    nat lo: paternal inheritance

ogagawa: "profit," gain

ogono (*bo*): the "head" (forepart) of a pig

ogono wat: "rockhead," raised former beaches

olagabo: ("gate of the pig"), entry stile of a *taun*

ololo: regimen of abstinence for those seeking power

olos: taro slices steamed in coconut grease

ora: benches in *taun* for feasters

orong: clan leader; "big," or influential, man

palik (L): heavy joking behavior or relationships
pan: women's cookhouse, adjunct to *taun*
pege: semen
pidik (T): a "mystery"; lodge devoted to a "mystery"
pram: ("fathom"), length of *mis* encompassed by outstretched
    arms

sabonu (*bo*): the "back" (hindpart) of a pig
sinam: the "second," or large, garden
songot bebe: feast to deconsecrate *bebe* shelter in *taun*
songot kalu: a "closed" mortuary feast
sugurno: the forswearing of siblingship
surumitik: a Taberan initiand

tabanat: ("giving to the *nat*"), feast honoring a clan's *nat*
Taberan: a large, contemporary *pidik*
tadak: a clan's tutelary place-spirit
Tago: the "Sea Hawk" moiety
talien dek: ("correct form"), traditional cultural practice
tanu: a ghost, human soul
tau: the paternal aunt, "female father"
taubar: the southeasterly trade winds
taun: the men's house
tege: the moon
tene pet (*bara*): a conjuror (of rain)
teve mangin arige: pooling of *mis* in clan alliance
tinie: coordinate musical and visual dance presentation
tongon: the human shade, or "body soul"
tonoe; Tonoe: self-releasing fish traps; *pidik* devoted to them
Tubuan: large, modern masking *pidik*
tunumat: September-November calm

unine: source, "at the base of" something
Usen: the (south)eastern, or "sunrise," Barok dialect

wewet: magic, conjuring
winawu: ritual adept, speaker
worowos: arboreal termite nest used for power

yii (trans.): to respect
yuo: vindictive spirits of the violently slain

BIBLIOGRAPHY

Barth, Fredrik. 1975. *Ritual and Knowledge among the Baktaman of New Guinea*. New Haven: Yale University Press.

Bateson, Gregory. 1958. *Naven*. Second edition. Stanford: Stanford University Press.

———. 1972. *Steps to an Ecology of Mind*. New York: Ballantine Books.

Bell, F.L.S. 1962. "Kinship Avoidance and Linguistic Evasion in Tanga, New Ireland." *Mankind*, 5:11:477-79.

Billings, D. K., and J. N. Peterson. 1967. "Malangan and Memai in New Ireland." *Oceania*, 38:1:24-32.

Biskup, Peter (ed.). 1974. *The New Guinea Memoirs of Jean Baptiste Octave Mouton*. Pacific History Series no. 7, general ed. H. E. Maude. Honolulu: University Press of Hawaii.

Brown, D.J.J. 1979. "The Structuring of Polopa Feasting and Warfare." *Man* (n.s.), 14:712-33.

Brown, G. Spencer. 1972. *Laws of Form*. New York: The Julian Press.

Buhler, Alfred. 1933. *Die Totenfeste in Neu Irland*. Verhandlungen des Schweizerischen Naturforschenden Gesellschaft no. 114 (Jahresversammlung):243-70.

Capell, A. 1967. "A Lost Tribe in New Ireland." *Mankind*, 6:10:499-509.

Chinnery, E.W.P. 1929. *Studies of the Native Population of the East Coast of New Ireland*. Territory of New Guinea Anthropological Report no. 6. Canberra: H. J. Green, Government Printer.

Clay, Brenda J. 1977. *Pinikindu: Maternal Nurture, Paternal Substance*. Chicago: University of Chicago Press.

Clay, R. Berle. 1969. "The Persistence of Traditional Settlement Pattern: An Example from Central New Ireland." *Oceania*, 43:1:40-53.

———. 1974. "Archaeological Reconnaissance in Central New Ireland." *Archaeology and Physical Anthropology in Oceania*, 9:1:1-17.

Errington, F. K. 1974a. "Indigenous Ideas of Order, Time, and Transition in a New Guinea Cargo Movement." *American Ethnologist*, 1:2:255-68.

―――. 1974b. *Karavar: Masks and Power in a Melanesian Ritual*. Ithaca: Cornell University Press.

Finney, B. R. 1973. *Big-Men and Business: Entrepreneurship and Economic Growth in the New Guinea Highlands*. Honolulu: University Press of Hawaii.

Geertz, Clifford. 1973. *The Interpretation of Cultures*. New York: Basic Books.

Groves, W. C. 1933a. "Divazukmit—A New Ireland Ceremony." *Oceania*, 3:3:297-312.

―――. 1933b. "Report on Field Work in New Ireland." *Oceania*, 3:3:325-61.

―――. 1934, 1935. "Tabar To-day: A Study of a Melanesian Community in Contact with Alien Non-Primitive Cultural Influences." *Oceania*, 5:2:220-41, 5:3:346-61, 6:2:147-58.

Hughes, Ian. 1977. *New Guinea Stone Age Trade*. Terra Australis no. 3. Canberra: Australian National University.

Jessep, Owen D. 1977. "Land Tenure in a New Ireland Village." Dissertation, Australian National University.

―――. 1980a. "Land Demarcation in New Ireland." *Melanesian Law Review*, 8:112-33.

―――. 1980b. "Land and Spirits in a New Ireland Village." *Mankind*, 12:4:300-310.

Jorgensen, Dan. 1981. "Taro and Arrows: Order, Entropy, and Religion among the Telefolmin." Dissertation, University of British Columbia.

Lewis, A. B. 1929. *Melanesian Stone Money in Field Museum Collections*. Anthropological Series vol. 19, no. 1. Chicago: Field Museum of Natural History.

Lewis, Phillip H. 1961. "The Artist in New Ireland Society," in *The Artist in Tribal Society*, ed. Marian W. Smith. London: Routledge & Kegan Paul.

―――. 1969. *The Social Context of Art in Northern New Ireland*. Fieldiana, Anthropology 58. Chicago: Field Museum of Natural History.

———. 1973. "Changing Memorial Ceremonial in Northern New Ireland." *Journal of the Polynesian Society*, 82:2:141-53.

Lithgow, D., and O. Claassen. 1968. *Languages of the New Ireland District*. Ukarumpa, E.H.D., Papua New Guinea: Summer Institute of Linguistics.

Peekel, P. Gerhard. 1908. "Die Verwandtschaftsnamen des Mittleren Neu-Mecklenburg." *Anthropos*, 3:456-81.

———. 1909. "Grammatik der Neu-Mecklenburgsprache." *Speziell der Palasprache*. Berlin: George Reimer.

———. 1910. "Religion and Zauberai auf dem Mittleren Neu-Mecklenburg," in Collection Internationale de Monographies Ethnographiques, *Anthropos*, tom. 1, fasc. 3.

———. 1926, 1927. "Die Ahnenbilder von Nord Neu-Mecklenburg. Ein Kritische und Positive Studie." *Anthropos*, 21:806-24, 22:16-44.

———. 1928. "Lang-Manu, Die Schlussfeier eines Malagan- (Ahnen-) Festes auf Nord Neu-Mecklenburg," in *Festschrift Publication d'Hommage Offerte au P. W. Schmidt*, ed. W. Koppers. Vienna: Mechitharisten-Congregations-Buchdruckerei.

Peterson, J. N., and D. K. Billings. 1965. "A Note on Two Archaeological Sites in New Ireland." *Mankind*, 6:6:254-57.

Powdermaker, Hortense. 1931a. "Mortuary Rites in New Ireland." *Oceania*, 2:1:26-43.

———. 1931b. "Report on Fieldwork in New Ireland." *Oceania*, 1:3:357.

———. 1931c. "Vital Statistics in New Ireland." *Human Biology*, 3:351-75.

———. 1932. "Feasts in New Ireland: The Social Function of Eating." *American Anthropologist*, 34:236-47.

———. 1933. *Life in Lesu: The Study of a Melanesian Society in New Ireland*. London: Williams & Norgate.

———. 1966. *Stranger and Friend*. New York: Norton.

Salisbury, R. F. 1964. "New Guinea Highland Models and Descent Theory." *Man* (o.s.), 64:168-71.

Schlaginhaufen, O. 1964. *Anthropologie von Neuirland (Neu-Mecklenburg) in der Melanesischen Südsee*. Zurich: Orell Füssli.

233

Schmitz, C. A., P. C. Laufer, and P. K. Neuhaus (eds.). 1962. *Beiträge zur Ethnographie der Pala, Mittle Neuirland*. Vol. 2. Cologne: Kölner Ethnologische Mitteilungen.

Schneider, D. M., and K. Gough. 1961. *Matrilineal Kinship*. Berkeley: University of California Press.

Scragg, R.F.R. 1957. *Depopulation in New Ireland: A Study of Demography and Fertility*. Territory of Papua and New Guinea Health Monograph. Port Moresby: Government Printer.

Strathern, Andrew. 1970. "Wiru Penthonyms." *Bijdragen tot de Taal-, Land-, en Volkenkunde*, 126:1:59-74.

Tischner, Herbert. 1965. "Bemerkungen zur Konstruktion und Terminologie der Hausformen auf Neu Irland und Nebeninseln," in *Festschrift Alfred Buhler*, eds. C. A. Schmitz and R. Wildhaber. Basel: Basler Beiträge zur Geographie und Ethnologie, Ethnologische Reihe, Band 2.

Wagner, Roy. 1967. *The Curse of Souw: Principles of Daribi Clan Definition and Alliance*. Chicago: University of Chicago Press.

———. 1972. *Habu: The Innovation of Meaning in Daribi Religion*. Chicago: University of Chicago Press.

———. 1974. "Are There Social Groups in the New Guinea Highlands?" in *Frontiers of Anthropology*, ed. Murray Leaf. New York: Van Nostrand.

———. 1977. "Analogic Kinship: A Daribi Example." *American Ethnologist*, 4:4:623-42.

———. 1978. *Lethal Speech: Daribi Myth as Symbolic Obviation*. Ithaca: Cornell University Press.

———. 1980. "Cultural Artifacts at Omara and Kistobu Caves, New Ireland." *Oral History* (The Institute of Papua New Guinea Studies), 3:8:59-63.

———. 1981. *The Invention of Culture*. Second edition. Chicago: University of Chicago Press.

———. 1983. "The Ends of Innocence: Conception and Seduction among the Daribi of Karimui and the Barok of New Ireland." *Mankind*, 14:1:75-83.

Zuckerkandl, Victor. 1973. *Man the Musician*, vol. 2 (trans. N. Guterman) of *Sound and Symbol*. Bollingen Series. Princeton: Princeton University Press.

INDEX

ararum, 170-75, 187-88, 191, 203; defined, 171
astronomical lore, and food quest, 43-
44
avoidance, xvi, 52, 54, 79, 215; elicitor
of relationship, 55-58, 69-70

Bakan Village, 3, 8-23, 33, 45, 101,
104, 114, 116, 119, 137, 149n.,
157n., 195, 196; map, 16
Baktaman people, 218
Ballingall, C. E., xxi
Barok people, 3-8, 14, 46, 215; dialects,
4-6; language, 4-6, 26, 26n.; north-
ern (Nabo), 65-66
Barth, F., 133, 218
Bateson, G., xi, xii, 49, 52-54, 76-77,
176, 215
Benedict, R., xii
blood (*a de*), 62-63, 219
Boluminski, F., 13, 33
Bradburd, D., 208n.
bride-price, 56-58, 83, 93
Brown, G. S., 158
Brown, Rev. G., 6, 21
burial, xviii, 152, 154, 157, 158, 209,
211, 217-19; described, 179-81

calendar, indigenous (*awat*), 28, 36-43,
221; as *kastam*, elicitation, 44-45;
table, 39
Castaneda, C., 140, 142n.
Chimbu people, 208n.
Chinnery, E.W.P., 13n., 71
clan (*a bung marapun*), 7, 21, 50, 79-
98, 168, 175, 197; described, 84-86;
and *tadak*, 99n., 102
Clay, B. J., xxi, xxiii, 26, 29n., 50n.,
63n., 65, 98, 153
Codrington, R. H., xii
conception, Barok ideology of, 62-63

condensation, symbolic, 154, 175, 210,
219
containment, xiv-xv, xvii-xviii, 49, 64,
89, 104, 131, 155, 156, 168-70, 174-
75, 187-88, 191-93, 197, 217-19,
224, 226; image of, 146, 153, 154,
177, 197, 206-207

Damon, F. H., 171n.
Dampier, W., 12, 12n.
Daribi people, 48, 107n., 152n.
dawan, 203
deception, as means to knowledge, 133-
34
divination, 182-84
Dousset-Leenhardt, R., 100n.
Duke of York Islands, 4, 141
Dumont, L., 169
Durkheim, E., xii, xiv, xviii, 134
Dyaul Island, 81

elicitation, xv-xviii, 44-45, 48, 50, 52,
54-75, 103, 131, 176, 215-17
ethos, 28, 45, 48, 52, 79, 97, 112, 147,
159, 189, 210, 215; defined, 45;
transformed into meaning, 216-17,
220

feasting, xvii-xviii, 28, 45, 50, 80, 123,
146-75, 209-12, 217; described, 162-
66; "closed" feast, 187-91, 197, 205,
207, 209, 211; as image, 167-70;
mortuary, 185-213; "open" feast,
187, 191-93, 197, 207, 209, 211;
preparations for, 159-62, 194-97
Finney, B., 20
Fortes, M., 87
Freud, S., 154

gardening; and calendar, 40-43; and
gender, 29, 32; moral significance,
29, 32-33, 44; staples, 33; techniques, 33-36

235

INDEX

Mead, M., xii

meaning, cultural, xviii, 214-16, 219-21

men's house (*a taun*), xvii-xviii, 14-17, 21-22, 45, 48, 50, 57, 71, 72, 77, 80, 83, 84, 86-90, 121, 146-59, 166-76, 178, 187-201, 206-207, 209-10, 215, 224-25; *ararum*, 170-79; and clan, 88; described, 148-52; *mis* used in decorating, 82; as *nat lo*, 63-64, 116n.

metaphor, xiv, 103, 120, 154, 216

mis (*a mangin*), 7, 9-11, 47, 56-58, 65-66, 84, 93, 120, 137, 164, 172-75, 199-203, 205, 208; and clan, 88-90, 223; described, 80-84; kinds of, 81-83; "pooling," sharing of, 10-11, 86, 88, 90-91, 116n.

modernization, 20-23

moiety, xvi-xviii, 48-75, 79, 90-98, 147, 168, 169, 172, 187, 190-92, 197, 201-202, 207, 210, 216, 219; cross-moiety relationship, 54-55, 92-98; exogamy, 55; inception of, 62, 68, 147; regulator of marriage, 61-62; in *Taberan*, 129-31, 133; totems, 50

Moka, 225

moon, eclipse of, 37-38, 38n.

Moroa, 24, 27, 136, 177

Mount Hagen, 225

Mouton, J.B.O., 12, 76

Namatanai town, 7, 11-13, 20, 83, 118-20; described, 118-19, as "direction" (*mara bo*), 24-25, 26n., 196

naming, personal, 106-10

nat (paternity), 54, 63-66, 68, 70-75, 97, 169, 187, 191-93; defined, 63-64; indemnification of, 65-66; and lineage, 86-87; *nat arige*, 72-73; as payment of *mis*, 172, 174, 187-88

Needham, R., 100n.

New Ireland, 24, 29, 222; map, 16; origin of, 24-25

Nietzsche, F. W., xii

Notsi people, 6, 98

nurturance, xvi, xviii, 28, 49-50, 64-66, 75, 83, 97, 131, 146, 169, 170, 187, 191, 217-19

obviation, 211-13, 217, 219-20

orong, 17n., 21, 57-61, 80, 84, 86, 97, 102, 137, 149, 157, 168, 174, 177-78, 192, 198-204, 207, 210, 217-20, 223-26; and clan, 88-89; in naming practice, 106-109; maternal uncle as, 71, 113; the need of, 178, 210, 213

Patpatar; language family, 4, 11; people, 101, 114

pidik, 122-36, 140-47, 176-77, 186, 216-21; defined, 122-23; *Kanut*, 180-81; resemblance to *kastam*, 122-23, 217-19; *tinie* as, 125-28

Pleiades, 40, 40n., 42

polyandry, 59-60

polygyny, 59-60

power (*a lolos*), xiv, 45, 80, 90, 99, 103, 121-26, 128-45, 149-50, 216-21, 223, 225; described, 135-36; *iri lolos*, 121, 206; as meaning, xviii, 216-17; spells (*mameng*), 35, 136-38

preferment, in marriage, 55-56, 61, 69, 92

Rabaul, 4, 6, 139, 141

Radcliffe-Brown, A. R., xii, 52

residence, postmarital, 18-19, 61

respect, xvi, 45, 48, 52, 54, 64, 71, 79, 215

Rivers, W.H.R., xiii

Salisbury, R. F., xiii, 95

Satele, 29-32, 138, 169

Schechner, R., 219

schismogenesis, xii, 49, 215

Schneider, D. M., 69

Schopenhauer, A., 184n.

Seligman, C. G., xii

Seneviratne, H. L., 126n.

237